VOLUME TWO: CHRONICLES–MALACHI

THE WORD MADE FRESH

compiled by
ANDREW EDINGTON

JOHN KNOX PRESS
ATLANTA

Library of Congress Cataloging in Publication Data

Edington, Andrew.
   The word made fresh.

   CONTENTS: v. 1. Genesis-Kings.—2.   Chronicles-Malachi.
   1. Bible O.T.—Paraphrases, English.   I. Title.
BS895.E33   221.5'2   75-13457
ISBN 0-8042-0076-9 (v. 2)

The text is reproduced from type set by
the Herring Printing Company, Kerrville, Texas

CONTENTS

I CHRONICLES

Chap.
1-8

The names of the people of God with the genealogies of selected families.

Chap.
9-15

The genealogy of the tribes of Judah and Israel with particular emphasis on the lineage of Saul and David and the names of people associated with them.

Chap.
16

When the ark of the covenant was finally brought to the city of David and proper rejoicing was had, then David gave to each person present a loaf of bread, a piece of meat, and a bottle of wine.

On the first day after the presence of the ark of the covenant and after David had appointed special priests from the tribe of Levi to minister to the people from the place of the ark, then David composed a psalm of thanksgiving to God in the general manner as follows:

"Thanks be to God, spread abroad the name of God, call upon him, tell people of the mighty acts of God, sing praises to the Lord and mention frequently his mighty works for man.

"Let anyone that praises God do so joyfully, seek the strength of the Lord, remember his great works, his mighty judgments, and the words of his mouth.

"You children of Israel, you descendants of Jacob, be certain that He is the Lord our God, his authority covers the whole earth, and he has a covenant with his people, commandments that are made to last thousands of years and the Lord is the one promising and He is the keeper of the promises. The promises that he made to Abraham and Jacob are still good.

"God said that he would give the land of Canaan even though you were but a handful of people, but God cared for you his people and he protected the children of his Israel for the sake of his promise.

"So sing to the Lord. Declare his glory. Proclaim his might. The Lord is to be praised and He is an awesome god. Gathered around the Lord is glory and honor as well as strength and gladness.

"Not only should you give glory and honor to God, but bring offerings to his temple and worship the Lord in the spirit of beauty and holiness. Encourage men everywhere to say that the Lord reigns over the earth and the heavens, for this is surely true.

"The roar of the sea is an acknowledgement of God, and ripe fields testify to his goodness, and the wind in the woods sings of the glory of God, announcing the presence of God.

"Be grateful to God, for he is good and his mercy endureth forever.

"Pray that God will deliver you, that he will save you from the ungodly nations and that he will gather you together as a nation so that as a united people you may worship the Lord and glorify his name forever."

Then the people shouted, "Praise the Lord!"

The assembly was then dismissed and everyone returned home and David returned to the palace and the ministers of the tribe of Levi were left in charge of the ark of the covenant.

One day David was talking to Nathan the prophet and said, "Nathan, it has occurred to me that I live in a mighty beautiful and fancy house while the ark of the covenant of the Lord is simply stuck behind some draperies."

"God is with you, David," said Nathan, "and if you want to correct this situation I'd say have at it."

During the night, however, the word of the Lord came to Nathan telling him that it was not God's will for David to build a temple and Nathan visited David and repeated to him the message he had received from God, saying, "David, the Lord has revealed to me that you are not to build the temple we were talking about yesterday."

"In fact," continued Nathan, "the Lord would remind you and everyone else that no dwelling has been erected for God since Israel left Egypt, but the ark of the covenant, the symbol of the presence of God, has been shifted from tent to tent.

"God never requested from any of the leaders of his people a house of cedars. The Lord would remind you, David, that he took you from a small boy, acting as a sheepherder, and made you ruler over all the children of Israel."

"The Lord reminds you, David, that he has been with you and he has handled your enemies and made a great name for you among all peoples. The Lord has also determined that he shall provide a place for his people and the Lord has promised to increase your power, David, and to provide from you a great descendancy. In fact, David, God promises to raise up children and grandchildren and one of the children will be given the privilege of building a great temple to the Lord."

"I will bless this boy and not depart from him and I will show him great mercy."

After hearing this, David went into the place of prayer and knelt in the presence of God and prayed saying, "Who am I, or what have I done to deserve such a great blessing? Your promises may seem to be a small thing to you because of your greatness, but to me they mean everything. How can I thank you?"

"O, Lord, there is none great except you. What one nation in all the earth is blessed as is Israel? It is wonderful that the people of

Israel are your people, and that you have made them great, and that you are their God."

"May your name be magnified forever. Surely the Lord God of hosts is the God of Israel as well as a God to Israel. May you also bless my family as you have said that you would and may the lineage of David always be worshippers of the true God. Bless my house, O Lord, and may it always be faithful to you."

In uniting the tribes and establishing the kingdom of Israel David found it necessary to subdue the Fascists, who had captured Gath and some of the other towns previously held by the Israeli. David also made war on Mississippi and these people then befriended David by bringing him expensive gifts, which actually amounted to tribute money.

David also took his army north toward Syria and conquered Hap,[1] king of Zobah, and in the process captured a thousand chariots and a great number of soldiers.

When the Syrians heard of this they were afraid that David was getting too close for comfort and they sent an army to fight David near Zobah, but David defeated their army and began collecting tribute from these people also. The Lord was with David and the real cause of his success.

Among the many valuables captured by David were many solid gold shields, and David brought these back, to Jerusalem and placed them in the church treasury.

Now when word of all David's greatness and success reached the ears of Big Toe,[2] king of Harvard,[3] he sent his son, Little Toe,[4] to visit David. Little Toe came to David and congratulated him on his great success and he brought David many presents of gold and silver. David added all this loot to the church treasury, which was, of course, under David's control.

David ruled Israel wisely and with justice and he served the Lord. David organized his government and delegated authority, naming Tuffy,[5] Commanding General of the Army.

About this time Nahas, the king of Annum, died and his son Hanun became king. David heard of this and he decided to send a visiting committee to call on Hanun and express sympathy to him because of David's friendship with his father.

The committee of young men called on Hanun and conveyed David's messages.

Some of the advisers to Hanun, however, told the king that they thought the committee was a spy group and that David was seeking information rather than sending condolences.

[1]Hadarezar   [2]Tou   [3]Hamath   [5]Joab   [4]Hadoram

As a result, King Hanun became very upset and took the members of the visiting committee, shaved their beards off, cut their hair, cut the seat of their pants out, and sent them out bare tailed and clean shaven.

David heard of this and knew the committee was ashamed to be seen; so David sent word to the men to stay in Jericho until their beards and hair grew and also he told them to get some new pants.

Word of all of this came to Hanun and he realized he had been wrong and that in David's opinion he was an unappreciative stinker; so Hanun gathered together a great sum of tax money and signed up an army of paid soldiers from the surrounding areas and paid these soldiers to declare war on David.

When David heard of this, he sent for Tuffy and told him to get the army together and handle the situation.

Tuffy did this, but when he saw that the invaders were divided among themselves, the Syrians being in one group and the men of Ammon in another, then he divided his army and put one section of it under his brother's command, a man named Flip Wil.[1]

Tuffy explained to Flip Wil that while he attacked the Syrians Flip would attack the Ammonites, and if Tuffy needed help Flip would come to his rescue and if Flip needed help, then Tuffy would come and help him. Tuffy then invoked the blessing of God on the whole procedure.

When Tuffy and his crowd approached the Syrian mercenaries they decided that they had already earned their money and so they began to flee. When the children of Ammon saw the Syrian army fleeing they decided the jig was up and so they fled also.

Hearing all this, David decided to put the lid on the Syrians for good and so he took the combined armies and sought the Syrians and defeated them, making them surrender numerous people as servants and paying great tribute to David in the form of gold and silver. David always enjoyed receiving tribute. The Syrians also agreed never to make another deal with the children of Ammon.

After a year of inactivity it was time to give the army a work-out; so Tuffy took the army on live maneuvers in the land of the Ammonites. David did not go on the trip but enjoyed receiving some of the spoil, particularly the heavily jeweled crown which was removed from the head of the Mayor of Rochester.[2]

The prisoners taken from the city of Rochester were worked long and hard with saws and axes to discourage any further trouble.

Trouble soon arose again also from the Fascists around Austin and one of the group was a giant who was killed by one of David's warriors who was quick as lightning and known as Sly Mike.[3]

[1] Abishai   [2] Rabbah   [3] Sibbechai

6

Later in the year another champion from Austin began to talk big as he was also a giant and carried a spear that looked like a vaulting pole. Again one of the trained warriors of Israel, this time a man named Sharpy,[1] fought the giant and killed him and the disturbance died down a bit.

Finally, a giant who was great in stature, but a bit freakish in having 24 fingers and toes challenged the people of Israel and one of David's nephews[2] named Delli[3] met him in combat and killed him. This ended the season on a winning note.

There was now an idle time for David and the devil in the form of vanity suggested that David might take a census to learn how mighty a king he was and how many people he controlled.

As a result David called Tuffy to him and said, "I want you to be in charge of taking a census as I want to know how many people are in the kingdom."

Tuffy, who was a warrior not a census taker, said to David, "Why count the people? All the people are under your control so why worry about how many? Why cause all this stir and trouble?"

David, however, insisted on the census being taken and so Tuffy grudgingly went to work. Finally Tuffy returned to Jerusalem and reported that there were 1,000,000 men of draft age in Israel and 470,000 in Judah. The figures, however, did not include the tribes of Levi or Benjamin as Tuffy had gotten disgusted with the matter and didn't count them, thinking no one would know anyway.

God was displeased with David's vanity and with the counting of the people without the Lord's blessing.

David soon realized that he had sinned and he asked the Lord to forgive him.

The Lord spoke to David's religious advisor, a man named Oral[4], and told him to tell David that since he had repented then the Lord would give him a choice of three punishments.

Oral came to David and said, "The Lord offers you a three year famine for the land, or three months of trouble from the enemies of Israel, or a three day run of sickness in the land. Take your choice and I will relay your decision to the Lord."

David then said, "Oral, any way I decide is tough, but I would rather be at the mercy of God than left at the hands of enemies; so I'll take the three days of sickness for Israel."

As a result there was great sickness in the land so that about 70,000 people were stricken.

God also was so displeased that he sent an angel to destroy Jerusalem, but God then decided against this and stopped the angel who was standing in front of the barn of a man named Deere[5], who

[1] Elhanan   [2] He had hundreds   [3] Jonathan   [4] Gad   [5] Ornan

7

was the leading grain thresher of the area.

David saw the angel of the Lord and he appeared to have the sword of destruction in his hand and David and the leaders of Israel who were with him fell on their knees in front of the angel.

David then prayed to God saying, "It is all my fault, Lord, why punish the people? I had the nutty idea of counting everybody. Punish me, and my family, but do not punish the people any more on my account."

The angel of the Lord then spoke to Oral and told him to tell David to build an altar and make a sacrifice in Deere's barn.

Now Deere and his three sons looked out and saw the angel with the sword and they hid behind a threshing machine until David entered the barn, then Deere came out to speak to the king, and bowed down to David.

Then David siad, "Deere, may I have a corner of the barn to use as a place for an altar in order that I might make a sacrifice to God? I will pay you a proper price."

"Anything you wish," said Deere, "but it is not necessary to pay me. I will even furnish the meat, the wood, and anything that is needed. It is a pleasure."

"No, Deere," said David, "I wish to pay the full price. It is not proper to make an offering that is not mine."

As a result David paid Deere about $4,500 for the equipment and the space.

David then made the proper sacrifice to the Lord and the angel put his sword away.

David then continued to use the place for his regular worship instead of going to the tabernacle which was at this period of the year in the hills. David was also still a little nervous about the angel with the sword and he felt at ease in Deere's barn.

Chap.
22

Now David felt that there should be constructed a magnificent temple, a great house for the Lord, a proper place for the offerings of the people to be received and for the altar services and worship services of the people.

David then ordered that all the non-Jews be conscripted for work if they were able to labor or had skill as masons or carpenters.

David began to purchase construction supplies, iron for nails, and brass for fittings, and great quantities of cedar.

Since David realized that he did not have much time left to live he concentrated on preparing plans and equipment so that Solomon, his son, could build the temple. David then sent for Solomon and instructed him and charged him with the responsibility of building the temple.

"My son," David said to Solomon, "It was in my mind to build a house to the Lord, but the word of the Lord has forbidden me, for

I have shed too much blood and made too many wars. The word of the Lord, however, has promised me a son who should be a man of peace who will be protected from his enemies. The son will be Solomon and he will build a house for the Lord and the Lord will carefully look out for him. Now may the Lord bless you, Solomon, and prosper you. You must, of course, build the temple. I pray that God will give you wisdom and understanding and I pray that you will observe the commandments of the Lord.

You will succeed, Solomon, if you observe the laws of God. Be strong, son, and of good courage, and do not be impatient or discouraged.

As a practical matter, I have saved and set aside well over two billion dollars in gold bullion, about two million dollars worth of sterling silver, and so much iron and bronze that we haven't even been able to weigh it, as well as enough timber and stone for all the walls. Already you have enough on hand for a good start.

There have been assembled and organized innumerable workers, hewers of wood, stone masons, skilled craftsmen of all kinds, with great abundance of gold, silver, brass, and iron for ornamentation. All you need to do is get with it!"

Then David gathered together the main leaders of the house of Israel and he spoke to them saying, "You are to help Solomon. The Lord has prospered you and protected you. There is peace in the land, direct your heart and soul on the Lord, work together, and build the temple to the glory of God. When the temple is finished, bring the ark of the covenant into it and all the holy vessels consecrated to the Lord."

Chap. 23

David had become very old and so he made Solomon king in his place, and David retired. David had also just before his retirement made a survey of the tribe of Levi and set apart 24,000 of the priestly tribe to supervise the building of the temple, some to be foremen, some to act as guards, and some to furnish music to soothe the workers while the building was in progress and to praise God.

The specific division of the tribe of Levi by name and duty is recorded for scholars in I Chronicles 23:5-32.

Chap. 24,25, 26

Further divisions of the tribe of Levi by name and duty for the building of the temple.

Chap. 27

The Israel army was organized on a basis of 12 regiments with 24,000 men to each regiment. Each regiment was called up for active duty one month out of each year. The names of the regiments and their leaders are recorded in I Chronicles 27:2-33.

Chap. 28

David, old and near death, called a convention of all the leaders of Israel, the heads of the tribes, the army leaders, the mighty men of valor and he caused them to be assembled and David made the keynote address to the convention saying,

"As most of you know, I have desired greatly to build a temple to the Lord, but I have had to be a man of war and have shed too much blood, but the Lord has blessed me with the privilege of uniting the tribes of Israel and establishing the kingdom of Israeli. The Lord has also blessed me with sons, and the Lord has told me to appoint my son Solomon as king in my place and he has told me that Solomon is to build the temple to the Lord.

God has further promised to make the kingdom strong and durable, provided the people adhere to the commandments of the Lord.

In the presence of God and in the sight of the leadership of Israel I charge you all to keep the laws of God, adhere to his ways and his judgments. If you do this, you will keep this land."

Then David turned to Solomon and in the presence of the leaders of Israel, he said to him, "Solomon, my son, worship the Lord God of Israel, the God of your fathers. Serve him with a willing heart and an active mind. Seek God and you will find him. Forsake him and he will cast you aside. Be exceedingly careful, for the Lord has chosen you to build his temple."

David then made a public presentation to Solomon of all the blueprints and plans for the temple, all the contracts, a list of all the supplies, the equipment, all the specifications, even to the size and style of the candlesticks, the altar table and all the decorative touches. David told Solomon that all these things had been planned and blessed by God.

Again David impressed on Solomon the need to be strong and courageous, dedicated to his work, and he again reassured him of the availability of money, materials, and labor.

Chap. 29

David turned again to the assembled leaders and said, "Solomon, my son, whom God has chosen, is young and green, and the job he has to do is immense, for this building is not for a man, but for God. Now I have done the best I could in gathering together all the material and working on plans and letting contracts. I have also raised plenty of money through conquest, and gifts. I have also shown my own zeal by making a gift of about $100,000,000 in gold and silver as my personal donation.

"Which ones of you are now willing to pledge his service to the accomplishment of this wonderful work?"

The leaders of Israel responded to David with enthusiasm and pledged their time and interest. In support of this they also made great contributions, amounting to over $145,000,000 plus a great quantity of jewelry. The people found great happiness in their giving, and their generosity and sincere interest brought a deep joy to the old king David.

As a result, David praised the Lord, and offered a prayer of thanksgiving saying, "Blessed is the Lord God of Israel. Praise ye the Lord."

Thine is the true greatness, O Lord, and power and glory and majesty are yours, for all that is in the heavens and on the earth is yours.

All riches, all power, all honor has its beginning in God. We thank you, God, and give you all the praise and all the glory.

It is humbling to stand in your presence, to willingly pledge ourselves to your work, when we know that all things, and all people are yours anyway. Man, in a way, is insignificant, for we are merely temporary visitors on this earth, and our lives move like shadows and are gone.

It is interesting to note that all that we have gathered for the building of this house of the Lord is just stuff, that has been yours all along anyway. I know you examine the hearts of people and it is a great joy to give so willingly to this temple and to behold my people giving so willingly.

Now, O Lord God of Abraham and of Isaac, and of Jacob, prolong this inspiration, keep our hearts in strong dedication to you, give Solomon a perfect heart, help him to keep your commandments, to follow your statutes, and to properly build the edifice which I have so carefully planned. Amen."

David then turned again to the assemblage and said, "Bless the Lord!"

Then the whole group bowed their heads and prayed to the Lord.

Following this there was a great feast and the offering of sacrifices to the Lord and great gladness and abundant joy on every hand. Solomon was again anointed as king and Solomon arose and sat upon the throne in his father's place and all Israel obeyed him.

There then came before Solomon all the mighty men of Israel, the leaders of the tribes, also Solomon's brothers and they all pledged allegiance to him.

This was the beginning of 40 years of the reign of Solomon and he died in his old age, full of honor and great riches, and his son took the throne after his death.

Now all the acts of the great king David are recorded in the books of Samuel, and in the book of Nathan, and also in the book of Gad, with many details.

Solomon, the son of David, was strengthened in his kingdom and the Lord his God was with him and encouraged his development.

Solomon spoke to the leaders of Israel and invited them to accompany him to Westminister Abbey where the ark of the covenant resided and there Solomon worshipped God and offered sacrifices in accordance with the liturgical commandments of Moses.

That night the Lord appeared in spirit to Solomon and inspired Solomon to pray. As a result, Solomon prayed and said, "O Lord, you blessed greatly my father and now you have chosen me to take his place. Continue the promise you made to David, my father, and since I must rule over a multitude of people grant to me wisdom and understanding that I may be competent to rule and judge this mighty nation."

God was greatly pleased with this prayer and because Solomon had not asked for wealth or power for himself, but had asked for wisdom and knowledge that would be beneficial to others, the Lord not only granted the request of Solomon but added to the blessing of Solomon wealth and honor in excess of any that anyone had ever had.

Solomon returned from this place of worship and reigned over the people of Israel. Solomon instituted a great activity program and he gathered horses and chariots and specified certain cities for the training and maintenance of the chariots and crews, and Solomon promoted so much business around Jerusalem that gold was as plentiful as stone and cedar trees were like scrub oaks.

Solomon imported horses and linen yarn from Egypt, purchasing all things at wholesale prices and selling them at a great profit.

Solomon then set forth to build the temple of God, designed by David, but destined to be built by Solomon.

Solomon then sent a message to Hiram, the king of Tyre, and reminded him of all the purchases arranged by David and he asked Hiram to continue to work this time with David's son, until the great temple was completed. Solomon reminded Hiram that he was building a house in honor of the one great God of all, that it was to be a place for worship and for observing all sacred feasts and customs. Solomon then humbly mentioned to Hiram that he was in great need of a true craftsman, a master builder, a man exceedingly gifted in decorative detail, skilled in the use of gold, silver, and brass. In addition, Solomon requested a contract for more cedar trees, fir trees, and algum[1] trees. The need for timber experts, log rollers, and

[1] I think Hiram found a substitute wood in this case

other laborers was mentioned. Solomon offered Hiram a tremendous sum for all these things, including 20,000 sacks of grain, 20,000 barrels of olive oil, and 20,000 barrels of wine.

Hiram was greatly pleased to receive such a fat contract in the mail and wrote Solomon by return mail as follows:

Dear Solomon:

Surely the Lord loves Israel to provide such a wise king as you. I, myself, bless the Lord God of Israel, who made heaven and earth, for he has given my friend David such a wise and understanding son that he might build a suitable house for the Lord.

For this reason, I am sending Crafty Wright,[1] who is an exceedingly talented artist as well as a knowledgeable builder and decorator. All you need to do now is send the payment to me. Incidentally, we will cut the cedars in Lebanon and float the logs down to Tel Aviv[2] and you can have them easily transported to Jerusalem.

Hope to see you soon,

Sincerely yours,
Hiram

Solomon then initiated a vast conscription enterprise and drafted into a giant labor battalion all the men living in Israel who were not Jews and were able-bodied. There were over 150,000 such in the land and he made 70,000 of them common laborers, 80,000 loggers, and 3,600 he appointed as foremen to supervise the work.

Chap.
3

At last, in the fourth year as king, Solomon actually began the construction of the temple on the mountain of Moriah, an area chosen by David because this was the area of the threshing floor of Mo Ranch where the Lord appeared to David through one of his angels.

The central foundation of the temple was 90 feet long and 30 feet wide with the roof 180 feet high. There was a covered porch attached, the ceiling and inner walls of which were covered with solid gold.

The main portion of the temple was paneled with gold beaten into the wood and then plated with gold and engraved with many figures and artistic renditions. Jewels and various precious stones were also inlaid into the wood.

The Holy of Holies, which was 30 feet square, was overlaid with solid gold and bejeweled. It was estimated to be worth over $15,000,000 unfurnished. Various other ornamentations were placed in and around the temple and two huge pillars reaching over 50 feet in height were placed in front of the temple.

---

[1]Hiramubi   [2]Joppa

13

A bronze altar was constructed 30 feet square and 15 feet high. A huge tank was forged that was 15 feet in diameter and 7 and ½ feet deep. This water tank was placed on the backs of two rows of oxen, all the oxen made in one cast. There were 12 oxen made all in one piece, with 3 oxen facing in each of the four directions. The tank itself was about 5 inches thick and was made to bulge out like a water lily, and the tank could hold 3,000 barrels of water.

There were 5 vats constructed on each side of the tank as the priests were to use these vats for washing of offerings.

All manner of tables, lamps, pedestals, and other fixtures were made and Crafty Wright made shovels and various devices and utensils used in working the sacrificial offerings.

At last Crafty Wright completed his work, having used polished bronze to construct the two pillars, the vats, the bases for the vats, the huge tank, the oxen, the fleshhooks, shovels, pots, the 400 pomegranates hanging from the chains around the tops of the pillars, as well as the tops of the pillars.

In the temple itself, only gold was used. Solomon commanded everything in the temple proper to be solid gold, the main door of the temple, the inner doors, the lamps, basins, spoons, even the candle snuffers — everything solid gold.

When the temple was finally completed Solomon had all the treasures saved by David brought into the temple and then he had a meeting with all the leaders of Israel to plan for the transfer of the ark of the covenant. As a result, the chief priests of the tribe of Levi took the ark and brought it to the temple and Solomon and the people sacrificed on this occasion with offerings too numerous to be recorded.

The ark of the covenant itself was placed in the Holy of Holies and only the supports of the ark could be seen by members of the congregation, for only the high ranking priests were allowed to enter the place of the Holy of Holies. There was nothing in the ark but the two tablets of Moses, and at the time of the writing of these Chronicles the ark was still intact in the temple.

There gathered then a great choir of the priests in pure white robes and they sang and played instruments to the glory of God. The singers sang a song saying "The Lord is good, and his mercy endures forever."

Then the glory of the Lord filled the house and it seemed as if the glory was a cloud that filled the temple and the priests left the temple for the glory of the Lord was so intense.

Solomon prayed then saying, "Lord, you will no longer have to dwell in darkness or be homeless, for I have made a temple for you, and may you live forever."

Then Solomon turned to the gathering of people and said, "Blessed be the Lord who has kept his promise to David, for he told David that he had postponed choosing a place for his temple until the people were united and Jerusalem was accepted as a holy city. It was in the heart of my father David to build the temple and the Lord assured David that it was satisfying to him that David had this great desire, but God would not let David build his temple, but left it to me, his son, to do. The Lord has kept his promise, for I have taken my father's place and have built the house for the name of the Lord, and in it have I had placed the ark of the covenant."

Solomon was standing in the presence of the people on a platform which had been built in front of the temple for such a purpose. Solomon then kneeled down and again voiced a public prayer in the presence of the crowd of people saying "There is no God like the Lord, in heaven or on earth, for God is the keeper of the promises, and he is merciful to all that turn to him. Even this day we witness the promise of the Lord to David being kept. For my father David's sake, keep the throne of Israel intact as you have promised if the people walk in the law of the Lord. Verify here today your promise.

"Yet I know that God is too great to be confined to a temple, for his dominion includes all of heaven and earth, yet listen, O Lord, to the plea of your servant. Always hear the prayers that are made in this temple, look down now and bless this building and make it holy.

"When we are here and seek forgiveness, hear our prayer, O Lord, and forgive.

"Let the innocent find a place of comfort and acquittal here and let the guilty be punished by you.

"If the people of Israel sin and forget you, and are defeated by their enemies, and then they come here and pray for forgiveness and help, hear their prayer and restore them.

"When skies are closed and there is great need of rain because of the sins of the people, hear their prayers when they come here to find you. Forgive them and teach them what is right.

"If sin produces poverty and hunger, if there are crop failures, and insect problems, let the people come here to pray, and hear them, O Lord, and heal the land. Give to each man that which he deserves, but forgive them and heal them.

"May our people always reverence the Lord and walk in the ways which you have directed.

"Even in the case of foreigners who come from strange lands to see your temple and to pray, hear them and answer their prayers, then all men everywhere will begin to know that you are the one true God.

"If our people of Israel go forth to war and pray here at your temple before going, grant to them victory over their enemies.

15

"If the people sin and forget you, Lord, and as a result are captured and scattered in various nations, and then repent and face toward this temple and pray, I plead with you to forgive them and restore them.

"Be constantly, O God, mindful of all the prayers offered in this place.

"Now, Lord, enter your temple, and let the priests of the Lord be clothed with understanding and righteousness, and let all men rejoice in goodness. Remember, Lord, your love for David and turn not aside therefore from me, your anointed one. Amen."

After Solomon finished his prayer, fire descended and consumed the sacrifices and the glory of the Lord was meaningfully present. The glory and the smoke was such that the priests did not even feel competent to enter the temple, and all this so impressed the people that they bowed down and worshipped God, saying aloud "The Lord is good and his mercy endureth forever."

Solomon donated a tremendous amount of beef for this occasion as he was very rich and there was held one of the most impressive outdoor church bar-b-ques ever recorded. The skilled musicians from the tribe of Levi brought guitars and furnished music for the occasion, using the special guitars made by David for the church. Solomon participated in further services, dedicating each part of the temple to the glory of God.

The observing of these ceremonies lasted a full eight days and at the end of the time the people returned to their homes and to their tents full of joy, and hope, and bar-b-que.

This marked the completion of Solomon's plan to build the greatest of all temples to the glory of God.

The Lord then appeared to Solomon in a dream and said to him "I, the Lord, have heard your prayer and I have chosen this temple as the symbol of my presence, and a place of sacrifice. If I close the heavens so that there is no rain, or if I send pestilence to devour the land, then if my people who are called by my name, and who know me, if they will humble themselves, and turn away from their evil ways, and pray to me, then I promise that I will hear and will heal their land. My eyes shall be open and my ears particularly attentive to the prayers made in this holy place, for this is my chosen place, and I shall be related to it forever."

"As for you, Solomon," continued the Lord, "if you will conduct yourself as David your father did, and observe my statutes and my commandments, then I will establish the throne of your kingdom and there will always be a Jew available to rule my people. If, however, you turn away from me and serve strange gods and follow weird customs, then I will remove my people from this land which I gave them and I will cause the land to be abused by other people, and people of strange origins will ask why the great temple was destroyed and the people scattered, and it shall be told them that the people deserted God, and were unfaithful to the one Lord who brought them from Egypt, and for this reason they were punished."

The building of the great temple and the completion of the palace and related buildings all took about twenty years, and then Solomon turned his attention to rebuilding the cities which had been given to him by Hiram and he placed many of the children of Israel in these cities in positions of authority.

Solomon built Phoenix[1] in the desert and Tampa[2] in the swampland and also he built Fort Knox[3] as a city of storage, and he also built places like Little Rock[4] and North Little Rock.[5]

Solomon also used all the immigrants, foreigners, and non-Jews as forced laborers, and others who were not Jews but who had always lived in the land and were natives, these Solomon taxed heavily.

The children of Israel, however, were never used by Solomon as servants, but they were made warriors, or horsemen, or white collar workers.

Solomon then moved one of his wives, who was Pharaoh's daughter and not a Jew, away from the holy city Jerusalem and put her in a country palace near the city. Solomon stated that he did not want his pagan wife to live in touch with the holy places and the holy objects in Jerusalem.

Solomon continued to strictly observe the proper religious practices and he appointed various priests to handle various obligations of the church and he devised a wise and orderly manner of religious practices.

After all this was done, Solomon took a trip to San Francisco[6] and there he met with the representatives of Hiram who had a fleet of ships. Solomon arranged for some of his own men to sail with the men of Hiram and they went to the Klondike[7] and returned with great quantities of gold for Solomon.

The Queen of Sheba became curious about all the reports she had heard about Solomon and so she decided to come to Jerusalem to see for herself, bringing a great caravan of gifts and many evidences of being rich herself.

Sheba and Solomon had many talks and she was tremendously impressed with his wisdom and appalled at the wealth and the cultural advancements so obvious in the temple, the palace, and all

---

[1]Tadmor   [2]Hamathzobah   [3]Baalath
[4]Lower Bethhoron   [5]Upper Bethoron   [6]Eziongeber   [7]Ophir

around the city.

"All the things I heard about you are true, Solomon," said Sheba, "and the reports are not even equal to the real thing. You are greater than I had imagined and your possessions more abundant than I thought possible."

After this Sheba prepared to leave and presented Solomon with many magnificent gifts and received from Solomon everything she desired and more than she asked was added to the loot she took home.

After this Solomon had a period of making some very expensive things, including 300 solid gold shields, worth about a quarter of a million dollars each, plus some smaller versions, worth in the neighborhood of 15 million dollars all told. Solomon also ordered a new throne and considerable new equipment of unbelievable expense. Solomon even decided to have all the dinner plates, salad dishes, coffee cups, knives, forks, and all dining room stuff made of solid gold.

Every three years ships returned from Africa and the Klondike with gold, silver, apes, and peacocks.

Solomon also encouraged all the neighboring kings to bring him riches from their countries in exchange for protection and trading favors.

Solomon built 4,000 stalls for horses and he established regular chariot cities for the training of the horsemen. The king's handling of the finances of the country was so astute that silver became commonplace as cedar trees. Solomon reigned for a total of 40 years and then died and was buried in the city of David his father, and his son Roger became king.

Chap. 10

Roger then went to Baltimore where the leaders of the people had gathered to make him king. Jerry, who was in Egypt at the time, heard of this so he came back to Israel to attend the gathering.

Jerry and the other leaders then handed Roger a petition which read "Your father went too strong on the taxes and the burden that he put on us was too fierce, but if you will agree to a policy of easing up on us a bit we will loyally serve you and recognize you as king."

"I'll think about it," said Roger, "and you can come back in three days for an answer."

Roger then called for a small group of wise, experienced men who had been associated with Solomon and explained the request to them and asked them for their advice.

The old, experienced men then said to Roger, "If you will be kind to these people, ease up on them a bit, and speak good words to them, then they will support you as long as you live."

Roger then summoned a group of his own cronies and asked their advice and they said to Roger, "Tell the people that the taxes and work load imposed by Solomon was nothing compared to what you will do to them. Tell them that your little finger will seem bigger to them than your father's legs, and where your father beat the slothful with whips you will beat them with scorpions."

When Jerry and the leaders of Israel returned the third day Roger spoke to them roughly and answered them in the identical manner suggested by his young cronies.

As a result of this, all the members of the tribe of Israel refused to acknowledge Roger as king and each man went his own way, and Roger found himself only king of the tribe of Judah.

When Roger sent a tax collector to Israel the people stoned him to death and refused to support Roger in any way or to pay the taxes. Roger had to flee to Jerusalem, the stronghold of Judah, for Israel rebelled against this portion of the house of David.

When Roger was safely in Jerusalem he began to organize an army from among the men of Judah and Benjamin in order that he might make war on Israel and see if he could obtain control of the entire kingdom.

The word of the Lord, however, came to Stewart, a man of God, and he was inspired by God to go to Roger and tell him not to start a civil war. Strangely enough, Roger listened and refrained from declaring war on Israel.

Roger did, however, decide to begin building up the cities in his area, fortifying them, and making them strong against attack.

At this time there also began to gather in Jerusalem and place themselves under the administration of Roger a large number of priests of the tribe of Levi, for Jerry had abolished them and no longer used the trained priests of God. Jerry made some of his own friends priests and put them in charge of strange rites and let them lead in the worship of pagan gods.

The kingdom of Judah was further strengthened by the arrival of many refugees from Israel who did not wish to worship strange gods, but wanted to worship and serve the one great Lord of all. These people had a good influence on Roger and for about three years he walked uprightly and acted more nearly like the great kings, Solomon and David.

Roger was a great ladies man and he desired many wives and so he married a great number of girls, but he apparently loved Marjorie,[1] the daughter of Absalom, more than any of the others. Roger also began to re-locate his children in other cities, and to strengthen thereby his relationships in many different communities.

Roger, having organized Judah and strengthened his position,

[1]Maachah

19

became careless and started wandering from the law of the Lord, and he no longer properly worshipped God, and the people followed him.

Because of this the Lord allowed Clyde, an Egyptian leader, to make war on Jerusalem and Clyde had with him a large and impressive army. Clyde captured the neighboring towns and then laid siege to Jerusalem.

Then the prophet of the Lord, Stewart, spoke to the king and the people and told them that the trouble was their neglect of God. Upon hearing this, the princes and the leaders of the people recognized that it was true, and they fell on their knees and humbled themselves before God.

When the Lord observed this, then He spoke to Stewart and told him that because of the people's good attitude the Lord would not totally forsake them, and that even though they would suffer losses and be punished, the Egyptians would not sack the city of Jerusalem.

After this, Roger made a separate peace with the Egyptians and agreed to let them take away many people as servants and workers and he let them take many valuables in the form of gold and silver.

Since the shields of gold of Solomon were taken by the Egyptians, Roger had shields of brass made and he then went into the house of prayer and repented to God. As a result, the Lord preserved Roger and the main body of the people of Judah and the kingdom began to become organized again. Roger reigned for 17 years and he died in Jerusalem after a fairly evil and disruptive reign, involving constant war with Israel and wandering from the worship of God. Tab, the son of Roger, then became king.

Chap.
13

Tab reigned for three years and spent most of the time at war with Jerry. Tab gathered a large army and defied Jerry and the people of Israel. Tab stood on a hill top and spoke to Jerry and the people of Israel saying,

"Didn't you know that the Lord God of Israel gave the kingdom to the sons of David? Why is it that Jerry, the son of one of Solomon's warriors, has rebelled and is causing so much trouble? In fact, he has assembled a lot of mercenaries, and evil men, as well as pagans. Now you think you can defy God, who is on our side.

"You are a great multitude, you are also infiltrated with idol worshippers, you have dismissed the ordained ministers of God. The Lord, however, is with us, we have not forsaken him, and we conduct regular services and as a result we consider God himself as our ruler and the leader of our army. I warn you not to fight against the forces of God."

Jerry, however, had decided to trick the men of Judah and the army of Tab with an ambush, and had large forces slip around in back of the army of Tab so that they appeared to be surrounded.

When the soldiers of Judah saw there was an army in front of them as well as one behind them, they called on the Lord for help, and the priests sounded the trumpet, and the men of Judah charged with a great shout and the Lord was with them and discomfited the enemy, and delivered the enemy into the hands of Tab. There was a great slaughter on that day, but the children of Judah won because of their faith in God.

Tab and his army pursued Jerry and captured many cities. Jerry fled to the point of exhaustion and was never able to recover his strength. As a result, Jerry died. Tab reigned in a fine manner, but did not live very long.

Chap.
14

Tab's son Asa became king and he was a righteous man and he did right in the eyes of the Lord and the kingdom was quiet and prosperous for ten years. Asa had all the false idols removed from the land and he implored the people to turn to God and to obey the Lord's commandments. The Lord encouraged Asa and gave him rest from his enemies during these times.

During this period Asa introduced a public works program and began to rebuild cities and strengthen those that needed attention. Asa also organized a regular standing army that was well trained and it discouraged most plans for invasion.

There came from Egypt, however, a leader of an Ethiopian group whose name was Highly[1] and he attempted to invade Judah. As a result, Asa took his army and when they were near to the Ethiopian army Asa spoke loudly through a megaphone, praying for the benefit of all to hear,

"Lord God of hosts, it is of no consequence to you whether there are few or many on your side, we know your power, help us, O Lord, today, for we are depending on you as we battle this foreign multitude. You are surely the Lord God, and don't let a bunch of heathen men defeat you."

The Lord heard the prayer of Asa and the men of Judah had a mighty victory and pursued the defeated Ethiopians and completely routed them. While they were at it, they captured a great number of cattle and took much spoil and brought home captives and many valuables.

Chap.
15

Elmer, a prophet of the Lord, moved by the spirit of God, called on Asa and said to him, "You must remember that the Lord is with you as long as you are with him. If you search for God, you will find him, and if you forsake him then he will forsake you.

"Now Israel has gone a long time without the true God and worship has been sadly neglected. The people have tried to live

[1]Zerah

without law and without the leadership of the priests. Israel has always found, however, that when they do turn to God, then He is prepared to receive them and to help them.

In the midst of all these things there inevitably is trouble and confusion, and jealousy between nations, and enmity between cities, but you be strong and persist in the work of the Lord and your efforts will be rewarded."

After hearing these words, Asa was encouraged and he initiated a great clean-up campaign and conducted an impressive type of 'mission to the nation.'

As a result, the people began to renew their worship and to offer sacrifices to God and the people shouted and blew trumpets and made great promises re-affirming their faith. Their enthusiasm went to the point of decreeing the death penatly to anyone who did not serve the Lord and the entire tribe of Judah was joyful. As a result, the Lord gave the people rest from their enemies.

Asa even demoted his mother from being honorary queen because she was found with an idol which she had made and placed on the patio. Asa had the idol destroyed. Asa also returned to the house of God the precious vessels of gold and silver that had belonged to his father, and peace settled on the land and with the people.

Chap. 16

During the 36th year of the reign of Asa in Judah the neighboring king of Israel, called Baldy, decided to create some problems; so he built a blockade on the major access point to Judah and wouldn't let anybody come or go without his permission.

Asa then decided to buy some help in Syria and so he sent a large sum of money to Robinhood who was living in Damascus and entreated him to start a war with Baldy and relieve Asa of the problem he was having.

Robinhood liked the price and so he sent various ones from his merry band to start hacking away at the borders of Israel. Just as Asa thought, word of this came to Baldy and he quit trying to blockade Judah and Asa sent some of his men to tear down the blockade which Baldy had constructed.

Along came Criswell,[1] however, a fortune teller, and said to Asa, "You really blew it! You decided to rely on Robinhood, a pagan, to help you in your troubles and you should have come to the Lord God of Israel. What happened to your faith? It was certainly strong when you withstood the Ethiopians and relied on the Lord, and the Lord delivered you. Didn't you know that God wanders over the earth day and night keeping in close contact with all that goes on everywhere? Because of your lack of trust, you shall be plagued with

[1]Hanani

22

a bunch of petty little wars as long as you live."

Asa didn't like to hear this word at all and so he had Criswell put in jail and he also began to get tough with some of his workers, all because he had gotten up tight over being reprimanded.

Asa died not very long after this, probably from phlebitis. Because he had in general been a very good king he was given an exceedingly elaborate funeral, even putting flowers and all kinds of spices in the casket with the body prior to cremation.

After the death of Asa, Fatso,[1] the son of Asa, became king and he immediately began to develop the army and resources of Judah as a threat to Israel. Fatso did this by fortifying the more vulnerable cities and placing armed garrisons in strategic locations.

Now Fatso served the Lord and walked carefully in the commandments of God, and he did not turn to Baal, but followed the Lord of his father and also took David as an example. The Lord, therefore, strengthened Fatso and as a result people seeking his favor and protection brought him valuable gifts and he gained in honor and in wealth.

Fatso not only did away with the constantly recurring sin of the people in the weird rites conducted in the groves, but he actually sent missionaries to instruct the people in the ways of God. These wandering missionaries taught the law of the Lord. As a result, the fear of the Lord came upon all the bordering nations and they were afriad to attack Judah.

Even the people from Mississippi brought gifts and sent cattle and sheep to Fatso as a sign of friendship. Fatso became a very powerful ruler and began to build new towns and to promote business, but he kept the army in Jerusalem. In charge of the various divisions were mighty men of valour and skilled generals, like Stonewall Jackson,[2] Douglas MacArthur,[3] and Pershing.[4]

Fatso in time acquired more wealth and influence and he brought about a truce with Ahab by sending a daughter to marry into Ahab's family. Sometime after this Fatso visited Ahab and was entertained with bar-b-ques and special feasts.

Ahab succeeded in promoting Fatso to join him in a venture against the city of Buffalo and Fatso said to Ahab, "I am with you, and my people and my army are at your disposal."

Fatso, however, was a man of faith and he said to Ahab, "Let us ask of God about this matter."

As a result Ahab sent for the various ministers of all groups including his own fortune tellers and he said to them, "Shall we attack Buffalo?"

[1]Jehosophat   [2]Aduah   [3]Amasiah   [4]Elradaa

"Go, man, go," they said, "for God will deliver the enemy into your hands."

"Ahab, I'm not too certain about this group. I didn't recognize any of the ordained ministers or any of the genuine prophets of the Lord."

"Well, Fatso," said Ahab, "there is one, but I don't like him. In fact, he never says anything good to me. His name is Fosdick."[1]

"You are imagining all that, Ahab. Send for Fosdick."

As a result Ahab turned to the sergeant at arms and said, "Get Fosdick for me on the double."

The two kings then sat side by side on separate thrones and awaited the arrival of Fosdick. While they were waiting, some of the fortune tellers and public relations representatives of the sword manufacturers began to put on some acts and make like a pep rally.

One of these men, Big Bird,[2] had secured a piece of iron shaped like a steer's horns and began to shout "Hook 'em, horns! This is the way you will push the Buffalo crowd out of the stadium."

The other prophets and associates all supported this and kept yelling, "Go get 'em."

The messenger, in the meantime, came to Fosdick and said, "The king wants you to come and give him the word. Let me suggest that for a change you agree with him, as all the other representatives are for the invasion."

"I'll go with you, Mac," said Fosdick, "but I will speak only the truth as revealed to me by the Lord."

When Fosdick stood in front of Ahab, the king said to him, "Shall we shuffle off to Buffalo or not?"

"Go," said Fosdick, "and everything will work out fine."

"Now Fosdick, don't pull my leg. I want the truth," said Ahab.

"The truth is," said Fosdick, "that I see your forces scattered as sheep without a shepherd and as a result, having no leader, each one returned to his own place."

Ahab then turned to Fatso and said, "See, I told you that I would only get a bad word from Fosdick."

Fosdick then spoke again saying, "In my vision I also saw a committee before God and God asked who would induce Ahab to go against Buffalo and various suggestions came from the committee members. Finally, one of the committee turned to God and said, "I have a plan to entice him."

"I will go down on earth and put a lying spirit into the mouths of the so-called prophets and they shall encourage Ahab to go to Buffalo."

"As you can witness," continued Fosdick, "this is exactly what has happened."

[1]Micaiah   [2]Zedekiah

24

This infuriated Big Bird so much that he ran up and socked Fosdick on the jaw and as Fosdick was getting up Big Bird yelled, "Which committee member proposed that?"

"All right, Big Bird, you will learn the source of such when you are trying to hide and your conscience begins to work on you."

Then Ahab said, "Take this man Fosdick to the Federal Prison in Atlanta, put him on bread and water, and leave him in prison until I return in peace."

"If you return in peace, a winner, Ahab, then I'll admit I no longer speak for the Lord, but I want everyone here to be a witness to my prophecy."

In a few days Ahab and Fatso and their armies headed for Buffalo.

"I am going to disguise myself," said Ahab, "and I will dress as an ordinary soldier and you, Fatso, wear the king's robes and the symbols of authority."

In the meantime, the commander of the Syrian force from Buffalo had given his men the game plan saying, "Do not worry about ordinary soldiers, but go only to kill the king or one of the leaders, as this is the quickest way to victory."

As a result, when the armies approached each other the chariot captains of the Syrians spotted Fatso in the king's robes and made a direct attack on him.

Seeing this, good ole Fatso called forth loudly, "God save me!"

As a result, the Lord enabled Fatso to find an opening and to flee at full speed. The chariot men in pursuit soon recognized that Fatso was not the king for they knew King Ahab was slim; so they quit chasing Fatso.

In the meantime, one of the ordinary soldiers who was behind a rock shooting arrows in the air accidentally hit Ahab who was riding disguised in a chariot.

"I'm shot," yelled Ahab to the driver. "Get me out of here."

The battle lasted all day and Ahab remained in the chariot badly wounded, and died about sundown.

Chap.
19

Fatso returned to Jerusalem and was met there by a fortune teller who came to sound-off publicly and the fortune teller yelled, "You have been helping the ungodly, that worthless Ahab, and God doesn't like that kind of thing, and so he is probably irritated with you. Of course, you have some good points, for you have destroyed the idols in the groves and you yourself are God-fearing."

Fatso soon began to promote a revival of religious interest and he also began to consolidate the kingdom.

One of the things Fatso did was to appoint judges to rule for him in the various towns and villages and he instructed them when appointed, saying to each, "Remember, you are judging not for man's sake, but for God's. There is no iniquity with God; so you must be just and blameless in your decisions. You must make no distinction of persons and you must not accept gifts."

In Jerusalem Fatso organized the ministerial association and placed the ministers in charge of controversies, telling them to make their decisions faithfully and in accordance with the will of God.

Fatso said, "When cases are appealed to you, be certain and examine all the evidence and rule without prejudice as part of your responsibility. I have placed Peter Marshall[1] over you in all matters pertaining to God. Be courageous, and God will be with you."

Somehow or other a bunch of men from the Mafia[2] got with an armed group from Mississippi[3] and decided to join together in an attack on Fatso and his kingdom of Judah. When this was reported to Fatso he called a gathering of the leaders of Judah and as many people as wished to attend and he told them the news.

On this occasion, which was held in front of the main church in Jerusalem, Fatso called on the people to kneel while he publicly prayed to God.

"Lord God of our fathers," prayed Fatso, "You are the ruler in heaven and on earth, in your hands there resides all possible power. We know you are responsible for us being here in the first place. We also know that when we stand here in front of your church you will help us when we have a great need. You have always delivered us when we have prayed properly in this place.

"Now we are in a big jam. It is reported that a big army of men from Mississippi along with a large group of outlaws and Mafia boys are headed our way and they plan to move against us and here we are with our wives and children and we don't know how to handle a tough outfit like this."

The spirit of the Lord then moved in one member of the congregation, an outspoken type of fellow named Big Ben[4], who was an ordained priest, and he said, "Listen, everyone of you, and also the king, don't be afraid! The forthcoming encounter is not yours, but it is God's. Tomorrow when these armies approach go down to meet them, but be certain that God will get the job done, for these people are defying God. You won't even have to do much fighting, if any, yourselves. You can be spectators. You will witness the deliverance by God, for God will be with you."

Then Fatso and all the people bowed down to the Lord and worshipped.

Early in the morning the people arose and in a great throng proceeded out of the city and marched toward the area where they expected to see the visiting armies. The ministers of the churches led

[1]Amariah   [2]Ammon   [3]Moab   [4]Jehaziel

the march and led in the singing of the Battle Hymn of the Republic.

In the meantime, the Mafia group and the Mississippi combine had encountered a large group of Kentucky mountaineers and had begun to kill them in a bloody battle. Shortly the Mafia group and the Mississippi bunch began to fight among themselves over the spoil and a great slaughter took place, which resulted in such disorder that those who weren't dead or wounded soon went home. The men of Fatso then came and took all the spoil that had been gathered by the invading armies and considerable wealth was brought back to Jerusalem. In fact, it took three days to get all the cattle, jewelry, and miscellaneous valuables back to Jerusalem.

When all the spoil was safely stored or divided, then there was a big celebration, with much singing and dancing.

The word also went out that it didn't pay to try to attack a nation that was under God; so Fatso began to have another period of peace and quiet. Fatso continued to serve God as his father had done.

Sometime after this Fatso made a deal to join Thumbs, King of Israel, in buying a fleet of ships to make money, but Thumbs was an ungodly man and so one of the local ministers forecast the doom of the project. In fact, not too long after this a storm hit the fleet and most of the ships were blown into the rocks or cracked up by the storm.

Fatso died after a successful reign of some 35 years.

Spiro, the oldest son of Fatso, assumed the throne and he was 32 years old at the time, and mean. One of the first things that he did was to have all his brothers and half-brothers killed so there wouldn't be any mumbling in the family about who would make the best king.

Spiro had married a daughter of the wicked Ahab and she took after her father apparently and influenced Spiro to pursue the ways of evildoing.

Since Fatso had left each of his sons a nice nest egg, Spiro acquired considerable wealth when he had the other sons killed and absconded with their property.

The Lord did not destroy the wicked kingdom because of his promise to David, but he began to cause the people and their king a lot of trouble.

For one thing, the people of Alabama[1] revolted and to this day[2] they are not at ease under restraint or outside control. Georgia[3] also pulled out from under Spiro and revolted.

Spiro also instigated some heathen observances and encouraged the people in public and obnoxious orgies.

[1] Edom   [2] As of this writing   [3] Libnah

27

Not long after this the postman brought Spiro a letter and when he opened it he read as follows:

Dear Spiro:

The Lord God of David, your noble ancestor, has instructed me to tell you that you have refused to follow the good example of your father and your grandfather, but have followed the evil example of Ahab, even to slaying your own brothers, and so the Lord says that he will smite your people with a plague, and there will be a great outbreak of diarrhea and there will be an awful time for everybody.

Yours truly,

Elijah, the prophet.

About this same time also the Fascists became active again and troops from Ethiopia decided to stage a few raids and they came into the land of Judah and plundered, and took away the wives of Spiro and his sons, all except Jed[1] who was a teen-ager. Spiro was too sick to be moved and he was stricken with cancer and died in two years.

Spiro reigned for eight years and he died and no one mourned his passing. Spiro was buried in Jerusalem, but they did not bury him in the sepulchre of the kings.

Chap. 22

Apparently the kingdom was up for grabs for awhile, but by the time Jed was old enough to vote, the people made him king. Jed was under the influence of Reba, his mother, who was a wicked daughter of Ahab, and Jed followed the evil advice which she gave him.

For one thing, he joined Thumbs in making war unnecessarily against Billy the Kid and he was wounded at the battle of Buffalo. Jed returned to Jersey City and checked into the hospital there. Thumbs came to visit and Jay used this opportunity to get both of the potential threats to his revolution at one time, and he managed to kill them both at Jersey City, as the Lord had spoken against the descendants of Ahab.

When Reba learned of the death of Jed she went on a mad spree and had all the posible heirs to the throne murdered.

Florence,[2] a nurse of one of the boys, took the small boy Jap[3] and hid him so that he would not be killed. For six years the nurse kept him hidden in the church while Reba ruled the kingdom with an evil and violent hand.

Chap. 23

After Reba had been reigning wickedly for over seven years Matt Dillon[4] decided that it was time to act. Dillon was in charge of the tabernacle and head of all the priests and ministers.

First, Dillon quietly sent word to all members of the ministerial alliance[5] in the entire area and he assembled them secretly at the

[1]Jehoahaz   [2]Jehoshabeath   [3]Joash
[4]Jehoiada   [5]This has to be the trick of the week

church. Dillon explained to them that young Jap was now old enough to be at least a teen-age king. Dillon distributed many of the valuable weapons of the time of King David and arranged for separate groups to guard each entrance to the temple.

The plan was put into effect the first full worship Sunday and when the people gathered in the temple, there they saw Jap standing in the king's spot, flanked by the armed members of the ministerial alliance. Dillon explained to the people that Jap was the legitimate king and the people began to shout, "God save the King" and to sing, dance, and generally create a disturbance.

Reba heard all the shouting and singing at the palace and so she hurried down to the temple to see what was happening. When Reba arrived she was amazed to see Jap, who she thought was dead, standing in the king's place.

"Treason, treason," she yelled and began shredding her Kleenex.

Dillon then stepped forward and quietly said to the army captain present, "Seize this woman. Take her to the stables and kill her."

After this was done, Jap was escorted to the palace and officially declared king, with Dillon as his chief advisor.

Dillon made a brief speech declaring that the people would now serve the one true God and that they would again be God's people. Whereupon he led them in a mission to destroy the places for the worship of Baal, and the people tore down the idols and destroyed the pagan ritual images and for good measure killed the priest of Baal in charge of the idols.

Matt Dillon then re-organized the church and there was a big celebration, and the king was praised and all the people rejoiced and peace descended on the area.

Chap.
24

Jap was seven years old when he began to reign, but he operated largely on the advice of Matt Dillon. When Jap became older, Matt Dillon arranged for Jap to acquire two wives and as a result he began to have sons and daughters.

Jap then decided that the church building needed a lot of repairs as the maintenance program had not been doing very well. As a result, he instructed the members of the ministerial alliance to put on a fund-raising drive and secure money for the rebuilding program, and to do it in a hurry.

The priests did not get into action fast enough to suit Jap and so he sent for Matt Dillon and said, "Are you getting too old to be tough, Matt? Why haven't you been riding herd on the building fund drive? Don't you know that the sons of the wicked Reba had damaged the church and stolen the valuables from it? Anyway, I hereby command that offering plates be placed in the form of cedar chests and I want the people to bring their offerings and get with it on this program."

The leaders and the people responded to this command and brought offerings until the needed amount was secured. Then the work started on the remodeling and the excess of funds which continued to come in were used for special vessels and ornaments.

Not long after this Matt Dillon, who had become very old, died and was buried in the plot reserved for kings, because of all the great things he had done in Judah.

After the passing of Dillon, some of the leaders of the people decided to return to the worship of material things and to act selfishly, forgetting the Lord and the promises made to observe his commandments and to worship him. As a result, the Lord became angry with the people.

The Lord inspired some of the ministers to preach to the people concerning the error of their ways and their forsaking of God, but they would not listen.

Finally, the spirit of the Lord descended on Zeke, [1] the son of Matt Dillon, and he began to admonish the people and denounce their leaders. As a result, some of the leaders secured the consent of the king and then had Zeke stoned to death. Jap, the king, sinned in permitting this.

As punishment, the Lord supported a small band of Syrians in their move against the people of Judah. The Syrians destroyed the leaders of the people and made away with many captives and a lot of loot.

The Syrians also left Jap severely wounded and so some of the associates of Jap who didn't agree with the stoning of Zeke decided to finish Jap off, and so they killed him while he was lying in bed.

Following the death of Jap, his son Greg became king.

Greg[2] was 25 years old when he began to rule and he attempted to observe the commandments of the Lord, but he did not have the compassion of David or the understanding of Solomon. The first thing Greg did was to have all the men killed that had been involved in the plot against his father, though he did spare the lives of their children.

Greg also did a thorough job of organizing Judah, and he secured 100,000 mercenaries to handle any unpleasantness that might arise from his neighbors.

A prophet of the Lord then came to Greg and advised him against the use of mercenaries and told him that the Lord would fight his battles if necessary and furthermore the prophet suggested that if Greg led the mercenaries into battle he would get killed. As a

---

[1] Zechariah   [2] Amiziah

result, Greg disbanded the group and sent them home. The mercenaries left mad and bitter.

"What about the money I paid them?" asked Greg, "Is all that wasted?"

"The Lord will make it up to you, Greg," said the prophet, "but for the time being the money is blown."

Greg then led his own army of his own people to fight a troublesome group of guerrilla warfare fellows who were doing some hijacking and robbing in the north. Greg defeated them thoroughly and returned with a great deal of spoil.

In the meantime, the mercenaries decided to go it alone since they had all sharpened their swords anyway, and so they laid waste a city or two in West Texas and cleaned out the banks and jewelry stores.

Greg had captured some of the images of the gods of the guerrilla group and brought them home and began to worship them instead of going to the tabernacle to worship the Lord God of Israel.

It was not long after this that a prophet of the Lord called on Greg and said, "Why have you started the worship of strange gods? In the first place, they are the gods of the losers."

"Who asked you to speak to me?" snapped the king. "In fact, you should be executed for criticizing your great leader."

"All right, I'll quiet down, but I know God has decided to destroy you for your wickedness."

After this Greg began to worry and so he sent for Jap and suggested to the king of Israel that they have a big battle, winner take both kingdoms.

Jap wrote a note back to Greg saying:
Dear Greg:
There was a thorn which asked the cedar tree for his daughter in marriage, but a wild beast came and stomped the thorn into the ground.

In short, just because you've won one tiny little battle, don't get the big head or you'll get clobbered. You'd better stay at home and cool it.

Cordially yours,
Jap[1]

Greg was not influenced by the letter, however, and gathered his army and marched to battle Jap and the army of Israel.

As Jap had suggested, Greg and his army was defeated and Jap took his outfit even into Jerusalem and sacked it, taking away spoil and captives.

Greg was left with a poor and unhappy kingdom over which he reigned another 15 years. Some of the local men finally became dissatisfied with Greg and they had him killed, but they did give him a proper burial.

[1]Another Joash

The people then decided to make Wayne,[1] the 16 year old son of Greg, the king of Judah. Wayne had a long reign of 52 years and he attempted to do all that was right in the eyes of the Lord. As a result, the Lord blessed Wayne and encouraged him.

Wayne did a fine job of organizing the kingdom and he built fine defenses for the cities and the Lord prospered him as long as he was faithful.

Wayne was a very active king and provided good equipment for his soldiers. Wayne also sent the troops forth in separate bands at different times with adequate rest periods and so he kept his soldiers content and yet vigorous.

Wayne finally became so successful, however, in his later years that he became arrogant, even to the point of thinking that he did not need the priests of the Lord to conduct worship services. Wayne, in spite of the long standing commandment of God, usurped the place of the priest in the burning of incense and began to do this himself.

As a result of this action, Wayne was asked to leave the tabernacle and he was furious over this. In fact, he raised a burning incense holder aloft in defiance of the priests, and on this occasion he was struck with leprosy. Consequently, he was banned from polite society and spent the rest of his days in seclusion.

Don,[2] the son of Wayne, then became king and he attempted to do that which was right in the eyes of the Lord, but he would not go to church for fear of being struck with leprosy. As a result, the people of Judah did not take their worship seriously and soon became corrupt in their ways.

Don was a successful king, however, for he was conscientious himself and he faithfully adhered to the commandments of God as well as he understood how to do so.

Ahaz was made king after the death of his father and he was 20 years old at the time. Ahaz immediately pursued evil ways and turned his back on the ways and admonitions of the Lord. The principle sign of the wickedness of Ahaz was the worship of Baal and the encouragement of strange services to strange gods.

The anger of the Lord was kindled by this and as a result the Lord permitted the Syrians to smite Judah and to carry many people into captivity. Then later the remainder of the people were overcome by the warriors of Israel.

The Israelites acquired many captives and great spoil and returned to West Texas with loot and captives.

Then a prophet of the Lord, a man named O.J.[3], stood before

---

[1]Uzziah   [2]Jotham   [3]Oded

the assembly and said to them, "You have overdone this thing. The Lord was angry with Judah and therefore delivered the people into your hands, but you went forth in anger and overdid the violence bit. You are even now planning to make slaves of the people of Judah. This is too much. The Lord is angry. You should return the captives."

Then some of the local leaders who had not been drafted chimed in saying, "Yea, man. Don't bring all those people in here. We are already in dutch with the Lord and now this will make things a devil of a lot worse."

As a result, the warriors walked off and left all the captives standing around in front of the civic group.

The men who had opposed receiving the captives then organized a small Salvation Army unit and they clothed the captives and fed them. Those that could not walk were put on donkeys and the others were all escorted back to Jericho, a city of palm trees, where their own people could attend to them.

Shortly after this, Ahaz contacted some of the Assyrian leaders in the hopes of getting them to join him and help rebuild the reputation of Judah, for the Capone gang, the Mafia, even the Daltons were raiding Judah as the kingdom was almost defenseless.

The Assyrian group came to Ahaz and in spite of the protection money which Ahaz gave them, they did not do anything for Ahaz, for God was punishing him. Instead of repenting, Ahaz began to denounce God and praise the gods of the Assyrians. Ahaz even destroyed the worship places where the faithful still went to serve the Lord. Ahaz was such a wicked king that after he died he was not permitted burial in the regular cemetery.

Chap.
29

Now Hez,[1] the 25 year old son of Ahaz, became king and he immediately initiated one of the greatest reform movements of all time.

The first thing that he did was to repair all the churches of the living God and he restored all the properly ordained priests from the tribe of Levi.

Hez reminded them of the failures of the previous generation, and of the loss of life and wealth that had resulted and he spoke to the ministers saying, "It is in my heart and is my basic plan to make a covenant with the Lord God of Israel and seek to cool his anger to us. Do not be negligent of your duties as ministers of God, for you have been historically chosen by God to lead us in worship."

The ministers responded wonderfully to this pronouncement and they immediately began to put the churches in order and they reported later in the year to Hez that all things were ready for the

[1]Hezekiah

33

proper worship of God.

For the occasion of launching the great reform, Hez had a great feast prepared and many sacrifices to God made ready. There was a great deal of singing and eating and celebrating for it was a great day of revival and renewal in the church and therefore an appropriate time for rejoicing.

Hez and all the people rejoiced and it was a great occasion on the earth.

Chap.
30

Hez, the next year, sent messages to all the worshippers of the true God throughout all the land, to all the places in Israel and Judah and the surrounding country, and invited the true believers to all come to Jerusalem during Passover week.[1]

This occasion was a tremendous success and so many more people came than the tourist bureau estimated that there were major housing problems and not everyone could properly prepare in order to meet the various liturgical requirements. Hez encouraged everyone to participate in the passover and Hez prayed to the Lord that those who did not follow the book would be forgiven, and they were.

The Lord heard Hez, and he healed the people and he blessed the occasion. There was great joy in Jerusalem that rivalled even the days of David and of Solomon.

Chap.
31

Following this renewal of the church, the men of Israel went out and destroyed all the places of idol worship and tore down the temples of Baal.

The Lord blessed the people and they began to bring gifts to the church and they again began to tithe and worship God regularly. Hez entered with enthusiasm in the development of the kingdom and in the worship and service for God.

Chap.
32

A year or so after all this had been happening, Big Hun, an aggressive leader of the hosts of Assyria, decided to go on a big raid, acquiring land, cities, and captives.

When Hez realized that Big Hun would not wait too long before storming Jerusalem, he ordered a lot of work to be done. One thing, of course, was to strengthen all the fortifications of Jerusalem and he also constructed conduits to handle the flow of water so that the attacking Syrians would not have access to any stream.

Hez reorganized the army and then he called for a public meeting and he spoke to the army and to the people saying, "Do not be afraid of Big Hun and his great multitude. Be strong and courageous. Big Hun has an army of flab, but we have the Lord our God to fight our battles."

[1]Years later this week was the one during which Christ was crucified.

The people relaxed after this and were comforted.

Big Hun at the time was besieging another city but he sent messengers to Jerusalem to tell the people there that Jerusalem was next on the list.

The messengers brought some leaflets which they posted around Jerusalem and on the leaflets was a message from Big Hun saying,

"Has ole Hez talked you all into dying or starving to death? Has Hez not taken away all your gods but one, and you are putting all your eggs in one basket?

"Check my record! I have destroyed everything and everybody that got in my way. You're next!

"Don't count on any god. I've been destroying gods by the dozens; so why should you figure that your God will be any different?

"Don't let ole Hez out-talk you!

"Surrender while you can!"

The men who came and nailed up the posters and leaflets were even more boastful in their talk.

On top of all this, Big Hun sent a number of hecklers who stood outside the walls of Jerusalem and taunted the people, and they denounced the Lord God of Israel.

Hez and Isaiah, a mighty prophet of the Lord, prayed to God over the matter.

The Lord sent an angel through the camp of the Assyrians and they became violently ill, and many died, and the others began to return home in miserable shape.

In fact, when Big Hun returned home a couple of his cousins killed him and took command. There was not a single arrow shot over the wall into Jerusalem.

The Lord saved Hez and the people of Jerusalem and there was again great rejoicing in the city and the people brought many gifts into the house of the Lord.

Hez became sick for awhile but the Lord extended his time because of the plea of Hez. Hez lived to build many fine things around Jerusalem, and the water conduits were among the best of the things he did.

When Hez died he was buried in honor in the place with King David and Lurch,[1] his son, took his place as king.

Lurch was only 12 years old when he became king and naturally he had to have a little guidance for awhile. The guidance counselor was a baddie and Lurch pursued evil ways, forsook the church and the worship of God, and re-established idolatry and pagan worship.

Lurch even put an idol in the tabernacle at Jerusalem. The Lord

[1] Manasseh

sent prophets and ministers to teach and warn Lurch and the people but they did not heed their words.

As a result, the Lord permitted the Assyrians to invade and capture Lurch and many of the people. Lurch was bound with chains and carried captive into the city of Babylon.

While in captivity, Lurch repented and humbled himself before God, and remembered the God of his father Hez, and he prayed earnestly to the Lord.

The Lord heard the prayer of Lurch and provided a means of escape and Lurch repented and humbled himself before God, and remembered the God of his father Hez, and he prayed earnestly to the Lord.

Lurch immediately went to work and did a number of things, for he had learned a lot of lessons. One thing he did was to restore the altar in the church and he commanded the people to serve God. Lurch also began to fortify Jerusalem and all the cities of Judah and to train a proper and dedicated army.

The reform movement of Lurch was not as successful as that of his father, as many of the people began to worship God but also retained their relationship to the idols in the hills.

When Lurch died his son, Brad, who was 22 years old, assumed the throne and he immediately began a reign of wickedness, forsaking the worship and recognition of the Lord God of Israel.

Brad's rule was so evil that those working close to him murdered him. The people then had the murderers executed and placed Jose on the throne. At this time Jose was only eight years old and not quite ready to run a kingdom.

Chap.
34

Jose[1] was under good influences, however, and when he was 16 he began to study for himself the laws and statutes of God. By the time he was twenty, Jose initiated great reforms and started another renewal within the church.

Jose also began a great remodeling program of all the churches and many of the cities. In the process of remodeling, one of the priests found the original laws of Moses and these were returned to their proper place, but not until Jose had spent a great deal of time studying the law.

After reading the commandments in their original form, Jose was tremendously impressed and greatly penitent for the unfaithfulness of his people.

Jose was truly terrified that the wrath of God would consume them and he sent priests to seek the word of God. The priests returned from visiting a prophet who turned out to be a female, and also a coed in Jerusalem U.

[1]Josiah

36

The young lady told the priests to tell Jose that the Lord was indeed angry with the people for their years of neglect and that all the curses and punishments written by Moses would be placed into operation.

"However," the young lady said, "tell Jose that the Lord is pleased that he has humbled himself and that he has studied the word of God and the Lord therefore will allow Jose to complete his reign in peace and he will not punish the people during the lifetime of Jose."

Upon hearing this, Jose called for a day of compulsory chapel and he made a public confession of his own faith and urged the people to be faithful to the laws of God and to worship the one true God.

Jose kept the passover feast each year and he worked diligently on the reform movement and the Lord blessed his work and prospered him. The annual passover feast of Jose was the greatest of all, and the word was that this year was the biggest event of all and the people felt that there had never been in the past nor would there ever be in the future, passover feasts in the same class as those provided by Jose.

During the later years of Jose, a leader from Egypt brought a marauding group to fight some of the neighbors of Jose, primarily seeking captives and jewelry.

The leader of Egypt asked Jose to remain neutral as he did not wish to have any trouble with Judah and its army.

Jose agreed not to send his army, but Jose was a brave man and he felt he should support his neighbors and so he disguised himself and fought against the Egyptians. During the skirmish a stray arrow caught Jose in the chest and he was transferred to a Red Cross chariot and returned to Jerusalem where he died.

There was great mourning for the passing of Jose, and there were several days of singing and lamenting, and a whole new bunch of folk songs and ballads came into existence.

Jeremiah, the prophet, led the services of mourning.

Chap.
36

The people then declared that Jed, the son of Jose, was the new king. Jed did not last three months, as he was captured by the leader of the Egyptian forces and he was taken prisoner to Egypt.

The king of Egypt placed his own man on the throne of Judah and declared his name to be Sad Sack. Sad Sack did evil in the sight of the Lord, as might have been expected, and it was not long before Big Ned came down and captured Sad Sack and took over the kingdom.

Dru, who was eight years old, was made king and lasted only three months. In fact, he never really learned that he was a king.

Anyway, Big Ned sent for him and with the usual touch of

patronage put one of his half brothers in charge of the kingdom, a man named Harpo, who ruled the kingdom poorly and wickedly for 11 years.

Although Big Ned had made Harpo promise before God that he would be loyal, Harpo decided to rebel. The people continued to wander from God and to worship idols and the prophecy of Jeremiah, echoing the words of the years, warned the people of the wrath of God.

The people were then captured and taken into Babylon and surrounding areas as captives.

Cyrus, king of Persia, then made a famous decree and published abroad a great statement, saying, "The Lord God of heaven has given me control of all the kingdoms of the earth, and he wants me to rebuild his house in Jerusalem. Who is there among his people who will go and do this thing?"

EZRA

In order that the word of the prophet Jeremiah might be made valid, the Lord moved the spirit of Cyrus, the king of Persia, so that he made a proclamation and then had bulletins posted in public places throughout his kingdom saying, "The Lord God of Heaven has supported me in worldly conquests and He wishes me to acknowledge Him by having a church built again in Jerusalem. Who is there among the believers who will do this job?

The man who undertakes this job will have my support and I expect the people of the land to support him. Everywhere this man stops with his helpers en route to Jerusalem, I expect the people to make a free will offering of gold, silver, beasts, or whatever possessions may be available. This is the order of mine, and I am Cyrus, king of Persia."·

When this notice was posted many of the leaders from the tribes of Judah and Benjamin, and many of the priests descended from Levi, were encouraged and full of the spirit of God and they were determined to return to Jerusalem and re-build the house of the Lord. The people responded with gifts and Cyrus made several large contributions as well as giving the group some of the valuables originally stolen from Jerusalem. The total gifts from Cyrus were in excess of a million dollars.

The names of most of the families involved in this undertaking are listed in Chaper 2:1-63.

The total number was in excess of 42,000, not counting the servants, maids, folk singers, popcorn vendors and other miscellaneous travelers. There were 736 horses plus 245 mules and 435 camels as well as some donkeys.

This great caravan returned to their previous places of residence in the area of Jerusalem and after seven months of getting moved into new dwellings and adjustments, the people turned to the matter of the construction of the house of the Lord.

Even before the foundation of the church was poured, an altar was built in order that the people might worship God, for the people were afraid of the unfriendly natives who did not desire the return of the refugees to Jerusalem. The people felt that only God's blessing and help would protect them and so they worshipped God faithfully.

After two years time, under the strong leadership of J. Newton[1] the work on the church began with the laying of the foundation. It was a tremendous occasion when the foundation was laid and the singing and the shouting of the people could be heard for miles.

[1]Zerubbabel

There were many laughing and singing for great joy and there were some old timers crying because they could remember the days of the great and glorious temple of the early years.

The building of the temple was such a stimulating and exciting activity that the pagan natives came to J. Newton and asked to join in the project and be part of the great job of construction.

"You are not really interested in serving God," said Newton, "but you only wish to get in the business and be part of the success." Newton refused to employ any of these people and as a result they began a program of sabotage and the creation of many difficulties for those laboring.

The native objectors were employed agitators to relay distorted accounts to King Cyrus and to complain and criticize.

After Cyrus died Artie[1] became king of Persia and no sooner was he on the throne than the aggravated group around Jerusalem wrote a letter and had a bunch of people sign it.

The letter said: 'Dear King Artie: A great number of us who support you in your kingdom want you to know that the Jews that were sent here from your kingdom instead of building a church are building fortifications and preparing a big revolution. We want you to know that if Jerusalem is rebuilded you'll never get it again. These people are troublemakers, and we want you to do something about it.

Sincerely yours,

Nader[2] and others.'

The king then wrote an answer. Dear Nader:

The letter which you sent has been read and I have checked the history of Jerusalem and you are right in noting that it has a history of defects and revolts. The record also shows that there have been some great kings and rulers in Jerusalem and this is a dangerous thing.

You have my permission to put a stop to all the work being done, until you hear from me further.

Cordially yours,

Artie (The King)

This letter and the authority it represented brought the building program and the public works to a sudden halt, and the condition remained until a new king came to the throne in Persia, a man named Darius.

Again J. Newton, encouraged by the urging and preaching of Zig[3] and Zag[4], organized his work forces and started the restoration of the temple a second time. There was a new head of the puppet

---

[1] Artaxerxes   [2] Rehum   [3] Haggai   [4] Zechariah

government in the next county under a man named Spot[1] and he came to J. Newton and the workers and wanted to know if they had permission to build and who were they anyway.

Nothing came of this conversation and the work continued; so Spot wrote a letter to the new king, Darius.

Dear Darius:

Peace to you! As a matter of information, a bunch of us went into the province of Judah to do some sightseeing and we saw the Jews there rebuilding the temple to their God. The work is progressing rapidly and well.

We asked the leaders who gave them permission to do this work and they said they were working for the God of heaven as they were his servants.

They also said that the original temple had been built by one of their ancestors before Big Ned had come and carried the people away captive into Babylon. The leaders also reported that Cyrus, the Great, had commissioned the Jews to return and rebuild the temple and they even said that Cyrus had donated to the cause.

Since then J. Newton, who says he was sent by Cyrus, is still trying to rebuild the temple and he may succeed at the rate he is going.

Would you be kind enough to check the files and see if all this is true, and then tell us what in the devil to do about this problem.

Yours truly,

Spot and Friends.

Then Darious the king ordered one of the secretaries to check the files and some months later a scroll was found which had been misplaced in a Highway Department folder and the scroll contained a record of the order of Cyrus even to the point of including mention of the plans and specifications.

In the scroll was also an admonition to the neighboring county commissioners to help and not hinder the project, helping primarily by staying out of the way.

The penalty, mentioned in the scroll, for tampering with this order was fairly stiff, stating that any man who stood in the way of this project would be hung and his home be destroyed and turned into a garbage heap.

Darius then took the words of the scroll and the penalties and endorsed the writing and sent the order over his name back to Spot and his friends.

As a result, the elders continued to work and the temple was completed and the children of Israel dedicated the temple with great joy and with a great celebration.

[1]Tatnai

The priests organized proper worship services and the people joyfully worshipped God, and were grateful to God for their deliverance from captivity and for the fact that God had melted the heart of the king of Syria so that he supported the Jews in their rebuilding of the temple. The people kept the passover and observed the proper and appropriate services.

Chap. 7

The most influential spiritual leader in the entire program of re-building the temple was a man named Ezra, who was a scribe of the Lord, a dedicated church leader, and one who had been appointed by Artie to select as many volunteers as he could find among the captured Jews and to return to Jerusalem with them.

King Artie gave Ezra a letter of authority granting to Ezra the right to employ people and Artie also gave Ezra a letter of credit to the tax officers in the neighboring counties which amounted to something over $200,000.

King Artie in his letter and decree mentioned that he did not want any trouble with the God of Israel and that the commandments of the God of Israel were to be respected. King Artie also declared all the ministers to be tax exempt. Ezra was also instructed to establish a system of courts and to punish with death any Jew who failed to observe the laws of God.

Ezra then said, "Blessed is the Lord God of our fathers who has put such a plan and such thoughts into the mind of the king. Fortunate am I to be strengthened by the support of God and to be given this wonderful opportunity of leadership."

Chap. 8:1-20

List of the leaders who helped lead the people from Babylon.

As the end of the journey neared and the area was near where robber bands and thugs were apt to rob a caravan, Ezra debated what to do. Having proclaimed to the king the belief that God would protect his people, Ezra hated to ask for an armed escort. As a result, Ezra dispatched the ministers with the money to go on a different route to Jerusalem and Ezra went the regular way with the main body of refugees.

The Lord delivered the caravan safely to Jerusalem and also protected the priests as they made their way.

Ezra, a descendant of Aaron, rejoiced in the success of the trip and he praised God.

Chap. 9

After all this was accomplished, the temple restored, and the regular worship services of the people put back on a regular schedule, then Ezra began to receive unfavorable reports about the activities of the people of God. It was reliably told to Ezra that the people were chasing the foreign women, neglecting the church, and attending worship at pagan rites.

When Ezra heard these things and was convinced that they were true, he wept openly, tugged at his beard, and pulled on his own hair. Ezra then called for an assemblage of the people and Ezra sat in silent meditation until the people were gathered in his presence.

When the people were quiet and ready to listen, Ezra spread his hands in a sign of prayer and with all the people listening he said, "O God, I am ashamed and I blush to even pray to you for we are a sinful people who have done evil and who are acting wickedly. All of us have sinned and fallen far short of the expectations for the people of God.

In spite of all our wickedness, we have been given the great privilege of restoring your temple, or escaping the captivity in Babylon. We know that even in our bondage the Lord God did not forsake us and extended mercy to us, even to softening the heart of the Persian king.

What can we say? In the face of all your kindness we have forsaken your commandments. You told us not to mix with the strangers who served weird gods and observed shameful practices. Yet you have not punished us in proportion to our sin else we would have all been consumed and there would be no remnant left.

In the face of all of this we can only say that you are the essence of righteousness and understanding and we stand before you today acknowledging our sins and we are deeply ashamed."

Following this prayer the people wept and confessed aloud their sins.

Then a man named Wilson[1] arose and spoke to Ezra in the presence of the people and said, "You are right in all that you prayed. Let us now make a promise to God that we will do away with all the additional wives that we have added from among the pagans and to send all the children of these wives away to school in the mountains."

All the leaders agreed and a great pledge was made before God to do this very thing.

Ezra went into a period of mourning and fasting and meditation for he was grieved over the sins of the people and he was grieved for the pagan wives and children who were suddenly cast-offs with no visible means of support.

A great convention was then announced so that all the men who were not present at the first meeting could attend. It was a three day convention for repentance and the people at this convention also agreed to separate themselves from all their pagan attachments.

The practical matter of providing for the separation and all the arrangements were placed in the hands of the leaders and a time began of dealing with the problems, for there were many people and many arrangements to be made.

The leaders sat in council and the men of the nation were

[1] Shechaniah

43

required to report and to pay a fine for each pagan wife and to agree on plans for dismissing her. A list of some of the men who came before the council and declared themselves to have an excess number of wives from among the non-Jew population is recorded in the book of Ezra, chapter 10:20-43.

NEHEMIAH

My name is Nix[1] and this book is an account of my activities, thoughts, and prayers.

At the time of this writing I am recalling the circumstance of my being in good standing in Babylon with King Artie, as I was one of his favorite friends and consultants.

One day a fellow and a few of his friends came to me and said that he had recently been to Jerusalem and I asked them about the conditions of the remnant of the Jews that had escaped, and also about the city itself.

"There is nothing but bad news. The remnant of the Jews that are left are not doing well and also are being abused by their neighbors. The walls of Jerusalem are torn down, the gates to the city are burned, and there is nothing going for Jerusalem," said Hoby,[2] the leader.

When I heard this I just sat down and cried.[3] After sneezing and putting the Kleenex in a wastebasket, I then prayed to God saying, "O God, the keeper of the promises, yet full of mercy particularly for those who obey your commandments, hear my prayer, which I expect to repeat almost day and night because of my distress. First, I confess that all of us are sinners, our people have not observed your commandments. I have sinned and so have all my family. We have not been good, but corrupt.

You remember, God, that you told Moses that our people would be scattered if we were disobedient, but you also said that if we turn to you and begin to keep your commandments, and genuinely reform, you will enter the picture again, restore us to our land from widely scattered places. Remember, please, that these people are your redeemed people.

Grant, O Lord, mercy and guidance to me today and be with me tomorrow when I call on the king, for I will need courage."

Always when I was with the king I was a happy, pleasant person and this was one reason the king enjoyed having me around socially. On this occasion, however, I was intentionally sad and was truly down in the mouth.

"What's eating on you?" asked the king. "You're not sick; so you must be carrying some grief."

"I am sad, O King," I said, "because my hometown is in trouble. The place where I was reared and my parents are buried is in pitiful shape. The walls of the city have been torn down and even the

---

[1]Nehemiah   [2]Hanani
[3]Remember, this was men's fashion in those days.

gates have been burned to pieces."

"All right, Nix, what do you want me to do? Do you have a request?"

At this point I made a quick, silent prayer to God saying "help."

"If I'm in good standing, King, and you really want to help why don't you order me to go home and rebuild the city of my fathers," said Nix.

The queen was sitting by the king while this conversation took place and the king asked, "How long will the trip take and when will you return to Babylon?"

To make a long story short, the king decided to send me and I agreed to set a time for returning. The king gave me his Master Charge card to use for purchasing materials for the wall and for a house for me, and the Master Charge also was useful in showing the various government representatives the support of the king. The king also sent an armed escort to provide me safe conduct to Jerusalem.

Not everybody was happy with this arrangement as Sandy[1] and Toby[2] did not approve of any relief for the Jews and I was immediately made aware of this when I came to Jerusalem.

After being in Jerusalem three days without making myself known I decided to do some sightseeing or inspecting on the sly; so I selected two or three trustworthy men and went out in the middle of the night to see the city. I found the walls completely torn down as reported and also the gates burned to ashes. None of the fountains were working and there were no pools for watering animals, and I found all Jerusalem in ruins.

Now I had been careful not to let any of the rulers or leading citizens know of my plans or what I was doing in town, but now I was ready to call a meeting, which I did.

When I had a good, representative group assembled for a town meeting I made a stirring talk to them, telling them that I was inspired of God, authorized by the king, and determined to lead the people in the restoration of Jerusalem.

As a result, a great enthusiasm for the project arose and the people shouted, "We will build the wall."

Sandy and Toby heard about this and they were red hot about it and began to make fun of the project. In fact, they began to taunt those of us interested and even intimated we were rebelling against the king.

"God will help us," I told them, "for we are servants of God. We will arise and build, but you lip artists will do nothing and you will leave no memorial for yourselves."

---

[1] Sanballat   [2] Tobiah

Everybody seemed interested in getting into the act. A group of ministers, for instance, started rebuilding the old sheep gate and various groups began to restore areas or sections close to them or in which they were particularly interested. The King James version of the Bible lists all the names of the people and families involved.

Sandy and Toby shortly heard news of the building of the wall and the remodeling of the old business places and they got real hot about the matter.

In fact, Sandy stood in front of a band of his soldiers and shouted, "What goes with these feeble Jews? Do they think they can protect themselves with a wall? Do they think that something can be accomplished by some magic prayer, or do they really have the idea that they can build something from the pile of rubbish and ashes that was Jerusalem?"

Then Toby put in his two-bits worth saying, "Yeah, man, some wall they'll build from that rubbish. If a fox crawls on it during the night it will tumble down."

Then I prayed to God upon hearing this and said, "We are despised, O Lord, in the eyes of these strangers. Do something about it. Turn the reproach back onto them. Surely they have provoked you as well as those of us who are building."

As a result, the workers became even more interested in building and the wall was soon joined all around the city.

When Sandy, Toby, and their associates learned that the wall was joined together and that even the personal openings were being closed and fortified, the gang decided to band together and fight against Jerusalem and prevent any further accomplishment.

As a result, we set watches day and night and the long hours and constant need for alertness began to weary the builders and they became discouraged.

Also rumors began to spread among the workers to the effect that their enemies would come into the city quietly and begin to kill the Jews one by one. Word also came that the workers would be mugged and killed on the way home at evening time or on the way to work early in the morning.

Because of all of this I stationed special guards as lookouts and I saw that every man and every family was armed and I told the people not to be afraid. I reminded them that God was with them and that God would support them as they fought for their homes, their families, and their friends.

When the neighboring gangs heard of all the preparations for resistance they became discouraged and the workers returned to full time labor on the walls.

To continue the precautions, however, I decided to let half the workers all the time stand by as an armed guard, with spears, shields, and big clubs, and this was impressive and very comforting to the laboring group. Every worker carried a knife or a sword on a belt around his waist and the whole look was formidable.

As a further exercise of care I announced that I would have trumpets placed at regular intervals around the wall and if the enemy appears at one place the trumpet will be blown and our forces will converge on the spot.

Furthermore, I ordered the men to no longer reside outside the walls of the city, but to stay in motels, apartments, tents, or private homes so that going and coming to and from work would be within the security as established.

As for myself, my associates as leaders, and our special administrative helpers, we never took off our clothes during this time except to take a bath.

Chap.
5

Everything went well for awhile until it developed that some of the greedy-minded among the Jews began to take advantage of the situation. Certain motel owners raised their rates, and food costs arose for those supplying the needs of their families outside the city. The bankers also raised the interest rates, and many of the workers had had to mortgage their lands and vineyards in order to pay the taxes due to the king.

In fact, many of the workers claimed that their children were being used as servants because of their debts and that their own Jewish businessmen were responsible.

When I heard all this I really blew my cool. After thinking the matter over carefully, however, I called a meeting of the rulers, the bankers, and Chamber of Commerce group and I spoke to them saying, "You are taking advantage of your friends and neighbors. I join them in being against you completely for this.

"What do you think you're doing? After we have redeemed the captives from Babylon you are making bondsmen of them yourselves. Will you sell your brothers? Will we have to buy brothers from brothers?"

There was nothing they could say to this forthright talk and they had no answer to the charges.

Then I decided to add a few more things to my speech saying, "Don't you fear God? You are acting like the heathen who is our enemy. Did it ever occur to you that I could have been getting a rake-off as well as some of the foremen, but we haven't. Now, shame on you.

"Furthermore, I urgently request you to restore what you have taken. Do it today! Return the mortgages and free the bonded servants and as much of the money, corn, wine, and oil that was an excessive charge."

The men did as I suggested. Then I called the ministers of the churches together and made a promise of all this in their presence. Then I took the apron which I had on and shook the cookie crumbs out in every direction saying, "May God be a witness, and may God do to any man that fails in his promise as I have done to the cookie crumbs."

Then the people who were witnesses shouted "Amen!" Then the people praised God.

All of this work on the wall took 12 years and even though I was the governor appointed by King Artie I did not eat the fancy food allowed a governor, nor did I collect anything from the people for myself, for I respected God and observed his commandments.

I didn't even buy any land although I knew that when we finished the wall the values would rise, but it was not for profit that I was acting as governor.[1]

Not only did I observe such ethics, but the 150 members of my administrative staff also followed my example.

Then I prayed to God and said, "O Lord, think well of me for my actions and bless all that I have done for the people."

Ole Sandy and Toby began to plot again, and this time they brought Jocko,[2] an Arab terrorist, into the picture. As a result of the meeting they sent a messenger to me at Jerusalem suggesting that we have a meeting at Joe's Bar and Grill about 10 miles out on the road.

I sent a messenger back to them saying that I was too busy with the work of rebuilding and fortifying Jerusalem and there was no profit in stopping a full day just for some beer and a grilled cheese sandwich. I knew, of course, that their invitation was just a plot to get me killed.

This didn't seem to discourage Sandy and his henchmen as they sent messengers four times with the same request, and each time I sent the same answer.

Finally Sandy wrote me a letter and had it delivered by hand. The letter stated that the word was being spread that I was plotting a revolution and that the building of the wall was to protect me when I declared myself king.

It is also reported, the letter said, that you have contracted with a P.R. firm to glorify your name, even to the point of having the ministers preach an occasional sermon supporting all that you do. It would be unfortunate for you, the letter said, if the king heard about this; so Sandy suggested a private meeting.

I then wrote a letter in reply.

Dear Sandy:
Thanks   for   your   letter,   but   you   are   completely

---

[1] A governor or so like this today would be a blessing.
[2] Geshenn

49

misinformed or you've made up a bunch of lies for your own purposes.

Yours truly,

N-

After this the word came that the mugging and sneak attacks would be renewed and many of our people became afraid again. Then I prayed again for strength from God.

One of the local leaders felt we should have an emergency meeting and that it should be held in the temple and that the doors there should be bolted and guards stationed as a security measure.

Then I said, "Am I the type that runs at every sign of danger? What man in a position as governor such as I am would go into the temple to save his life and escape danger? I will not go!"

It turned out that all this had been contrived as a threat sponsored by a bribe from the Sandy camp. The idea was to make me look bad before the people and to sin by worrying about God's ability to protect me.

"O God," I prayed, "Think about what Sandy and Toby and a few irresponsible ministers have been doing and fix them for me, Amen."

As a result the wall was completed in every detail and when all our enemies heard of it and the non-Jews around us saw what had been done, they were greatly impressed and they understood that all this was the work of God.

Not everything was rosy, however. There were many nobles who didn't care for me and the methods of fair business practice that I enforced, and they wrote letters frequently to Toby, who had married into a Jewish family, and they then expounded to me on the greatness of Toby and tried to intimidate me. Even Toby wrote me a threatening letter or two, which I just put in file 13.

Chap.
7

Now when everything was completed, even the doors properly hung, there were appointed the proper people for supervision, the singers named for the church choirs, and the ministers given their assignments.

Then I gave my brothers Bobby[1] and Teddy[2] complete charge of the palace and all Jerusalem and I instructed them saying,[3] "Don't open the gates of the city until the sun is well up, and even when the gates are closed keep them guarded. Furthermore, train every man to be alert as a watchman at his own home or business."

At this time, the city was large but there were not too many people living within the walls and re-building of homes was just beginning.

God then moved me to make a record of the families and the

---

[1]Hanani   [2]Hananiah   [3]I still don't care for nepotism.

names of the people who would be called "charter members of the new Jerusalem."

I did this and they may be found recorded in Nehemiah 7:6-65.

There were numbered 42,360 not counting servants, horses, and the 245 members of the Jerusalem Singers Association. From all these were received offerings to pay for the materials used in reconstruction and for the work of the church.

On one occasion, most of the people gathered in a great assemblage on the street and Ezra, the scribe, who was responsible for keeping the books of law, arose and read to the people from the book of laws compiled by Moses.

Ezra started reading at 9 a.m. and read straight through to twelve noon. Some people didn't stay for the whole thing, but many did. There were a number of prominent people who were on the speakers platform, and none of them could leave, and they heard all the law.

At the end of the reading I stood up and announced that this day was to be considered a holy day and that the meeting counted as attending church. Also I told the people to leave the meeting in a joyful frame of mind, thankful to God, and to go forth and do something in God's name for someone else. Take food to someone who is in need, and let the joy of the Lord be your strength.

That evening there were a whole bunch of private parties and social gatherings.

On the second day the ministers began to review the reading of the law of Moses and they arranged for the institution of the seventh year of forgiveness to be reviewed, and for the establishment of booths for people by families and by groups for merchandising, as was the way of the wilderness. The law was periodically read for the next seven days and at the end of the eighth day the celebration ended.

Toward the end of the month a day was set aside for special service and at this time the children of Israel stood apart from all the non-Jews and they spent part of their time worshipping God and part of the time confessing their sins, and then they also used a good bit of time confessing the sins of their fathers and grandfathers.[1]

At the end of the service the ministers began to bless God and to praise him, and each doing a part, they recounted the summary of God's relationship with the people.

"There is only God, the one God," the summary started, "and the one God made the heavens and the earth and all things everywhere, and the whole host of heaven worshipped God.

[1] This came real easy

"God chose Abe and brought him from Palm Springs and gave him the land of Canaan, and Abe was faithful to God. As a result, God promised to establish the lineage of Abe as his people. God heard his people when they were in bondage in Egypt, and he heard their cry from the Red Sea, and after impressing Pharoah with signs and wonders, God opened the Red Sea and destroyed the army of Pharoah as a stone disappears in deep water.

"God also provided food, and meat, and water for his people, and in spite of all of this the early day Jews of that time were stiff-necked and hard-hearted.

"When the people made a golden calf and went wild with a big party, God forgave them and sustained them for the forty years necessary in the wilderness, as a penalty and a preparation for entering the promised land.

"God gave the Jews kingdoms, and fields, and vineyards, and fruit trees, and they were disobedient again, this time in a day of prosperity. Ultimately this led to the downfall of the people and the Jews fell to their enemies and were scattered abroad, and then again the Lord heard the cry of his people and a remnant was restored, and we are that remnant, again in the holy city of Jerusalem.

"We are servants today in our own land, under a stranger king who lives a long way from here, and we are under a foreign jurisdiction. We, therefore, make a great promise, to which we all ascribe.

"We agree to walk in God's law and to observe the commandments of the Lord our God.

"We will not intermarry nor allow our children to intermarry to those who do not serve the one true God.

"We will not conduct our regular business practices of buying and selling on the Sabbath day and we will observe the seventh year of repentance and forgiveness of indebtedness.

"We will bring a proper offering to God on a regular basis as well as special gifts for special occasions.

"We will agree to the system of drawing names out of the hat for those who will do the gathering of wood and the management of chores in connection with the work of the church.

"We agree to tithe, and this tithe shall be ten percent and it is to be paid before we do anything else with our profit.

"We agree to support the ministers, and the ministers are to be responsible for the conducting of the worship services."

Chap.
11

After this was presented as a covenant before God, it was explained that one out of every ten families would be required to live within the walls of Jerusalem and the families were selected by lot and the people blessed particularly those families who volunteered to do this service.

A list of these volunteers is recorded in Nehemiah 11:3-12:26.

I failed to mention earlier that in the dedication of the wall of Jerusalem I divided the leaders in two great companies; so that there would be thank expressions properly presented on all portions of the wall; so everyone would be a part of the celebration. I led in all the thanksgiving along with the other rulers and it was a great occasion.

Another thing that happened that day was that in the reading of the law mention was made of those particular groups that had failed to help the children of God in the wilderness and so a separation from these people was decreed.

This brought to my mind the fact that when I came to Jerusalem from Babylon I found that the Jewish leadership was in decay, and I had Toby thrown out on his ear, and I brought the ministers back into action, and I helped reorganize and renew the church.

There was great sin among the people when I first came to Jerusalem. I found Jews working in the winepress on the Sabbath day, and I testified against them, and against the men of Boston[1] who brought fish for sale on Sunday. I closed the gates of the city on Sunday and made the Blue Law work. I threatened to physically throw off the wall any merchants who tried to sell on Sunday by climbing the wall.

I recall the horrors of those early days when I saw so many of our young people marrying into anti-godly families and having families that couldn't speak Hebrew or read the word of God.

I gave them a fit. I admonished them, I pulled some of them by the hair, and I knocked some of them in the head.[2] One of the head ministers had a son who married an anti-godly woman and I chased him out of town.

My prayer is that God remember this, remember the evil that these people have done, and remember the offerings that I have brought and all the good things that I have done.

[1] Tyre   [2] A real active evangelist

There was a king by the name of Aha[1] who ruled an extensive kingdom, covering an area from India to Ethiopia, comprising 127 satellite nations.

During the third year of his reign, Aha staged a huge celebration, bringing representatives from all over his widespread domain to behold his glory, and to be entertained. Aha exhibited his riches in the form of beautiful tapestries, reclining couches of red, white, blue, and black marble, as well as beautiful linens, with some bedspreads made of fine woven gold and silver threads.

After the distinguished guests had spent many days viewing these wonders, Aha provided a seven day feast period. Royal wine was served in abundance in gold cups, although the drinking was done by law, which simply provided for abstainers, as the law merely stated that a person could not be compelled to drink.

At the same time the queen, an exceedingly beautiful lady called Vash[2] was entertaining all the wives and girl friends in a similar manner.

By the seventh day of this, many of the men and certainly the king were overly merry because of the wine and the king began to brag about the beauty of his queen, and decided to send for her in order that all the princes and the people could admire her beauty. The king therefore appointed a committee of seven men to go to the queen's palace and bring her for display. The queen had been belting a few herself and certainly did not want to appear without getting a shampoo and a set; so she refused to come.

When the committee returned and reported that the queen had rejected the order of the king there was great consternation. The king asked his advisors for counsel. The chief aide of the king, a man named Mem[3], spoke eloquently on the subject.

"The queen has not only wronged the king, but the whole kingdom, every prince and every married man from India to Ethiopia has been wronged. For certainly this great act of disobedience will be noised abroad unto all women and we will have a woman's lib movement. In fact, the ladies of Persia and Media shall refuse to obey their husbands and their boy friends, and all men shall be held in contempt."

There was much murmured agreement in the assemblage; so old Mem continued, "I therefore recommend that the queen be displaced, that this be an irrevocable ruling, and that another lady be chosen to take her place." The motion apparently passed unanimously, and so the king sent letters to all the provinces, with bulletins to be placed in all public places ordering every man to rule

[1]Ahasuerus   [2]Vashti   [3]Memucan

Some few days later, after Aha had sobered up and recalled the banishing of Vash, he asked his advisors for a plan to select a new queen.

The plan proposed was very simple, as it only called for a beauty contest. The idea was for each province to select its own beauty and send her to the palace at Shushan and there all of the finalists would be carefully screened and a winner selected by the king. This meant that every province had a chance to provide the girl who would be Miss Syria and then the Queen of the land.

This action was initiated and some months later all the contestants were assembled at Shushan and put under the care of Birt Perks[2], the Dean of Women.

Now it so happened at this time that there was a Jew named Mort[3] who had been captured by a previous king, and who had brought with him into captivity his much younger cousin, and since she was an orphan, Mort had reared her as his own daughter. Esther turned out to be an exceedingly beautiful young lady.

Esther won the local beauty contest very easily and was taken to the palace where she immediately made a big hit with Perks; so that he gave her the best room in the women's building, and also helped her with her cosmetic selections. Esther had been careful, however, not to let it be known that she was Jewish, and brought to the area as a captive.

Now Mort, who apparently did not have regular employment, checked daily on Esther and her progress and hung around outside of the palace a great deal, and often sent messages to Esther.

Each finalist spent one night with the king and then was referred to the girls' dormitory for boarding and availability should the king decide to send for one of the girls for an additional interview. Esther's time to be with the king came in October, over three years after the contest started. Esther obtained great favor with the king and he was so completely delighted and entranced with Esther that he assembled all the finalists and proclaimed Esther the Queen and placed the crown on her head and published the news in all the provinces.

Mort, for lack of anything else to do, always sat outside the palace gate and kept in touch with the news and gossip. Mort learned one day that Black John[4] and Mike the Mouse[5] were planning to assassinate the king; so Mort slipped the word to Esther, who told the king, giving credit to Mort. The king investigated the matter and learned that the report was true and he caused the two hoods to be

[1]I cannot help but wonder about the percent of compliance.

[2]Hegai   [3]Mordecai   [4]Bigthan   [5]Teresh

arrested and hung. The matter was recorded in the king's diary which his secretary faithfully kept.

Time marched along and the king promoted a man named Heyman to be the general manager of the kingdom and relieve Aha of most of his duties; so he could have more time for play. Since Heyman was quite an egotist, the servants and others around the palace began to bow to him, as this pleased Heyman very much.

Mort, however, who was always hanging around, would not bow or reverence Heyman, and the others thought it looked bad for them to be bowing and Mort, a self-confessed Jew, to remain aloof; so they reported Mort.

Heyman was infuriated to learn that he was not properly revered by a Jew, but he felt it beneath his dignity to deal with the matter personally. Heyman determined to use an indirect approach.

When in counsel with the king one day, Heyman said, "There is a people scattered abroad throughout the land that are known as Jews. These people do not obey the king's laws and their own laws are different from ours. I propose that we set aside one day, the 13th of December, and let it be an open season on these people. On this day let all the real natives destroy, kill, or cause to perish all Jews, both young and old, women and children, and to rob them of their possessions. From this day I will collect enough to pay $100,000 into the king's treasury, and we need the money."

The king then published the decree, and sent it to all the provinces, and had it posted on all public bulletin boards, using the words of Heyman. The people were perplexed and most of them wondered what brought on this nutty announcement.

Now when Mort read the bulletin he howled like a stuck pig for he knew what was back of it and he knew that the whole plan was simply a way of legally getting him killed. Mort put on his hippie type clothes as an expression of mourning and since such clothes could not be worn around the king's gate, Mort began hanging around only at night.

There was also great mourning among the Jews throughout the provinces as there seemed to be no way of escape. The Jews, as captives, had no means of resistance and sadness was everywhere.

Esther was told of Mort's hippie clothing and she sent a new suit to Mort to cheer him up, but he refused to wear it and continued to lament. Esther then sent messengers to Mort to learn of the details and Mort relayed the whole business, his refusal to bow, the planned vengeance of Heyman, the plight of the Jews. Mort urged that Esther go immediately to King Aha and make a plea for some help.

Esther sent a message then to Mort reminding him of the peculiar office arrangement devised by Aha to keep down the number of visitors. The arrangement was that the king sat on his throne and unless you had been previously invited by the king, you took great risk in appearing. If, for instance, you appeared and the king was feeling good and wanted to see you, he would hold forth the golden sceptre, but if he didn't, you were immediately executed, without further trial.

The reply of Mort to Esther was some truly great wisdom. Mort said, "In the first place, you are a Jew, and for all you know someone in the palace might take the notion to kill you. Ultimately, of course, God will himself deliver his people, but you and I might go in this purge. Speak up! Go to the king. How do you know but what you were born for such a time as this?"

Esther replied by messenger saying, "I will go to the king, and if I perish, I perish, but pray for me, and ask all of God's people everywhere to fast and pray for me."

Three days later Esther put on her best purple outfit, went into the king's house and stood in the inner court, looking her very, very best. The king looked upon her and held out the golden sceptre and Esther advanced and touched the top of the sceptre, as the custom was.

Then the king said, "What is your request, Esther? I'll give you about anything you want."

"I have come to invite you to dinner, and I would like for you to bring Big Cheese Heyman with you."

"Send for Heyman," said the king, "and we will dine with Esther."

During the cocktail time before eating, Aha asked Esther further about her request as he knew that something was behind the entertainment approach. Esther told Aha that she would tell him the next night, if he and Heyman would come again for dinner.

The next day found Heyman beside himself with joy, until he noticed Mort at the gate and Mort did not so much as look up when Heyman paraded. When Heyman came home later in the day, however, he assembled some of his friends, his wife and family and he spoke in his bombastic fashion saying, "I've got it made! I am rich, I have many children, I have been promoted by the king, and I am the only man who has ever had dinner as the guest of the queen in company with the king and eaten a meal prepared by the hands of the queen. What's more, I'm invited again tomorrow. Yet as long as old Mort sits at the gate, my ulcers act up and I'm despondent."

Then some of the friends of Heyman suggested that he build a gallows and he prepared to hang Mort in the palace yard on the morning of December 13. The idea excited Heyman so much that he caused a gallows 50 ft. tall to be erected the first thing the next morning.

For some reason, however, the king had insomnia that night and so he decided to catch up on back matters and read the diary of the kingdom for the last few preceding months. In reading this he was refreshed in mind about Mort saving his life by reporting the assassins.

The next morning the king asked his servants what had been done to honor Mort, the man who had saved the king's life. The servants told him that nothing had been done.

"Where is Heyman?" asked the king.

"He is standing in the courtyard," was the reply.

"Get him," said the king.

When Heyman appeared, the king said, "What would be a good thing to do for someone that I would like to honor?"

Now Heyman, of course, thought the king had Heyman in mind; so he replied, "I would suggest that the royal apparel that the king normally wears be brought, and the king's horse, and the king's crown, and let the man to be honored put on the king's apparel and ride the king's horse down Main Street, and have an announcer with a megaphone going in front saying, 'The king is honoring this man.'"

Then the king said to Heyman, "Make haste and do as you suggested, and get Mort the Jew and array him, and put him on my horse, and don't omit a single detail."

When this had been done, Heyman returned to his home mourning, with his hat pulled way down on his head. After telling this to his friends and his wife, the gathered company sympathized with Heyman, but expressed the belief that the signs indicated the fall of Heyman. About this time the escort came to take Heyman to dinner again with the queen.

Again during the drinking time before the meal the king asked Esther, "What is your big petition? Just name it, and I'll do it."

Esther then said, "If it please the king, spare my life and that of my people." Esther explained about the open season and the bad day of December 13th.

The king said, "Who is responsible for this terrible thing?"

Heyman was terrified. The king went into the garden to think over what he had heard and Heyman prostrated himself by the couch on which Esther was reclining and was begging her for mercy. When the king suddenly returned, he saw Heyman kneeling by Esther and thought that he was making a pass at her. The king shouted for the bodyguards who immediately put the clamps on Heyman.

Harry,[1] one of the bodyguards, suggested that since there was already a gallows just finished in the courtyard that it could be used to hang Heyman; so they hanged Heyman on the high gallows.

---

[1] Harbonah

As an expression of appreciation, and by authority of the king, Aha then cancelled Heyman's will and gave all Heyman's property to Esther. The king gave Mort one of his rings and Esther made Mort the overseer of all Heyman's property.

Esther came again in a few days to the king and when he held forth the golden sceptre, she advanced and asked the king to do something about Dark Monday, December 13.

"I know," Esther said, "that you cannot change an irrevocable law of the Medes and the Persians, but why not pass a new law, giving the Jews on the same day the right to defend themselves."

"Brilliant idea," said the king. "Let the writers prepare a letter and a law, let it be put on all the bulletin boards, and spread abroad through all the provinces, taking the message by horseback, by riders on mules and camels, and young dromedaries and let the law and letter say, 'The king grants to the Jews to gather themselves together, to stand for their lives, to destroy, to slay, to cause to perish anybody who assaults, both little ones and women, and to take any spoil they can."

And so it was done and it was published at Shushan, the palace. Mort left the palace in a flashy blue and white suit and a cloak of fine purple linen, and the city rejoiced and the Jews had gladness, and joy, and were respected by the people. The Jews throughout the provinces rejoiced and had feasts and many of the people of the land became Jews, figuring that if you can't beat them, join them.

As the day approached, the Jews began to have some pep rallies, to gather themselves together, and organize for resistance. Most of the public officials began to act favorably toward the Jews because of the high position of Mort, who was in high standing with the king and managing most government contracts. When the day came, there was much fighting but not as much as anticipated. There were some 500 killed in the capitol. The queen petitioned the king the next day to have the ten sons of Heyman hung and he gladly obliged. There were reported some 75,000 persons slain throughout the entire area from India to Ethiopia. The days following the one big day of fighting were days of feasting and celebration. This time became a national holiday by the decree of Mort and he published this information throughout all the provinces.

A name was given to the holiday, the name of Purim, because the day was picked by lot, and the word for lot was Pur. The two days of feasting following the December 13 uproar were therefore made national holidays.

To make the whole matter official, Esther wrote a letter to the same effect.

There is much recorded about King Aha, his taxes upon the

land, and upon the isles of the sea, and many versions of his power and also his declarations about the greatness of Mort, for Mort was second only to the king. It was noted that Mort was accepted by the multitude of his brethren and that he worked seeking wealth for his people and he spoke words of peace to all his followers and descendants.

JOB

There was a man from Utah[1] named Job and he was a God-fearing, righteous man, law-abiding and opposed to evil.

Everything in connection with him seemed to be ideal, and he represented the American dream. Job was rich, he had more sons than daughters, plenty of servants, a huge ranch, good health, friends who didn't live too close, and his only worry seemed to be that his children would not follow exactly in his footsteps.

When Job was at his peak there appeared one day before the Lord in heaven the spirit of evil, old Satan, or the Doubter, and told the Lord that he had been traveling on earth.

"Did you see my man Job, in Utah?" asked God. "Job makes me glad that I created man."

"Sure I saw him," said Satan, "and he is mighty righteous but who wouldn't be at the price he's getting? You have put him in the lap of luxury so why shouldn't he worship you. You start causing him trouble, though, and he'll quit you quick."

"I think his faith is sound, but to prove it, I will let you bother him. You can do anything you want to do but you are not to touch him personally. No arthritis, backache or the like," said the Lord.

Shortly after this one day Job was having dinner. During the meal a messenger came bursting into the room all out of breath and shouted, "Job, there's big trouble. The West Side gang[2] attacked the ranch, killed all the ranch hands but me and then drove all the livestock away with a well run rustling job."

No sooner had he finished than another runner came and said, "Job, there's big trouble. I've just come from the sheep ranch and lightning has struck the sheep and killed the shepherds. I'm the only one left."

In a few minutes another messenger came charging in and yelled, "Job, the camel corps is gone. The Pittsburgh Pirates[3] divided into three teams and came pouring down on us, captured all the camels and killed all the helpers except me, and I'm scared half to death."

Before Job could absorb all the news another messenger appeared and said, "Job, I've got bad news for you. All your sons and daughters were having dinner together enjoying wild turkey when a tornado came and struck the house, tore it down, and killed all your sons. In fact, I'm the only survivor."

Then Job went through the proper procedure of mourning, which in his day was to shave his head and tear his clothes to shreds. Then Job worshipped God and prayed, saying, "I was born naked and

[1] Uz   [2] Sabeans   [3] Chaldeans

61

I guess I'll die naked. I was born broke, and I guess I'll die broke. Sometimes the Lord gives, sometimes he takes away, but blessed is the name of the Lord."

In no way did Job blame God or refute him.

Sometime after this the various angels began reporting to God and old Satan came along with the crowd and God said to Satan, "What are you doing here?"

"I've been traveling around on your earth," said Satan.

"What did you think of my man Job?" asked the Lord. "Didn't you notice that he stood fast under adversity and did not fold or turn against his creator?"

"Yeah, man, old Job is pretty tough and a good one, but man is basically selfish and he can in time of stress stand anything as long as it doesn't physically bother him. You let me mess with his digestion and such and he'll turn bad."

"All right," said God, "You can test him, but you will not be permitted to kill him."

As a result, Satan headed for Job full speed and socked him first with boils. Job was immediately miserable, as there was no penicillin or good medication and he sat in hot ashes.[1]

Job's wife came to him then and said, "Why don't you quit, Job? Curse God and die.[2] That will relieve you of your miseries."

"You speak like a poorly informed female. Don't you have any reasoning ability? God is in charge of everything, both good and bad, and sometimes He dishes out one and sometimes the other, and who are we to say He doesn't know what He is doing?"

Word, of course, of all Job's troubles spread around and some of his cronies from neighboring ranches and towns heard of his problems and some of them got together and decided to visit Job and offer their sympathy.

When Job's friends approached him they hardly knew him for his sad condition and they were shocked to the point of tearing their clothes, putting ashes in their hair, and generally putting on an act.[3]

The three visitors, friends of Job, sat down with him for seven days and seven nights and no one said a word.[4]

Finally Job broke the silence and spoke to his friends saying, "It would have been a great help if I had never been born. How nice if the day of my birth could be cancelled. I wouldn't be here.

"No more birthday parties for me. Every time I think of my birthday I will cry and groan.

"It would have been a real break if I had been born dead. I could then have slept instead of living.

---

[1] Recommended by a neighbor   [2] Job had good insurance policies
[3] No longer stylish   [4] The early orientals didn't rush things

"In fact, it would have been great if I had been born in prison and killed on birth as is the custom under these conditions. Now all I can do is long for death, and it does not come. Why should I be living when I want to be dead? Great trouble has come to me, everything I didn't want to happen has happened. In spite of being in good shape, I have been stricken with awful ailments."

"Now Job," said Vince,[1] "I hope you don't mind an opinion or two from a close friend. I know you have been a source of great strength to many people and that you are a highly respected citizen. You are hit by trouble yourself for a change, and you can't take it.

"As little as I like to mention it, I feel I must remind you that the innocent never suffer. Trouble comes to those who deserve trouble. It is God's punishment that you suffer.

"I know these things because of a clear vision from God. God surely is not going to make it tough on the righteous.

"It occurs to me that God cannot completely trust his angels, let alone man. Man lives briefly and then his life is snuffed out, why should you think you are above all this?

"A person can get by a little while without God, but not for long. God gets to a fellow and misery comes to punish a man for his sins.[2] Man sins very easily, we understand that.

"My advice to you, Job, is to confess your sins. God might change everything for you. He certainly can, for He controls the rain, and helps the poor, and attends to sufferers. God constantly wars with the crooks. In fact, He makes the crooks act like men who can see no better in the day than at night.

"The poor have hope, for God will look out for them. Actually, you are honored to be afflicted by God and you should be pleased with the attention. For when you sin and then confess, God heals and He will help protect you from further sins. God will protect you from starvation, and war, and gossip,[3] and you will be safe from wild animals and thieves and your sons will become leaders and so will your grandsons. I know from experience that all this is true; so admit your sins."

"You know what I wish?" said Job, "I wish that there were some scales to weigh my troubles. I believe my troubles would outweigh one thousand seashores.[4]

"The Lord has struck me down with poisoned arrows. Everything and everybody is against me.

"If all was well I wouldn't be howling, for surely a jackass

---

[1]Eliphaz   [2]I'm glad this isn't true
[3]Only God can do this   [4]You've got to believe he hurt

doesn't bray unless his food is gone. A man gripes when there is no salt on his potatoes. To me now nothing has any taste and I can't stand the thought of eating.

"All I ask of God is death while I still acknowledge him. Why am I strong enough to live? I am helpless, I feel there is no hope, but I seem to be as tough as brass, and I can't die.

"On top of this you accuse me of sin, without any facts. What kind of a friend are you? Don't you fear God yourself? You are proving to be highly unreliable.

"Any hope I had of help from you is gone. I feel like a caravan that has stopped at an oasis and found that the well was dry. You act as if you are ashamed to be my friend.

"Tell me now, Vince, what have I done that is wrong? Give me a reasonable answer. You are wrong about me. I am still a righteous man. You have no basis for your accusations. I know the difference between right and wrong, and if I were wrong I would gladly admit it.

"I know a lot of things. I know life is long and hard and man often yearns for the day to end. Just like it must be for a slave who works hard and only looks ahead for the week-end day of rest. I realize I have been allotted months of frustration and long and endless nights.

"When I go to bed at night I long for the morning and when morning comes I wish it was already night. My skin is infected, it aches and it itches. My boils fester and are painful, my life is passing by, and I fight for breath. Maybe I'll die soon, I certainly think so.

"When I die I shall disappear as a cloud and be gone so let me sound off a bit here at the end.

"Oh God! What's wrong? Am I some grim monster that you must torture me all the time? Even when I finally get to sleep I have nightmares.

"I wish someone would choke me to death. God, please leave me alone and let me die in peace. Why spend so much time with a mere man? Let me alone, God, even if it is just long enough to spit.

"How did I get to be your big target? If it is a sin, why don't you pardon it and let me be whole again? It is only a matter of a few years anyway; so why not take me now?"

Then one of Job's friends called Short-stuff[1] spoke saying, "How long will all this windy talk keep going? What a lot of guffaw! The matter is simple. If a man is righteous God blesses him, and if he is wicked he gets in trouble. If you were forgiven and righteous again you would be made well again.

---

[1] Bildad, the Shuhite

"Isn't this the history of man? Hasn't this always been the rule? Granted that the wicked may prosper like a growing weed for a short time but the wicked are consumed just as a weed withers. That's life, man!

"The wicked have it tough in the long run. There is no security for them. God will not help evildoers nor will he desert a righteous man. When you are laughing and well again then you will be considered righteous and then the wicked will envy you, but now you are just one of them."

Chap.
9

"What you say," said Job, "sounds reasonable, but how can mere man be reasonable with God. Would you get into a question and answer game with the Lord? I agree that no one can eventually prosper who challenges God.

"God removes mountains, causes earthquakes, orders the sun to rise, and has put the stars on a definite schedule.

"In fact, God controls the winds, and all the weather and other wonders too numerous to mention. In fact, God comes passing by and he cannot be seen. God does as he pleases. Who can say to God, 'Why are you doing thus and so?'

"This being the case, surely you don't expect me to argue with God. No one could be righteous enough to argue with God.

"I admit that God is dealing me the real miseries. I can't catch my breath though I've never smoked. If I attempt to justify myself before God, advocating my own course would be a sin in itself. Even if I were absolutely perfect I could not be expected to understand my own soul.

"I am convinced that God knows everything and is in charge of everything. God destroys good people and bad people. It is only with God's permission that the wicked run everything.

"There are a lot of crooked judges and politicians[1] and God apparently lets them be unfair. It's got to be God that allows this. Who else could it be?

"My time on earth disappears swiftly, the years swish by like an eagle diving on a pigeon, or as a ship drops over the horizon. I wouldn't dare forget my troubles and act as if nothing were wrong or God would just crack down on me with even worse ailments.

"God has it in for me for sure. I don't know why, but being innocent isn't the answer. I don't think there is any use in my trying.

"If I made myself spotlessly clean, and used the best cleaning soap, God would just push me into a muddy ditch.

"My situation is terrible. I can't defend myself against God. If God were a mere man we could settle our differences by arbitration, or call on an official of some kind to make a ruling. Not so with God.

[1]Who said the Bible was out of date?

It must all be his way.

"Would to God that he would ease off of me long enough for me to recover, and maybe I wouldn't be so intimidated and I would say to God that I am innocent and not deserving of all this misery."

Chap.
10

"Woe is me. I am weary of life and sick inside as well as outside. Listen to me, Lord. Is this really a good plan, to give so much trouble to a good man and to let the wicked prosper?

"You know that I am not wicked. You made me, why are you trying to destroy me? You set a mold for me and poured me into it as if I were milk and curdled cheese, you put flesh on me and hung me together with bones and sinews, you breathed into me life.

"What is your secret plan? If I do any tiny little thing wrong you whack me down, and yet if I'm upright and law-abiding I get it in the neck even worse. What goes on? Why was I born? I know I don't have long to live for no one lives very long; so how about just leaving me alone for a while? Let me have a little breather here at the last before I go into the great unknown."

Chap.
11

Then Godfrey,[1] another of Job's friends, began to speak and he said, "All those big words and long speeches of yours ought to be answered. I can't let you get by with false statements.

"You have said that your thoughts and actions are good, but I bet anything that God knows about some sins of yours that you haven't mentioned to us. In fact, you probably deserve more punishment than you are getting.

"What's more, you can't figure out God. Don't you know that he is higher than the sky and deeper than hell. God can do anything and he knows everything. God doesn't have to read the morning paper to learn of the sins of man.

"In fact, insignificant man has as little chance of reasoning about God as a wild horse's colt has being born tame.

"You say you are ready to turn to God and reason with him, then the first thing you better do is confess your sins. You aren't really puzzled, you just don't want to admit that you have privately been a bad boy.

"After you have done this, then everything will come clear, you will have hope again, you will be able to sleep, and you will recover a feeling of security."

Chap
12

"Nuts to you," said Job. "You leave the impression that when you and a few others die there will be no wisdom left on earth. Well, I know just as much as you birds do. Furthermore, you haven't brought out anything new. Your comments have been often

---

[1]Zophar

discussed.

"What I am saying is that I have called on God for help and the result is that I am suddenly a big joke to my friends. My argument is that I know some rich people who despise the poor and who have no sense of mercy and they are well and happy, yet I have always been kind and I am in a mess. I know robbers who are doing well and I have never stolen a thing and yet I am suffering terribly.

"I know God does everything. I just don't know why. There's nothing great in knowing this. Every animal knows, the birds know, the earth knows, all nature obeys every wish and follows every plan of God. I know that the soul of every person and the life of everything is in the hand of God.

"This is not hard to understand. Just as I can tell good food by the taste glands around my tongue so my mind can tell the truth by the taste of what I hear. At my age, experience has made this possible.

"God can destroy and God can restore. God can cause floods or bring on a drouth. God is all strength and all wisdom, and all people, good or bad, are under his authority.

"God is able to control judges, make or break kings, overthrow the mighty or raise up the poor. God can confound a man's mind and often introduces senility into the aged. God builds up some nations and destroys other nations, and sometimes he confuses the leadership of a nation so that the people wander around without direction as if they were a bunch of drunks. I know all this. I've seen it, and heard it, and I believe it."

Chap.
13

"Actually, you birds coming here to advise me don't know any more than I do. You are flops as doctors. Certainly I would be pleased if I could talk this whole thing over with God. If you want to be helpful the best thing you could do would be to shut up.

"How about listening to my reasoning and my pleas. I'm the one in trouble. You talk as if God has given you inside information, which I seriously doubt. Dare you speak for God? Aren't you afraid of God? The talk you have been giving is worth less than ashes and your attempt to defend God is ridiculous.

"Risky as it may be, I am going to empty my mind, and take the consequences. I realize God may take my life because of what I am going to say, I must speak as I feel. You see, even if he kills me, I still trust him, and that is why I am going to speak my piece, for I trust God.

"I only ask you, my friends, to do two things. One is to take your cotton picking hands off me, and the other is not to appear so imposing and seem to be so shocked.

"Basically, my affirmation is that I am a good man. I defy any of you to name sins that I have recently committed, although you talk to me as if I were still a kid stealing watermelons. Man is a fragile creature for he is born, lives a little while, and then dies.

"Actually, he comes on the scene like a flower unfolding and disappears as a shadow fades.

"No one is pure. God knows that. How can one born impure be pure. Man is not a plant, nor is he like a tree. A tree can be cut down and then sprout new growth and new trees even where it falls, but man dies and is gone until the heavens disappear and an arrangement is made.

"It would be nice if I was in the grave now and forgotten, only to be remembered and called forth for judgment at a set time. I am willing to die and wait for the great change. You all are among those that make everything hopeless. You notice every little error, you gossip, and go great guns with nit-picking. You do to man what water does to a stone as it gradually washes it away. You talk as enemies of man, who insist on making him old and wrinkled before his time, and then dying a miserable death."

Then Spock[1] spoke saying, "It is strange to me that a supposedly wise man like you should utter such nonsense. Actually, you are being crafty and plotting under the guise of prayer, attempting to hide your sins.

"It is not mine, but your own testimony that gives you away. You talk as if you were the first man born and that you have been with God from the very beginning. Were you here before the hills, or do you know the secret of life? You don't know anything that we don't know. Yet you seem to argue with God and act very much like a know-it-all.

"No man is clean. How could he be and be born of woman? You swallow sin as if it were water, and what greater wrong is there than this?

"Now as for me, I know the truth. I learned it from my elders, it has been handed down, and the truth is that the wicked suffer just like you are suffering. Trouble, anguish, and hunger follow the wicked and finally the wicked are terrified. The bad people finally are separated and live lonely lives, and they also lose all their money.

"The people who attempt to deceive as you are doing are hypocrites and real phonies and God sees to it they don't have anything but troubles like you are having."

"A miserable bunch of comforters you fellows are. You make me feel worse," said Job. "I could make pious and objective statements myself if I were in your shoes, but I think that my

---

[1] Eliphaz

68

approach would be to attempt to give you strength and encouragement.

"Worn out and tired as I am, you come and make things worse. Even though I know I am innocent I receive no help. God is crushing me as if he were angry, my friends chide me, and my enemies take advantage of my sickness and my trouble. I am completely miserable.

"Yet I know that I am innocent. It is not sin that has caused all the trouble that has come my way. I still am turning to God in prayer and I am pleading with Him. I don't have long to live and all I'm asking is a little peace and ease as I near my end.

Chap. 17

"Here in my sad condition my friends are making fun of me. I think God has actually prevented my friends from understanding my situation. I am a complete mess. People who used to know me don't recognize me when they see me.

"Nevertheless, I know that in the final analysis, the righteous will prevail. Good men gradually gather strength over the years, strength of spirit.

"But I have had it. I am weary. Please all of you leave. None of you have helped or made sense in any of your talk. There would appear to be no help for my condition. I must just hang on as best I can and hope to die. There is no other hope for me."

Chap. 18

"Now wait a minute, Job," said Short-stuff. "We are not animals, and we aren't so dumb, either. All this moaning and groaning and tearing your clothes doesn't cause the earth to shake or the wind to blow. The old time truth is still correct, and that is that the wicked are punished and the righteous prosper.

"If you are having such a bad time it is because you deserve it. The wicked will always catch it. Life will constantly deal the evil people a load of trouble. Finally, the wicked should be thrown into everlasting darkness, alone and lost. That is exactly what happens to sinners and to those that reject God."

Chap. 19

"You keep harping on the same theme. You've called me a sinner umpteen times. All right, name one of my sins. What has actually happened is that God has forsaken me, though I have not forsaken God. God has deprived me of everything and left me with absolutely nothing.

"My wife and brothers don't even recognize me. I call my servant and he doesn't come. My best friends have deserted me. Please have pity on me. Can you not see that God is inflicting all manner of torture on me? Why add to my torture with your own criticisms?

"Oh, how I wish I could write what I know so that it would always be read. I wish I had an iron pen that would write on a big rock, then I would write for all to read forever. I would inscribe on the rock the assurance that in spite of everything I know that my redeemer liveth and that when all is said and done, He reigns, and He will reign forever. After I die I expect to see God, and then God will be with me, and I will not be forsaken. In fact, I will see God not as a stranger, but as a friend.

"How do you dare continue to pick at me, one who sees such a glorious hope even in despair. You act as if I were a condemned man and I am not, and you had better watch for yourselves, for your attitude will get you in trouble with God."

Chap.
20

Then Godfrey spoke forth and said, "I can hardly wait to answer your charges. I heard you and my own good sense calls on me to reply.

"In the first place, don't you know that from the very beginning the plan of God has been for the wicked to prosper only a short time. Even though a wicked man may rise to great heights it is a short trip with him and he will disappear as an overnight dream. Even though he might outwardly seem to enjoy his wickedness, even then he suffers inside and is fearful. The wicked may get rich quick, but God will soon take it all away. This is done as punishment to the wicked ones who have been selfish and ignored the poor and the needy.

"God will definitely give it to him here on earth. God will strike him while he is enjoying things the most and he shall be reduced to misery and poverty. That is exactly what happens to the wicked."

Chap.
21

Job said, "Hear me once again, and then you can mock me to your heart's content. I have no complaint against man. You are going to be astonished at what I am going to tell you, for I even tremble myself that I say these things.

"I observe the wicked. Some of them grow old, still rich and in power, some of them dance all the way to the grave. They defy God. They even say there is no need of God for them. I have never been influenced by such evil men. I know they are struck down in death, and then if not before they will taste the wrath of God.

"No one teaches God anything. Everyone dies in his own time as God wills it. Some die quietly, some in suffering, and some in bitterness. Don't you think for a minute that everything is settled on this earth. The wicked die, sometimes in the height of glory and wealth, but they will be summoned from the grave at a proper time to face the judgment of God.

"You are no comfort to me, for you are misinformed about the ways of life."

Chap.
22

Then Vince spoke again and said, "You are wrong about man

being worthwhile to God. God couldn't care less. What is one fellow to Him, whether he is wise or foolish?

"Do you think that it is important to God that you claim to be a good man? You are bound to be wicked somehow. You have welched on a bet, taken clothing from the needy, failed to provide bread and water to the starving, or stolen some little old ladies social security check. God is high in the heaven and He looks down and He sees you do things that we don't see or know what has happened.

"What you need to do is to confess and repent. Return to God in humility and He will restore you. In fact, if you are sincerely penitent you will no doubt get rich again and all will be well with you. Once you have fully repented you will be able to pray again and your relationship with God will be satisfactory."

Chap. 23

"I still say I'm getting worse treatment than I deserve," said Job. "My condition is so bad that my feeble attempt to find God fails. If I could just sit down and talk with God all this business would clear up promptly.

"I just can't find God. I look ahead and He is not there, I look behind and He is not there, right and left I search, but I cannot find him. God will find me though. God knows where I am and where I go. When He is through testing me, I will be all right. God knows I try to be a good man and faithful. God knows what He is doing and He won't be persuaded to change His plan. For this, I am afraid. For I know God knows about me and my problem, and He knows my thoughts. For some reason God is keeping me alive, weak, helpless, blind, and miserable, but alive.

Chap. 24

"The bad people do not think this way. These people mistreat God's creation, they pollute the waters, erode the soil, and shamelessly destroy God's creatures.

"The wicked care only for themselves. They never leave grain in the field for the needy and they pay no attention to the lonely, the poor, the naked, and the starving.

"The bad people take advantage of the ignorant, they cheat the people who work for them, and they take advantage of minors, yet God doesn't stop them at once or bring their activities to a screeching halt.

"Many of the wicked are only concerned to see that man does not catch them stealing, or falsifying reports, or committing adultery. All these people try to do is to avoid being caught by man. They do not consider that God knows all that happens.

"One thing for sure, though, the grave catches the wicked like a hot drought catches the snow. The wicked may rise in great power and with great show for a little while, and then they tumble. Who thinks now that I am not telling the truth?"

71

"Aren't you terrified of God?" asked Short-stuff. "How can man justify himself in the sight of God? God orders the stars, commands the moon. Do you think that God concerns himself with man, who is really just a worm in his sight?"

"What a brilliant bunch you birds turned out to be," sneered Job. "You have brought me no comfort and you think you are wise while all the time you tell me stupid things.

"Have you never really thought of the majesty of God, how He stretches the north over the empty place and hangs the earth on pure relativity, not to mention the marvelous arrangement of carrying the rain around in clouds. God made everything from the highest heavens to the tiny little crooked snake. There is no way of understanding all of God.

"Even though God himself is responsible for my troubles, I promise you I will not speak evil or act deceitfully, as I will retain my faithfulness. I am not a bad man and I am not going to be one. I will not succumb to pressure and if you don't believe me you can hardly be considered friends," continued Job.

"Men know how to do a lot of things. They know how to mine for silver, they build dams to contain streams, they find treasures in the earth, and they plant and sow, but man cannot discern the deep wisdom of God. Only God knows where complete wisdom resides and only God reveals this knowledge as it pleases him. To stand in awe of God, that is what God says is the key to wisdom, it is where man begins his search.

"Of course, I long for the good old days, when I was healthy and well to do, a respected member of society, surrounded by friends, and certain that God was helping me every step of the way.

"I was really something in the good old days. Young men stood aside for me, my opinion was sought by the highest council, I was even named Citizen of the Year, and enjoyed a fine reputation.

"I had even figured out that I would lead a long, fruitful, helpful life and then die a respectable death in my old age. It is hard to realize how successful I actually was.

"Now I am nothing. Young men spurn me, stupid young fellows with strong backs and weak minds. These young upstarts constantly make fun of me, they sing silly limericks about my sad condition, and my status is gone. No one respects me. I am despised and pitied.

"I can no longer sing or play the guitar, and I cannot sleep at night. Everything seems black and dismal to me. I know my end is death but I thought it would be a dignified arrangement.

"I helped the poor, I was always doing good things for others, and so I expected that good things would happen to me, but instead only trouble came my way. My heart is troubled and I am afflicted. All of my joy and gladness has turned to sadness.

Chap.
31

"You keep wanting me to admit to something that isn't true. I have been careful about women and have even refrained from looking at pretty girls so that improper desires would not arise within me. I know you fellows think I've been tom-catting around on the side, but it is not true. God knows it isn't true, even if you don't.

"You think maybe I've taken advantage of someone's wife, but that isn't true. If it were true, I'd want someone to take advantage of my wife. I insist that you think of me as a fair and decent man.

"You all may think that I have been unfair in dealing with the servants, but this is not true. I am fully aware of the fact that a servant is as much a creation of God as I am, and I have always treated my servants with this mind.

"Furthermore, I have not been unmindful of the poor, or the widows, or the orphans. I have earnestly tried to see that my success has not gone to my head, but in all things have acknowledged that everything has come from God.

"My problem is that I am baffled. I wish God would speak up and tell me what is wrong. It would be even better if the causes of my trouble were put in writing and I could begin to cope with them, but as it is, I only know I suffer, and I do not know why. Woe is me."

Chap.
32

Apparently listening to all this exchange between Job and his three friends was a young man named J. Namath.[1] When all was quiet, Namath spoke, "I can't stand listening to all this tripe any longer. I may be young, but I'm not stupid. Not every rich and famous man is wise, and as you have just proven, being old doesn't necessarily make you wise, either.

"It was obvious that none of the three of you got anywhere with Job, and you surely didn't make much of a case against him. Now the time has come for you all to listen to me.

Chap.
33

"I speak with no authority of title, except that I am a child of God, and I'll speak for him as nearly as I can. You say, Job, that you are righteous and that God is punishing you without cause. You are accusing God of being unjust. Let me remind you that God is greater than man, and the justice of God cannot always be understood by man. Why do you keep arguing with God? God is not accountable to anyone.

"You sit back and listen now to a little good, common sense, Job. God does not enter into philosophical debates with man. Now

[1] Elihu

73

listen carefully, fellows, for the ears can taste the truth, but you have to be really listening.

"Now Job should be called Absorbine Jr. for all that he has had to soak up from his friends. Yet he continues to declare his righteousness and asserts that delighting God does not necessarily bring any reward.

"Get this straight first, God does not initiate torment and he will not divert justice just for kicks.

"It is not proper to say to a king that he is wicked nor to top rulers that they are worthless, so how much less proper is it to accuse God of neglect?

"Everyone is the same in God's sight, rich or poor. God made them all, and no one lasts very long on this earth, whether they be weak or mighty. God sees everything and knows everything. There is no hiding from him.

"You have got to admit that God is fair. God knocks over the wicked in their time, He brings peace when He so desires to do so, whether it be to a person or a nation.

"As for you, Job, if you have committed no other sin, you are guilty of rebellion. The least you can say is that God is right and that you have deserved all your trouble. You can't possibly say that God is wrong.

"Think a little deeper, Job," continued J. Namath. "Do you think it makes a great deal of difference to God whether a man is good or evil? You have got to learn to accept God as He is. You are trying to make a gigantic case out of one little man. Do you think variety is a way of approaching God? You are just wasting words!

"Just keep quiet. I haven't finished yet. I haven't gotten to the part where I speak for God. You must understand that God is all powerful and the one mighty ruler. In the final analysis, he blesses the good and curses the wicked. It is just that simple!

"Are you aware of how great God really is? He makes the tiny little drops of water, and also the whole sea. God has covered the bottom of the sea and spread clouds in the heavens and he arranges for light to come and go on to earth. God roars in the thunder and crackles in the lightning.

"God has arranged for the snow, the light rain, and torrents. God sends the animals into caves to hide when He brings the hurricane from the south, and the clouds respond to the wishes of God, for watering the earth or for punishing the people with floods.

"Now, Job, you just stop a minute and think about the majesty and the power of God. How smart are you? Could you weigh a cloud? Were you working with God when He made the universe? The cloud covers the sun until the wind of God blows the cloud away and man has light again. Man can do nothing else but fear God, and arguing with God is unthinkable."

Chap. 38

Then God began to come through to Job and Job heard the reasoning of God, for Job understood God to say, "Where were you, Job, when I began creation? Where are the foundations of the earth and how is it suspended and held in place? Who enclosed the seas as if in traps, or arranged for morning to arrive on schedule every day?

"Have you walked the bottom of the sea to learn all the secrets there, and do you know about death, and its meaning? What is the origin of light? Do you know all about hail? Did you know that I am even reserving a lot of hail for a big battle some day?

"What about rain in desolate places where there is no man. Who is responsible for this? Do you think rain has a father and a mother? What about the stars? Does any man have any say-so about the course of the stars or the stability of the North Star?

"Did a man arrange for water to cause clods in a dusty place, or did man teach the lion to hunt food for the cubs?

Chap. 39

"What about lambing and calving? Do you think the 4-H Clubs decide on these matters? What about the wild horse? Did man free him?

"Do you think that man can train an animal to plant seed, harvest corn, cook, baby-sit, or can a man create a memory for the ostrich who has a hard time remembering where she has laid eggs? God deprived the ostrich of widom and there is nothing man can do about it.

"Have you ever tried to build a horse? What about the hawk and the eagle? Did man teach these birds to fly? Are you responsible for making the eagle blood-thirsty?

Chap. 40

"Do you now have any argument with me, Job," said the Lord.

"All I know now for sure, O God, is that I am nothing. I have nothing to say for myself."

"Face matters, now, Job," said God. "Are you wishing to question my judgment? Do you wish to appear righteous at my expense?"

"Maybe, Job, you don't realize your own inadequacy. Can you drag a whale ashore with a simple hook? Are you responsible for the strength of an ox? Are you the one who made the mountains provide food and shelter for the animals?

Chap. 41

"How can man expect to contend with God when man cannot create or completely control creation. It just isn't reasonable! There is no limitation to the power of God and there are none who can contend with Him or stand against Him.

"You are absolutely right, O Lord. I know you can do anything," said Job. "I have talked too much, and blabbed too much that I didn't understand. I have always heard you, O Lord, but now I can really begin to understand a little about you. I repent and bow down in shame and humility."

God then moved the friends of Job to be remorseful for their treatment of Job and they came to Job with food and gifts seeking forgiveness and affirming their friendship.

Job prayed to God in behalf of his friends and this pleased God and He returned to Job all of his glory and wealth and health and He blessed him so that he was in better shape after his sad experience than he had been formerly.

Blessed is the man who does not seek the advice of the wicked, nor hang around all the time with sinners, nor join in with bitter critics, but whose delight is in the law of the Lord, and much of his time is spent in thinking on God's law.

Such a man shall be strong like a tree planted by a good stream of water, that regularly bears fruit, and whose leaves do not wither. Whatever such a man does succeeds.

The ungodly are not so, but are as undependable as chaff which the wind blows away, therefore the ungodly will not be able to survive judgment, nor will sinners be allowed eternally in the company of the righteous.

The Lord blesses the way of the righteous, but the way of the ungodly shall perish.

Why do the heathen make such a racket and in rage defy God? Often great rulers get together and work against the Lord's plans and his workers, thinking they will be able to rule everything and everybody.

The Lord sitting in his heaven shall laugh and be amused at their folly. Then God will also act to confound them.

God has declared his own ruler in Jerusalem and God will place the heathen under his control. God warns the wicked that they shall be broken with a rod of iron and smashed like a piece of pottery.

If the rulers and the judges are smart they will begin at once to serve the Lord with great respect, and to bow down before the Son lest he be made angry. Happy are those who completely trust in Him.

Lord, there seem to be more and more people objecting to me. Some even write me off as hopeless, but I know, Lord, that you are my shield and my defense. When I cried unto the Lord, he heard me, and so I will not be afraid if 10,000 line up against me for God delivers, God will smite my enemies and break their jaws, for salvation is in the hands of God, and His blessing is upon his people.

Hear my prayer, O Lord, as you have helped in the past, have mercy on me again.

How long will men be vain and make shame of the glory that is mine in the Lord? God will hear those whom he has set apart for his work.

Stand in awe and sin not, be quiet and think about God. Offer to God your goodness for his use, and trust him.

There are some who think God is not interested. Show me your light and put gladness in my heart and I will then be able to go to bed and sleep in peace.

Hear another prayer from me, O Lord. This is a morning prayer.
I know the foolish will perish and that you have no use for
workers of iniquity, particularly those who are violent and deceitful.

As for me, O Lord, I will come to you asking for mercy and in
wonder will I worship. Lead me in the paths of righteousness because
my enemies work against me, show me the correct path to follow.

There is no faithfulness in the wicked, they flatter and mislead,
please destroy them, Lord. Let all those that trust in God rejoice and
shout with happiness, bless the goodies, Lord, protect them as with a
shield.

Lord, please don't blow your cool and punish me. Have mercy
on me. I am weak and I ache, my soul is disturbed, save me, please,
for I am afraid to die, or at least I'm not ready yet.

I am weary, Lord, with groaning and I cry all night.[1]

Tell my enemies to leave me alone. I feel suddenly that the
Lord has heard my prayer and I am confident my enemies will
retreat.

I put all my trust in you, O Lord. Save me. If I had done
anything wrong it would be different, but my enemies are stomping
me without cause. Settle a quick judgment on them, O Lord.

Lord, judge the people now, including me. Judge me according
to my righteousness and my integrity. Put an end to the wicked. I
know God helps the righteous and hates the wicked.

I know the Lord is fully prepared to handle the wicked. God
arranges for the wicked to fall into their own pits and to receive the
very trouble they intend for others.

Therefore, I praise the Lord because of his righteousness and I
sing praises to the most high God.

O Lord, how excellent is your name in all the earth. Your glory
exceeds the glory of the heavens, you have even managed to let
babies be more powerful than those who oppose them.

When I think about your heavens, the work of your fingers, the
moon, the stars, the planets which you made, it makes me marvel
that you have taken such an interest in man. You have really blessed
man and made him a wonderful creature, almost as glorious as the
angels. You have given man control of the earth, you have granted
him the job of managing the sheep, the oxen, and the wild game, the
fowl of the air, the fish of the sea, and all the creatures of the sea.

How excellent is the name of the Lord in all the earth!

[1] Definitely the back ache

I will praise God with all my heart and acknowledge all his wonderful works.

My enemies will be defeated by the presence of God.

God has always supported me, God has rebuked the wicked, and reduced them to nothing.

The day of the wicked is a short one. The Lord is a righteous judge and he will administer judgment on the people.

The Lord will always be a refuge for the oppressed, and God will support those who put their trust in him.

Sing praises to the Lord and declare to all the people the wonderful things that the Lord continues to do.

Have mercy on me, O Lord, and consider my troubles with my enemies. I will rejoice in the salvation of the Lord. The heathen are sunk down in a pit of their own digging.

The wicked, and all the wicked nations will be turned into hell.

The needy will not always be neglected and the poor will not be without help forever.

Be active, O Lord, scare the willy-nilly out of the evil persons, and let men be reminded that they are merely human.

Why do you so often seem remote, O Lord? The wicked are getting by with persecuting the poor. The wicked are even boastful about their success, and they disdain God.

The wicked think they are self-sufficient, they curse, deceive, they lie, and plot and cheat, they sneak up on the innocent and uninformed. Arise, O Lord, and whack them good.

God, you know how the wicked defy you, how they boast, please at least break a few arms here and there.

The Lord is king forever and forever, and the heathen shall perish. God will help the fatherless and the oppressed, and bring justice into being on this earth. Amen.

I put my trust in God. Why would I want to flee to the mountains or seek some escape?

The wicked are at work. Their arrows are constantly being directed to the righteous. Sometimes it seems as if law and order have collapsed.[1]

Don't worry, the Lord is in his holy temple, God is watching all the time, and the Lord enjoys the view of the righteous but the ways of the wicked are irritating.

Eventually the wicked will catch hell from the Lord, and God will smile on the righteous.

Help! Help! We need help, God. The righteous are having it

[1] So that's where the expression originated

tough. The wicked are undermining the good people with flattery and lies and talk of big profits.

The Lord will finally hush up the lip artists and bless the poor and the oppressed.

The word of God is sure, it is also pure as refined silver, O God, please preserve and protect the good people from the vile and evil persons who are everywhere, and who often are made rich and famous.

Chap.
13

Do you remember me, O Lord? When will I get a little relief from my enemies and comfort for my sorrows?

Lord, brighten my life a bit. You certainly don't want my enemies to get the best of me. I have trusted in God, though, and I know God's mercy. I will praise God, for God has been good to me.

Chap.
14

Only a grade A nut has said in his heart that there is no God. Such persons are no-good fools, who do abominable deeds. The whole crowd of them are a bunch of dirty bums.

You'd think they would know something, but they don't even say a blessing before the meal. They should be terrified, for the Lord is associated with the righteous.

What a great day it will be when the people of God are restored and the goodies rule the world under God.

Chap.
15

Lord, who do you want around you? I'm sure you wish a person who walks uprightly, who does good work, and thinks truthfully.

You certainly prefer a pleasant speaking person and not one who complains about his neighbors, or acts mean to his neighbors.

You desire, of course, someone who stays away from evil relationships, but loves and respects the righteous.

God also wants around him a person who tells the truth even if it penalizes him to do so, a person who loans money at a fair interest rate, and a person who does not take advantage of others.

There's a stable man for you!

Chap.
16

Protect me, O God, for I trust fully in you.

I know it will go hard for those people who seek strange religions and observe strange rites. I am most fortunate to have been reared in a godly environment. I will therefore continually thank God.

My heart is glad and my spirit is bright for I am dependent on the Lord. I know that God will keep me from hell, and will save my soul from torment. I know that the righteous way is far more pleasant and God will continue to guide me.

O Lord, check my record. See if I have not made every effort to adhere to your requests and to obey your commandments.

Make me secure. Hide me from the wicked. The evil ones are waiting for me like hungry lions. Arise and deliver me, Lord.

Save me from the wicked men around here, the fat, prosperous, power-mad, money-hungry scoundrels. As for me, I can go to sleep seeing the protective God over me all through the night.

The Lord is my rock, my strength, my deliverer. I will always call on the Lord, and he will save me from my enemies and deliver me from the flood of troubles, the sorrows of hell, and the snares of men.[1]

When I explained to the Lord about the evil ones, God heard my prayer and he shook the earth, he stirred things plenty with thunder, lightning, smoke, and fire.

God used hail and all types of natural powers to discomfort my enemies. In the midst of all the confusion, God delivered me, he made me stand in a safe place, he did this because the Lord was pleased with me. The Lord rewarded me according to my righteousness and in accordance with the cleanliness of my hands.

God did this because I have observed his laws and worshipped him. God shows mercy to those who show mercy. How simple it is.[2]

God has given me great confidence and I have the feel of success. All of this is a credit to God. It is not me, but God who acts and blesses. God has protected me, has strengthened my life, and enabled me to walk with confidence.

God has delivered me in battle and enabled me to be victorious. God has made it possible for me to be the ruler of a mighty kingdom, within which are many evil men. God delivers, and so I give thanks to the Lord for he has given great deliverance to his king, to his anointed one, to David, who is me.

The heavens exhibit the glory of God and all the expanse of sky testify to his handiwork.

Everything carries a message about the glory of God; the darkness of a silent night, the noise of day, the sun appears as if arising each morning from the tabernacle of God, the sun bursts on the world like a bridegroom on his honeymoon, or a great athlete being announced just before a game. The sun is marvelous on its rounds, there is nothing hidden from the heat of the sun. It is testifying to the glory of God.

The law of the Lord is exact and a real challenge to a man's soul. The statutes and regulations of God are right and pure, and makes man see life more clearly.

The respect for God is a clean and wholesome feeling and God's

[1]Sounds like he had been a dormitory supervisor   [2]Try it — you'll like it

judgments are always absolutely correct.

Life is really sweet to the one who obeys God and learning of God is much more to be sought than silver and gold. The standards of God are good guides and there is great reward for observing them.

Lord, protect me from the sin of thinking too much of myself, and so let me be a righteous person.

Let the words of my mouth and the meditations of my heart be acceptable to you, O Lord, my strength and my redeemer.

Chap.
20

I am confident that the Lord will hear me in time of trouble. We will all rejoice in the salvation God provides for the righteous. Yet God must do as God sees fit.

I, for one, know for sure that the Lord cares for those who trust him. Some people trust in chariots, some in horses, some in planes, and some in banks, but most of us trust in the name of the Lord.

The wicked fall, the righteous are risen, hear us when we pray, O God, the Lord of hosts.

Chap.
21

As king, I rejoice in the strength of God which is available for me. You have given the king everything he wants.

You have done everything for the king; a beautiful crown, long life, glory, honor, and majesty have been made a handy thing for him. The king trusts in God, and God willing, the king will not change.

The enemies of the king shall finally be swallowed up and disappear as if thrown into a fiery furnace. The enemies of the king were always plotting evil, but God was always watching.

Blessed is the Lord God, and we will sing his praises and recognize his power.

Chap.
22

My God, my God, why have you neglected me? I have been crying day and night and nothing has happened. O holy God, our fathers trusted in you and it worked. Make it work for me.

I am in trouble. The people boo me even before I get to bat. They make fun of me and call me a Bible thumper. They say, he trusted God, why doesn't God deliver him? I pass it on, why not help me? You are responsible for my being here in the first place.

My opponents are really organized. I feel as if I am surrounded by hungry lions. I feel weak, my strength is gone, my tongue sticks to my mouth, and the worst part is my back hurts.

Please help me. Deliver me from this sorry pack of human dogs. Be certain that I will praise the name of the Lord in public.

In fact, I tell everybody now to praise God. The Lord delivers, he never turns his back on those that trust him, always God knows and God cares.

Eventually, all the ends of the earth shall praise the Lord, all nations shall worship God, for all the kingdoms forever are the Lord's, everything is God's, from the smallest seed to the mightiest mountain, and from One shall come the word that shall cause a new kingdom of God's making to encompass the earth.

Chap.
23

The Lord is like a shepherd to me. I never need anything. God leads me by still waters for drinking and refreshment, he guides me along a good path in order that I might honor the name of the Lord. Though I face death or uncertainty I am without fear, for God is with me, he is ready to protect, I am at ease so that I can eat without worrying and I have a full life. I am respected, and I find goodness and mercy around me all the days of my life and I look forward to dwelling in the house of the Lord forever.[1]

Chap.
24

The earth is the Lord's and everything in it, including all the people. God built the earth. Who do you think he wants around him?

A man with clean hands and a pure heart, one who is no phony, such a person will receive the blessing of God.

The King of Glory appears. Who is the king of glory? The Lord strong and mighty, the conqueror of all, the Lord of hosts, he is the king of glory.

Chap.
25

I trust in the Lord. O Lord, don't let me down. Whack away at the wicked.

Lead me in a plain path, show me the truth, remember all thy mercies of old and make them presently available, forget my sins as a youth.

Teach all who need guidance, Lord. Those who fear God and seek him are in need of learning. Bless them all, Lord.

God will reveal his promises to those that trust him.

I am always praying to the Lord for it seems that I am always in trouble. Just like now. My enemies are many and they are plotting all the time. Deliver me, O God, and be certain that I trust in the Lord. Keep me on a straight path, and while you are saving me, Lord, save all Israel.

Chap.
26

Judge me, Lord. I've done absolutely the best I could. I have avoided phony people, I have kept your loving kindness before my eyes, I have stayed away from the wicked. I am really not a bad guy.

I don't mind speaking out in church in your behalf and telling of all your wonderful works. I enjoy being in your temple and associating with nice people and I really detest going with a crummy crowd. Redeem me, Lord, be merciful to me. I will witness to your greatness before the people.

[1] I definitely prefer the King James version of this psalm.

The Lord is my light and my salvation, whom shall I fear? The Lord is the strength of my life, of whom shall I be afraid?

When the wicked headed my way they stumbled and fell. I'm not afraid any more regardless of the numbers on the other side. I am not even worried in war.

My main goal is to live as close to God as I can, always trying to learn more. I know when trouble does come that God will protect me and shield me, and that I will finish way ahead of my enemies.

Hear me, Lord. Have mercy on me. Hide not your face from me, Lord, and put me not away in anger. Never forsake me, O God.

Even though my father and mother give up on me, the Lord will take my part. Teach me, Lord. Lead me in a plain path. Cheaters and liars have risen up against me, so much so that I would have fainted unless I had believed to actually see the goodness of the Lord in the land of the living.

Be patient. Serve the Lord. God will strengthen you, just serve God.

Hear me, Lord. Answer me. If you don't speak I will be as desolate as a fellow deserted in the pit.

Prevent me, Lord, from falling for the soft talk of those who would lead me astray. Punish those characters. See that they get theirs.[1]

I know God will finally destroy them. Blessed is the Lord who has heard my pleas.

The Lord is my strength and also the strength of all who trust in him. Bless your people, Lord.

Give glory to God. The voice of the Lord is powerful, his word controls the waters, the storms, the acts of nature, controlling fires, producing calves and fawns, the Lord is the king, the God of all, in charge of everything.

I will praise you, Lord, for all your goodness to me. You have given me birth and kept me alive. Sing, everyone, to the Lord and be grateful to him.

The anger of God is never very long and as weeping vanishes in the night and morning comes; so is the joy of the Lord.

Be helpful to me, Lord. Don't let me get killed, for if I'm dead I can't write songs of praise. I will always give thanks to the Lord who has turned my mourning into rejoicing.

I put all my trust in the Lord. The Lord is full of mercy. Ease my pain, O Lord. At present I am in great distress and I am full of

---

[1]Imagine a pit stop and no help

grief. I am getting old and creaky boned, people don't like to look at me, there is much slander out against me and some are plotting to take my life.

Save me. Brighten my life. Put the quietus on the liars.

Blessed is the name of the Lord who has shown me such kindness in his beloved city. Love the Lord, all you believers, be of good courage and God will strengthen your heart. Hope in the Lord.

Chap.
32

Happy is the man whose sin is forgiven and whose life is purified. I remember when I was burdened with sin, how miserable I was, I felt clammy, my bones hurt. Then I confessed my sin and God forgave me.

Don't be stupid like a beast and have to be guided by reins. Trust in the Lord and let him guide you. Be happy and shout for joy, for the goodness of the Lord is real.

Chap.
33

Praise the Lord. Rejoice in the Lord for the earth is full of the goodness of the Lord. It is amazing to consider the majesty of God's creation.

Let all the earth stand in awe of God. God spoke and creation came into being. The Lord confounds the wicked. Blessed is the nation that recognizes God and worships him.

No king is saved by numbers, no man saved by his own strength, all things are controlled by the Lord. God is our help and our shield and the more we trust in God the happier we get.

Chap.
34

O magnify the Lord, let us all exalt his name. I searched for God, and then he found me. A poor man cried and the Lord saved him even as the Lord delivered me. Taste and see that the Lord is good.

Depart from evil and seek good. Keep your tongue from evil and your lips from speaking guile, seek peace and pursue it.

God responds to calls. God is close to those who are contrite and he mends the broken-hearted.

The wicked finally wind up killing each other, but the Lord redeems the soul of the righteous and no one that trusts in the Lord will be lonely.

Chap.
35

Lord, listen to my plea. Get to work on my enemies. Blow them away like chaff, turn your angels loose on them, hound them to pieces for they are a great nuisance to me, always plotting my downfall.

When you have trapped them, Lord, in their own snares, then will I rejoice and praise your name.

It is really provoking to me that the men who slander me and make all kinds of false accusations are the very people that I have helped the most.

Judge me, O Lord. See for yourself that I am innocent. Don't give that bunch of crooks any satisfaction. Put them down fast. Confuse them and shame them and then will the name of the Lord be truly exalted and I will witness daily to the power and righteousness of God.

The wicked really puzzle me. They act as if they have no fear of God. On the other hand I see the Lord, the originator of righteousness, the ruler of man and beast, how outstanding is the loving concern of the Lord. All real pleasure stems from God and God's blessing goes to those who trust him, God is a fresh fountain to them.

Protect me now, Lord, from myself, from the pitfall of pride and conceit, and while you are at it, sock it to the wicked.

People, don't worry about evildoers and certainly don't envy the workers of iniquity.

Trust in the Lord and he will provide for you. Stick with God and his program. You must be very patient and do not worry about the flash success of the evil ones. Suddenly one day the wicked will be gone and there will not even be a historical marker to note where they had been.

The patient and the understanding shall inherit the earth and shall enjoy peace. While the wicked are plotting against the just and denouncing them God is merely laughing at the futility of their efforts.

The wicked prepare to shoot their arrows at the innocent, but the arrows will fall back on the wicked. The arms of the wicked will be broken and the righteous will be at peace. It is a promise that will some day become reality.

The law of the Lord resides in the heart of the righteous, so be patient. I have seen the wicked in great power, spreading themselves as a giant green bay tree, yet they disappeared and could not be found.

The man of peace is upright and he will witness the collapse of the wicked. The Lord is the strength of the righteous and he is their salvation. The Lord will help them, and deliver them, because they trust in God.

Don't criticize me any more, Lord. I know I have sinned. I am truly sorry. I smell bad even to myself because of my sin.

I am feeble and groaning. I hurt all over. Nobody will have anything to do with me and I don't blame them. Everyone is plotting against me.

Actually, I am trying to be deaf to all the complaints, for I put my hope and my trust in you, O Lord.

I am penitent. I am ready for a new life. One mistake and all the tongues started wagging against me. Forsake me not, O Lord, be my salvation and my help.

I determined to keep my mouth shut. I never said a word, but my insides shook, and my heart burned.[1]

Heal me, Lord. I have had a mild stroke, I can only mumble. What is in store for me? Am I near death? Refresh me, God, draw near to me. I feel deserted; let me have my strength return. Hear my prayer, O Lord.

The Lord has heard my plea and rescued me from the depths of despair and from the infirmity of my flesh. I sing now as with a new song. Blessed is the Lord and happy is the man who trusts in him.

There is no way of recounting the wonderful works of the Lord. Offering sacrifice or paying the church pledge has no great meaning unless a person gives of himself. So I am ready to be used. Surround me, Lord, with your goodness and your loving kindness. Make haste to help me and hurry to confound my enemies.

Bless those who seek you, Lord, and may they all together praise the Lord. I am weak and in need, O Lord, and you are my only help, but please hurry. Amen.

Blessed is the person who is concerned about the poor. The Lord will preserve such a person for God has real use for him.

I pray, Lord, that you will have mercy on me and heal me, yet my enemies are pulling for my death and can hardly wait. The baddies are really plotting together against me. They are passing the word that I will never get out of bed again.

I know you are with me, Lord. Heal me. This will reassure me about your power. Nevertheless, I continually say, Blessed is the Lord God of Israel forever and forever. Amen.

As a young deer pants for the water in a fresh running stream, so pants my heart for the Lord. My soul thirsts for further knowledge of God.

Yet here I am crying in bed, unable to arise. I can remember the great day of dancing and parading as we took the ark of the covenant to the temple.

Then I say to myself, why are you depressed, why is your soul in low key? I will hope in God for I will yet again be able to arise and praise him in his temple.

I admit my boat is swamped. The waves and waters of trouble

[1]This was before Alka-Seltzer

have washed over me, but the feeling of the presence of God, day and night, that is a great comfort.

My enemies keep taunting me. They say, 'Where is your God?' Again I say, my hope is in the Lord.

Chap.
43

O Lord, brighten my day a bit. All I hear is the complaints and plots of my enemies. Send out thy light and your truth, let them lead me, let them bring me to a good understanding. When that happens, I can again declare the glory of God in his temple.

Chap.
44

We know the record, O Lord. We know all you have done in the past. Our fathers did not capture the promised land by their own swords, but only through the power of God. Praise the Lord, and let us boast in the name of the Lord.

You have now, O Lord, let us get in bad shape. We have a poor image with other nations. Everybody picks on us. It is confusing. The enemies seem to be increasing, and yet we continue to declare your majesty.

You have really put us to the test. Judge now, O Lord. Haven't we stayed by you and continually declared thy name as Lord of hosts?

For your sake, O Lord, we are picked on all day every day, we are like sheep lined up before the slaughter pens. Wake up, God. Save us! Deliver us from our enemies and all our woes, and redeem us for your mercy's sake.

Chap.
45

A Song About King David

You are indeed a handsome man, and you have a friendly spirit. Put on your sword and ride majestically. Your presence will intimidate your enemies.

God has blessed you. God has wanted you on the throne of Israel, for it is God's throne. David, you are a righteous person, seeking to improve; so God has given you the crown.

You are really well fixed with a wardrobe full of up-to-date clothes and with a bunch of beautiful daughters. Everybody loves the king, even strange girls from foreign lands fall for David on sight.

It is a beautiful sight to see a wonderful daughter with her companions coming to pay homage to her father. What is more, God has promised to make the name of David a good name, to be treasured generation after generation.

Chap.
46

God is our refuge and strength, an immediate help in time of trouble, therefore we will not be terrified even if the earth seems to be in the act of moving, or mountains shake and suddenly slide into the sea.

Just remember that there is a place of eternal refuge, where a river flows by the throne of God, and God is ever present.

The heathen rage, God utters his voice, and the earth melts. It is good that the Lord our God is with us.

Take a look. See how God sometimes destroys and makes desolate, and then how suddenly he makes wars end, doing away with weapons and the implements of war.

Think about it. Know that the Lord he is God, he will be exalted in the heavens, he will be exalted in the earth, the Lord of hosts is with us, the God of Jacob is our refuge.

Chap.
47

Get excited! Isn't it thrilling to know that the Lord is a great king over all the earth? God plans everything that's necessary.

Sing praises to God, for he rules over all the earth, he reigns over the heathen as well as the people of God. God is greatly to be exalted.

Chap.
48

Great is the Lord and greatly to be praised. Particularly should this be the case in Jerusalem, for it is God's city.

Great rulers have often been terrified when they viewed the power and might of the Lord.

Let us declare the rule of God throughout the whole city, tell everyone you see, have the men in the towers to shout it to the passersby, for God is our God forever and forever. Amen.

Chap.
49

Now hear this, everybody, whether you be educated or not. I will teach you now with a parable. A rich man who depends on his wealth is in trouble, for none of them can buy a favor from God.

God deals death to the wise and the foolish, the rich and the poor. Often a rich man thinks he can leave arrangements to perpetuate his house or his wealth, but it can't be done. Time erases too much. No one can take his wealth with him, either.

Therefore, I place my soul in the hands of God, knowing that the praise of man perishes, but the favor of God is eternal.

Chap.
50

God has spoken and God shall continue to speak. Assemble the people, get a big crowd together and hear God.

"I have an announcement," said God, "for I am your God. I don't need all your puny little gifts. Are not all sheep mine anyway? If I were hungry I could eat anything, for everything in the world is mine.

"Come to me with thanksgiving in good times and I will come to your aid in time of trouble.

"I have also observed the wicked. They do not read my word. They encourage crookedness, they are those that commit adultery, they are deceitful and speak with an evil tongue. I know you, wicked ones. You thought you were getting by with all this, but you were wrong. I plan to fix you plenty! To those who praise me and who obey my laws, to them I will show salvation."

Have mercy upon me, O Lord, according to thy tender kindness and the multitude of your mercies, please blot out my transgressions. Wash me thoroughly, cleanse me from my sin.

I admit my sin. It is horrible for me to think about it.[1] My sin is truly against you, and you only.[2] I guess I am just a natural born sinner.

You want the truth, and the truth I'll give. Please clean me out but good, maybe even with Lysol. Let me again start to feel right about life. Don't discard me, Lord.

If you will let me speak, I will again speak your praises. I know you are not interested in my church pledge, or else I would double it,[3] but I know that what really appeals to you is a broken and a contrite heart.

Be good to Jerusalem, Lord. None of this was their fault. Bless the people and I am sure they will respond.

A Song about a Tattletale
Why do you boast about being a blabbermouth? You just prefer evil to good. God will fix you for this. God will destroy you, he will take you away from home and have you banished.

The good people will get a laugh out of this, even though it be a terrifying thing. They will say that that is what happens to a fellow who turns against God.

As for me, I feel safe. I am under God's protection, and I trust in the Lord. I will praise God forever, I will serve under the banner of God, and I will set a good example.[4]

The fool has said there is no God. They are corrupt and they think everybody else is. God looks down and sees evil everywhere, so much so that there is no completely pure and righteous man in sight. I can hardly wait for God to stir the people who trust in him so that they will become super active and committed to God, and then be able to rejoice in glorifying his name.

Save me, O God. Hear my prayer. Strangers and oppressors are rising up against me. They are really after me. I will sacrifice to you, O God, in a proper way, I will praise God's name for he has delivered me.

---

[1] It didn't do Uriah any good either   [2] I still think Uriah got a dirty deal
[3] I've always thought he should do this also
[4] This was probably written when David was a fugitive from Saul and pretty young

Hear me, Lord, as I moan and groan and complain. I am sick and weak and afraid of dying. I wish I had the wings of a dove, then I would fly and hide in the wilderness.[1]

There is such violence in the city, muggings every night. Wickedness is everywhere, strife and terror, but all these things I could face, but now it is you, Lord, you are indicating that my time of death is near, and I am afraid.

I still trust in you, Lord, I will pray day and night, and please deliver me now as you used to deliver me in battle.

God shall surely punish the wicked. Fellows with butter-smooth words but evil thoughts are not likely to deceive God.

I know that anyone who will cast his burden on the Lord will find support, and the righteous shall never be trodden under foot. I know the wicked will be cut short, while I will continue to trust in the Lord.

Be merciful to me, O Lord. I have many enemies,[2] but when I face terror I know you are with me and I will not therefore fear what any man threatens to do to me.

The fascists are working on me, every day, changing my words, trying to trap me. Why don't you trap them?

I know that God is for me, that if I had saved my tears there'd be at least a ten gallon jar full of them. I put my trust in the Lord, I will not be afraid of man, I will continue to praise the Lord, for it is only reasonable that as the Lord has delivered my soul from death he will certainly deliver my feet from falling and permit me again sometime to walk publicly in the view of everyone, with God's blessing.

Be merciful to me, O God. Help me. I am a fugitive from Saul, send guidance to me, O Lord, and look kindly on my predicament.

Although I am in great personal danger, I still can envision the greatness of the Lord. Let your glory, O God, encompass the earth.

A net is prepared for me, and a pit dug, but I perceive the diggers are even now falling in their own hole. My own heart is at peace, for I praise the name of the Lord.

Continually will I praise you, O Lord, even now as I strum on my guitar. I sing of your great mercies, I will sing of you in the presence of all nations, so let thy glory be over all the earth.

The wicked are truly a bad lot. Some of them almost seem to be born bad. Let them melt away, O Lord, for we have had enough of them for awhile.

It would be nice, O Lord, if you adjusted your system so that

---

[1] But not during dove season   [2] Everyone that was a fascist

the righteous would get all the good breaks. Then men would say that it paid to be good.[1]

Chap.
59

Lord, I am in hiding again. Saul's men are trying to catch me. They can't wait to capture me. Save me, please, God. Arise, O Lord, and whack away at the wicked, not missing a single one.

They are like a pack of dogs barking at each other, signalling and making all kinds of threats. Laugh at them, God. Show them who is the real boss. Scatter them, bring them to their knees, condemn them for their cursing and lying, burn them in your wrath, and show them that you are the Lord God of Israel.

No matter, even if they continue running around the city like mad dogs, I will still praise the Lord, I will speak of your power and praise your mercy, for you have always been my strength, for you are both my God of defense, and my God of mercy.

Chap.
60

Father, the battle is not won and we have not been doing well. This means that you are not with us. It looks as if at times you are even helping the enemy.

You are our only help. Help from man is useless. Through God, and only through God can we conquer.

Chap.
61

Hear me now, Lord, as I pray. I will always be praying, when I am discouraged I always turn to the rock that is higher than I am.

Always have you, Lord, been a tower and a shelter to me, I am at ease in your temple. I am blessed in being born in a line of church people. I will always remember to praise the Lord ever day.

Chap.
62

My soul rests at ease because of my faith in God. He is my rock and my salvation.

The wicked will not last very long. Learn to trust in God, people, for he is all that I say he is. Don't be influenced by circumstances, whether you are rich or poor, educated or not, all power belongs to God and all mercy. God blesses each person in the exactly proper measure; so don't be up tight, trust God.

Chap.
63

O God, thou art my God. I will continually praise you. As long as I live I will praise you, whether I be thin or fat, hungry or full.

At night as I lay in bed and think of you I am comforted, for I know that those plotting against me haven't a chance with you as my protector. Those that support me shall be blessed, and I know that those that tell lies about me shall be punished.[2]

---

[1] This is an example of unanswered prayer
[2] Just so God didn't have to do it all, David punished some himself.

Lord, I am praying again for protection. Be a secret place for me, O God, for my enemies are putting their fat lips out against me. They say everything you can imagine. Bounce it all back on them.

Would that all men would fear God. Surely the righteous shall be glad of their faith and the upright in heart shall find peace.

All the people praise you, O Lord. Some day all will turn to you in prayer. Particularly fortunate is any person called of you and inspired to serve under your care.

Let us learn to be satisfied to worship. We recognize that you have the power to calm seas, to quiet down people, to make the wind cease, you control the sun and the moon and their schedules, you control the rain, and all nature responds to your control. May we join nature in songs of praise.

Make a joyful noise to the Lord, everybody, serve the Lord with gladness, let God know how impressed you are with his power, come and see the works of the Lord.

Don't you remember how God opened the sea? God watches everything. Please, God, don't let the wicked prosper.

Bless the Lord, everyone. As for me, I have been through great strife, but I declare the Lord to be my salvation and I make public witness to the glory of God and I testify as to what God has done for me.

I prayed to the Lord and though he was a little slow, the Lord answered me, God showed mercy to me, and I bless his name.

God be merciful to us and bless us and cause his face to shine upon us, in order that we might recognize that there is help on earth through the Lord.

Would that all the people would praise God. Would that the nations would be glad and shout for joy, for God has judged the people fairly. Come on, everybody, praise the Lord!

Then shall the earth yield its full amount and God, even our own God, shall bless us, and all the ends of the earth shall fear him.

Let God arise and scatter all his enemies. I wish God would blow evil away like smoke or melt it like wax.

Praise ye the Lord. God is all powerful. God breaks the chains of the prisoners, he shakes the earth, he sends rain, he helps the poor, he defeats the kings.

The chariots of God are innumerable and wonderful to behold, God has led captivity itself away into captivity, bless the Lord who daily provides our needs.

God is surely the God of salvation, the ruler of rulers, and the Lord of all. Put an end to war, O Lord, and let all the people turn to praise the Lord our God.

Save me, O God, for I am depressed. My eyes are wet and my throat is dry as I serve God, hoping for some help against my enemies. I have more enemies than I have hairs on my head.

All that I have done, I have done for the sake of the Lord. I have endured shame, I have been a fugitive, and a rebel. All this for your sake.

Now, God, come to my aid. You know all about all my troubles. I have had to eat gall and drink vinegar.[1] I am heavy-hearted because of what I have done wrong and even more so over the things of which I am accused and am yet innocent.

Please do a little fixing of my enemies. One suggestion is the stomach ache. Try this on some of them. The troubles that you have brought on me I deserve, but not the extra punches of the wicked. Why not just take them completely out of the land of the living, particularly the ringleaders who plot so against me.

As for me, I will praise the name of the Lord, and I am certain that this is more desirable than sacrifice or a big plate offering.

The Lord will in time bless the needy; so let heaven and earth praise God, let all the people of God praise him, and may the name of the Lord be a sacred treasure handed down from one generation to another. God will provide an eternal place for his people.

Hurry, O God, with deliverance. My time is really crowding me. Let the people who seek the Lord prosper and let the wicked get it in the neck.

I am poor and needy,[2] O God, please no delay, just deliver me now.[3]

In thee, O Lord, do I put my trust. Deliver me from the unrighteous and the wicked. You have been with me from the very beginning, God. Some people admire my bravery, but I know it is because you are with me.

The talk is that the wicked are spreading, that God has deserted me and that now would be a good time to run me off the throne. Hurry with some help!

Confound and confuse my enemies. I continue to hope, and to praise your name. I move daily in the strength of the Lord. Stay with me, Lord, I know I'm old, but I need you all the more.

Praises continue to come from me. I sing to the glory of God, and my tongue tells of the righteousness of the Lord, but please bring quick confusion to my enemies.

[1] This is slightly exaggerated, but he made his point.
[2] He meant poor and needy in spirit.   [3] A spear had just come close.

God bless my son Solomon. Grant that he may judge the people fairly and with mercy and encourage him to help the needy and the disadvantaged.

Give dominion to Solomon, that he may increase the expanse of the kingdom, spread his name abroad in every direction.

Grant that Solomon may be widely respected and that many kings will come to him to acknowledge his greatness.

Make the name of my son Solomon memorable so that as long as there is history his name will be remembered. Let Solomon be a blessing to all nations, and may these things also be a means of glorifying the Lord God of Israel.

May the whole earth be full of the glory of God, Amen, Amen, as prayed by David the son of Jesse.

I know that God is really good to his people, but I was slipping. I had gotten where I was envious of the wicked and I resented their success. It just seemed that the wicked were always better off than the good boys.

The wicked wear coats of pride and breeches of violence, they are also usually fat and rich. They are corrupt and they defy God.

For instance, they ask how God knows anything. How can God see and not be seen? These are really an ungodly bunch. As for me, I behave myself, go to church, and I'm having a terrible time with backache and arthritis.

The only help I get is when I go into the sanctuary and pray.

I guess that you will suddenly put an end to all their wickedness just as a dream vanishes when a person awakes.

You are all I have, Lord. I am depending entirely upon you. My flesh and my courage are at a low ebb, but you come on strong as the strength of my life.

It is refreshing for me to draw near to God, it is stimulating and encouraging.

How long are you going to be angry with your people, O Lord? Remember us poor church people, for we are having trouble, right in our own congregation. There are some bigmouth people urging the doing of wicked things. They are doing crazy things in your sanctuary, even having a bar-b-que.

The church seems to be deteriorating. We no longer have great dedicated preachers and none of us seem to know how long the wicked will prosper.

How about doing something? You divided the sea, created the mountains, dried up rivers, started floods, made summer and winter, so why not do such a little thing as crack the heads of the wicked.

Save me, God, don't let the wrong crowd rule the church. Act now, for the baddies are on the increase.

Thanks be to God. Promotion or prosperity does not come from man, but from God. Only the Lord is able to render proper judgment.

The Lord prepares the wine for the righteous and the wicked get the dregs, so let me praise the Lord for he will bring justice to the earth.

The name of the Lord is greatly respected in Judah. God destroys the weapons of war, and demolishes the chariots of the wicked. When God is aroused there is no standing up to him, for God is fierce, he rules the earth. He will trim down unruly leaders to size, and he will save the humble.

I cried to the Lord in my day of trouble and he heard me. I'm glad I remembered to pray. I admit there are some puzzling matters.

Why does God often seem so inactive? Has God forgotten how to be merciful and helpful?

Surely there is no god like our God, and I will think of the wonders of the past, the dividing of the waters, the floods, the fire, the voice of God's thunder, the lightning, the storms at sea. I will remember and be comforted, for you have a record, Lord, of leading your people.

Let me remind everybody and let us tell our children about the commandments of God and his statutes. God's law is to be handed down from generation to generation. Teach the children to set their hope in God and forget not his commandments.

Tell the children to be an improvement on their parents. God has done many marvelous things and yet the old timers failed to obey the Lord.

Help us, O God. Forget our shortcomings, deliver us, and purge us for your name's sake.

Listen, Lord, to the pleas of the prisoners and balance the books with the wicked, and then we your people will give you thanks and we will show our appreciation down through the years.

Turn to us again, O Lord, bless us and restore our power. How long do you plan to be angry?

We were a great people, escaped from Egypt, and we began to cover the Promised Land as a vine and spread as branches of a tree. Then all of a sudden every beast of a heathen began to gnaw away on us and we are next to nothing.

Look down from heaven, Lord, and check on us. We need some help at once. Inspire us, renew us, and bless us. Let us seek your face again and then we shall be saved.

Sing to the Lord, make a delightful song to praise his name. The law of God was blessed in Joseph who controlled the land of Egypt when he didn't even know the language. God has been tested and we know that he delivers.

The Lord has declared that he is God and we have failed to listen. If the people will return to the Lord and obey his commandments then God's blessing will again reside with his people. If only the people had obeyed, then God would have long ago devoured their enemies.

God is the judge of all the earth. How long are you going to let the wicked get by as they do, O Lord?

Why don't you defend the poor and the disadvantaged? These people are in trouble and they don't understand. Get with it, God. Start your action!

Don't be quiet, God. Speak out. Your enemies are raising hell everywhere and saying all kinds of weird things. Some of them are saying there should be no nation of Israel.[1] In fact, they have organized a group of nations just to wipe out Israel.

Fix some of these people like you did the Moscow Muggers and the Capone Gang. Blow them around like chaff in the wind, burn them like kindling, terrify them, make them ashamed, humiliate them so that all men may know that your name is Jehovah, most high ruler over all the earth.

How pleasant it is to be in your church, O Lord. Often I yearn just to be in peace, quietly sitting in the sanctuary.

Just like the sparrows find a place to nest and the swallows a chimney down which to swoop, so it seems as a sanctuary to those of us who come to worship in your house.

Happy is the man whose strength is in you, a person who going through a difficult situation digs a well so the next person coming that way may be refreshed.

All such godly people finish their life in the presence of the Lord.

A day in your presence, Lord, is better than a thousand elsewhere and I would rather be a menial servant in a hut of yours that to dwell in the glamour suite of the Waldorf-Astoria.

The Lord is a sun for light and a shield for protection, the Lord gives grace and glory, and no good thing does the Lord withhold from those that love him and who obey his commandments. Happy is the man who trusts in God.

[1] Some of them are still saying it

Lord, you have been good to Israel and restored our unity, you have forgiven our sins, continue to be merciful to us, inspire us, and grant us salvation.

Certainly the Lord speaks of peace to his people and salvation is offered to those that fear him. Surely a new day is coming full of righteousness and peace and the Lord will bless our land and we shall glory in praising God.

Hear me now, O Lord, for I am in great need. Protect me, and encourage me. I know the Lord is good and ready to forgive. Have mercy on me, Lord.

Always when I am in trouble I call on the name of the Lord, for I am confident that God will help me. There is no other god except Jehovah and the words of God testify to his greatness.

Teach me continually your way, O Lord, and I will continue to praise you, and always will I depend on your mercy, for I know you are compassionate and considerate. It would be greatly helpful, Lord, if you would do something extra nice for me now, Lord, so that my enemies might be able to see that you support me.

The city of God is set upon a high hill and the Lord favors this city over all others. Many glorious things are spoken about Jerusalem.

I hear fellows brag about being born in Egypt, or the South, or California, but some day persons will be bragging about having been born in Jerusalem. Jerusalem shall some day be the key word in great songs widely sung throughout the world.

Continually, O Lord, do I find myself praying to you about all manner of things. Now I'm asking for relief from my troubles.

I find myself getting old and nearing death, my hearing and my sight are fading, and I feel that you are leaving me in the dark.

Don't wait too long, O Lord. There is no point in healing me after I'm dead as I'll be in the cemetery. I want some healing now.[1]

O Lord, don't you realize that I cannot praise you from the grave, nor from that dark hole can I tell of your loving kindness and mercy. I am really in bad shape and of no use to my friends or my family. Please heal me. Just a quick miracle, O Lord.

The time has come for us to sing of the mercies of God so that all generations forever will know that the Lord is good, that the throne of David will remain intact year after year, and the heavens shall carry the story of the wonders of God in the shifting clouds and twinkling stars.

---

[1] David's back was really hurting

The strength and power of the Lord is visible on the sea, and blessed are the people who recognize the power of God and who rejoice in praising him.

God is the strength behind David and the Lord will bless his works and strengthen his arm and the followers and descendants of David that serve the Lord will be blessed.

All these things being true, it is hard to understand why David becomes old and suffers, as if you had deserted him. At such times as this we wonder where the loving kindness of the Lord is, for is not his servant David in great distress? When will help come?

Nevertheless, blessed be the Lord forevermore.

Chap.
90

Lord, you have been a central concern in all generations. Before the mountains were formed or ever you had created the earth, always you were in existence, even from everlasting to everlasting you are the one God.

A thousand years seem but as a day to you from your scale of observation, it passes as if it were a half-time show.

Everything is under your careful control, you know everything, we daily face the tribulations caused by our own errors, and yet one whole lifetime passes as a story told around a campfire.

We are basically limited to 70 years anyway, give or take a few, and we never know all about your wrath or the use of your power, so teach us to try to make every day count, and daily bring us closer to you.

Have mercy on us. At least balance our hard times with good times.

Let the graciousness of the Lord be reflected in our lives, bless the work we do, and make it durable for your name's sake.

Chap.
91

Anyone who loves the Lord is able to live in the shadow of God's majesty, and so I think of the Lord as my fortress, for I completely trust in God.

Think of the Lord as a giant bird that will cover you with his wings and deliver you from the traps and the snares of life. There is no need then to fear the bullet that flies by day nor the violence abroad at night, for the Lord will protect as he pleases.

A thousand might die very close to you, but the Lord is able to save you, no evil will come to you, sickness or misery except with the Lord's permission.

It is really quite simple, for the Lord merely assigns a couple of angels to watch over his chosen ones, and they can even keep you from stumping your toe.

God responds to those that love him, he provides deliverance and honor, and the life of those who love God is a full life.

It is a good thing to give thanks to the Lord, to sing his praises, to comment on his lovingkindness and his faithfulness.

How great and wonderful are the works of the Lord. Brutes and fools can't see this, and they perish because of it.

The enemies of the Lord in time will be consumed, but those that love the Lord shall be refreshed and flourish as a well-watered tree. The Lord is my rock and there is no error in God.

The Lord reigns. The throne of God is established forever. The Lord is above the floods, above the mountains, above the noise and strife of even the storms at sea. The words of the Lord are true and holiness is the name of God's house.

Now, Lord, I think it is time for you to take action against your enemies. How long do the wicked get to do their thing? How long will you allow them to brag, to take advantage of widows, to murder? Did you know, God, that they think you aren't keeping in touch?

I know the brutish and cheaters are going to be punished, but they don't think so.

The Lord knows even the thoughts of man. Fortunate is the man that God teaches, even though God uses hardship and suffering as a means of teaching. Eventually all will be properly adjusted.

From my own experience, I know that I would have been lost if all I had depended upon was the help of some friends, but I trusted in God, and the Lord has supported me. The Lord is my rock and the Lord will destroy my enemies in his own way and in his own times.

Come, let us sing to the Lord, let us really belt it out in praises to the rock of our salvation.

The Lord is a great god and a great king above all gods, in his hands are everything, the deep places of the earth are his, the seas are his, for he made them, and God's hands formed the dry ground; so come let us worship, let us kneel before the Lord our maker.

Surely he is our God and we are the sheep of his pasture. I have been imploring you hard-headed people for forty years, please now turn to the Lord and depend on him.

Sing a new song to the Lord. Declare his greatness, describe his wonders to everybody. Honor, majesty, and strength all belong to the Lord our God.

Give to the Lord the glory due him, honor him properly, tell the unbelievers about God, witness to the power of the Lord, then watch the heavens rejoice, the sea roar, the field applaud, and the whole earth be glad, for the Lord will come to judge the world, to see that righteousness rules and that God's word is supreme.

The Lord reigns. There may be clouds, and darkness may seem to cover the earth, but God will go forth with fire from his mouth and consume his enemies.

Confused and baffled will be those that serve false gods, who worship money or science, for the heavens will declare the power of God in lightning and natural disasters, but the Lord will deliver from fear those that love him; so rejoice in the Lord, be grateful that God is holy.

How about even another new song? The Lord has done some marvelous things. The Lord has declared his salvation, he has remembered his promises of mercy; so let us make a joyful noise to the Lord, crack out all the musical instruments, let the sea roar and the waves clap their hands, for the Lord comes in great righteousness to rule the world in fairness.

God reigns. Let the wicked tremble and the righteous stand in awe. God is the king that loves justice, exalt the name of the Lord, for he is holy.

Moses, Aaron, and Samuel praised God and when they called on the Lord he responded. God replied with a cloud and a pillar of fire, for when they sinned they repented, and they observed the laws of God.

Exalt the Lord our God and worship him.

Make a joyful noise to the Lord, everyone; serve God cheerfully, realize that he is God, that it is God that has made us, we are not self-made, we are his people, so come with thanks to God and bless his name, for the Lord is good, his mercy is everlasting and his truth endures forever.

I will sing praises to God and bless the Lord for his mercies. I will no longer go to the girlie shows and associate with brawlers. I am definitely going to give up all wickedness. When I hear gossip start I am going to just walk away.

My concern and my interest will be with those who are faithful and I shall gather around me as helpers those that are honest and godly.

The liars and the deceitful are not to be tolerated and I plan to clean up Jerusalem.

Hear me now, Lord, for this is one of my trouble times. I am too upset to eat. Groaning and not eating have caused me to lose weight and I just sit around like a pelican, doing nothing.

I feel like a lonely sparrow on a rooftop with all the B.B. guns pointed at me. I cry in my beer.

God, you lift me up, then cast me down; but it is great to know that you endure forever. I look to the day when the heathen shall all fear the name of the Lord, when the kings of the earth shall see your great glory, and the kingdom of God will prosper.

For generation after generation shall the Lord look down from heaven and he will hear the prayer of the lonely and the destitute, he shall release the prisoner, and gather all the kingdoms of the world together in peace.

I wish I could live to see all this. I know God does not plan these things in my lifetime, but I know that the generations to come will behold his glory and the children of God shall be well established in the earth.

Bless the Lord, O my soul, and all that is within me, bless his holy name, and never forget all that God has done for us.

God forgives errors, he heals diseases, he equips believers in loving-kindness and tender mercies, he makes food taste good, and refreshes a person so that even the advanced in years feel young and spry and seek to fly like eagles.

The Lord has provided a basic system of justice. God revealed his plan to Moses and his activities were witnessed by all the people of Israel. The Lord is merciful and gracious, slow to anger and plenteous in mercy. God will not always be scolding nor will he always remain angry.

God has never punished us in relation to our sins nor rewarded us on a basis of what we really had coming. As high as outer space is above the earth, so tremendous is his mercy to those that worship him. As far as the east is from the west, that's how far God has separated us from our mistakes. Just as a loving father cares for his children, so the Lord cares for those that serve him.

God knows us. He remembers that originally we were a pile of dust. A man is really a lot like grass or a flower in the field, he grows up and then suddenly the wind blows him away, but not so with God's mercy, for it is from everlasting to everlasting, and his righteousness spreads from generation to generation among his followers, those that keep his agreements and remember to obey his laws.

The Lord rules over all the earth and all the kingdoms of the earth.

Bless the Lord. Let his angels that do his errands bless the Lord, let the ministers bless the Lord, and let all the good things that are being done in all the earth be a sign of the blessing of God. Praise God again and again.

Bless the Lord. Acknowledge the goodness of God and the greatness of God. God is clothed in light and God stretches out his creation like a curtain. Do you know who made all the seas?

What about the clouds and the winds? They are God's playthings. The Lord has angels for special work and also ministers to preach his word.

Creation is a marvelous thing. Imagine making something as permanent as the earth. Yet God separated the water and the land, furnished a little thunder for sound effects, and produced mountains and valleys. Then God put boundaries on all creation. Just think of all the details. The spring, the birds transplanting seeds, grass for cattle, herbs for the wild game, fields for food and wine to nourish mankind, oil for cosmetics and bread for body building. God thought of all these things.

Trees made so the sap may run, also providing a place for birds to nest, high hills for goats and rocky places for black squirrels, the moon to tell of the seasons and the sun to keep track of the days. God arranged for a period of darkness so the subtle creatures like coons could steal corn and lions could stalk young deer. When the sun rises the animals go to bed and man gets up and goes to work. I just can't imagine such wisdom and such planning.

The sea is a fabulous creation with all kinds of little things swimming around under water and man rowing a boat on top. The playful whale is a sight in itself.

Yet God continues to rule. When God so decrees all is well and when God decides otherwise, he complicates matters. The glory of the Lord is surely forever and the Lord shall rejoice in all his creations.

Now and then God looks hard at one place and causes an earthquake or he tumbles a mountain top and starts a volcano erupting. For all these things, I will worship God, I will sing songs of praise to him. I am satisfied with my belief in God and I also know that the wicked will in time be eliminated. Bless the Lord, O my soul.

Give thanks to the Lord and tell everybody about his wonderful works. Be glad to be one of God's people, search for the Lord, be mindful of all his wondrous works. Surely the Lord is God and his judgments are to be exercised all over the world.

God has made a number of promises, some to Abraham, some to Isaac, and some to Jacob, and God keeps all his promises. It never mattered to God whether his people were few in number or many, he protected them. God appointed prophets and leaders, he sent Joseph ahead of time to prepare a place for his people, and God always blessed his people.

God sent Moses to deliver his people, he gave Moses great

powers so that the Egyptians saw the waters turn to blood, the hail, the locusts, all the plagues were testimony of the power of God.

The Lord led his people in the wilderness with a cloud by day and a pillar of fire by night and he fed the people with manna from heaven and quail from a special migration.

God remembered his promise and finally the people crossed the Jordan with great singing and much pleasure as they came to claim the land of Canaan.

Praise the Lord for he is good and his mercy endures forever. Blessed are the good, for they can appreciate the mighty works of the Lord.

God, help our people. Inspire them. None of them saw the miracles of Egypt, and even our ancestors that saw these things forgot about them when confronting the Red Sea, yet God delivered them and swept away the Egyptian army in a flood.

Even after this, though, the people soon forgot about the power of God and his willingness to protect his people, and they disobeyed God and pursued the lusts of the flesh.

The whole history of the trip through the wilderness is a record of sin, repentance, and deliverance, then sin again. The patience of God is without measure. Time and again God delivered, and time and again the people rebelled.

Save us again, O Lord. Gather us together as one people. Blessed be the Lord God of Israel from everlasting to everlasting. Amen.

Give thanks to the Lord, for he is good and his mercy endureth forever. Certainly those that have been delivered by the Lord should give thanks for he preserved them in the wilderness, he has helped the hungry and thirsty, God has saved so many. Would that all men would appreciate the Lord and bless him.

God fills the hungry soul with goodness, and I wish mankind would continually praise God for his goodness and for his wonderful works to the children of men.

God has even delivered fools who have rejected him until they are at death's door, but even then God responds.

Some men are impressed, of course. Certainly those that go down to sea in great ships and travel on the great waters, for they see the power and majesty of God. These men learn of God in the raging storm when the seas are tumultous and the ships are tossed to and fro. At such times men call on the Lord and he delivers.

How I wish men would praise the Lord for his goodness and his wonderful works for the children of men.

The church people should also praise the Lord. Surely they observe the Lord turn a drought area into a lush green pasture, the fields are blessed, the land prospers. The Lord often helps the poor and the church people know this, so let them rejoice, and those who are wise should learn from this that the Lord is good and his loving-kindness is a working matter.

The time has come for me to sing, to glorify God, to take my guitar and sing first thing in the morning.[1]

God is merciful and to be praised. God always speaks in holiness and God has promised me success against the enemies of Israel. The Fascist[2] dogs will get it for sure.

Who else could guarantee such victories except the Lord? Help us now, Lord, and lead us in our battles. Although we are brave, it is only because we know that the Lord is with us.

Lord, it's time for action. The wicked are going full speed and they are mouthing about me something awful. I have tried to be considerate of my enemies, even praying for them, but they are worse than ever. Please smite them.

There are several things you could do, Lord. One is just shorten their time of life, cause them to lose their jobs, or let their children become instant delinquents. Another way is to let them start blackmailing each other.

Most of these wicked men seem to enjoy cursing others, how about encouraging others to curse them?

Deliver me, Lord, because of your mercy and because everyone knows that I trust in the Lord. Save me. Do it in such a way that everyone will know that it is done by your hand.

Continually do I praise the Lord, trusting in him, and being assured that God will always help the needy.

The Lord has spoken to the Savior who is to come, who sits on the right hand of God,[3] and has promised that under the Messiah will the world grow in righteousness and the wicked gradually be removed.

The Lord has promised the Messiah. He shall judge the heathen, he shall be the glorious high priest over the one great church idea under his direction. Someday he shall be the real king of kings.

Praise the Lord. Note his wonderful works. The Lord is gracious and full of compassion, he has fed his people when they were hungry, the works of his hands are true and his commandments are upright. God has provided a means of redemption for his people. The Lord is holy, reverence the name of God, and stand in awe of the

[1]Neighbors were not allowed to complain about kings
[2]Philistines
[3]This interpretation seems quite clear to me

105

Lord, for this is the very starting point of wisdom. The peace of God endures forever.

Happy is the man who respects God and observes his commandments. Such a man is blessed in himself and his descendants make a contribution in life.

Such a man as is godly considers himself rich, life is enjoyable to him and interesting, he is compassionate, he gives freely, he conducts his affairs with great integrity, and he shall not worry over bad news, for he trusts in the Lord.

A good solid Christian citizen gives to the needy, stands unafraid in the community, is honored by his peers, and the wicked observe him and are jealous.

Praise the Lord. Blessed be the name of the Lord from morning until night. The Lord is truly the Lord of all, he is in charge of everything, he is concerned about the poor, he sometimes relieves a barren woman so that she starts having kids, and he often elevates the lowly to a high place.

Long ago Israel made a break with Egypt and the promised land was waiting, the Red Sea opened to let God's people through, mountains and hills proved to be no barrier. Stand in awe, everyone, for the God of Israel brought water from rock and made the earth tremble.

Let all the glory go to the Lord. The gods of the heathen are really pitiful for they are made from metals by men's hands, they have eyes but see not and mouths but they can't talk. They have hands that do nothing and feet that don't take them anywhere.

O Israel, trust in God. The Lord has been great in our past and will bless our future. Blessings come to those that worship God. Let us bless the Lord while we are alive for it will be too late when we are dead.

I love the Lord because he has heard me. When I was sick and dying, when I was in great trouble, I called on the Lord and he delivered me; so naturally I praise his name and trust in him.

How can I possibly repay God for all that he has done for me. At least I can publicly witness to my belief in God.

Precious in the sight of the Lord is the death of his saints.

I am your servant, Lord. I will pay my church pledge and in the presence of the people I will praise the name of the Lord.

Praise the Lord for his merciful kindness, praise him all the nations, for the fact of God is an eternal truth.

Give thanks to the Lord for he is good, let all Israel say that God's mercy endures forever. I called on the Lord in time of great distress and he came to my assistance.

It is a lot better to trust in God than to depend on man. Even though I become surrounded by a multitude of nations, yet I will trust in God.

The Lord is my strength and my song. I shall live and declare the works of the Lord, even though he punished me, he did it for my own good.

The very stone which the builders refused has become the head of the corner. This is the Lord's doing and it is marvelous to behold.

This is the day which the Lord has made, let us rejoice and be glad in it. Along with this good day, Lord, please send some instant prosperity.

The Lord is my God, and I will exalt his name. Give thanks to the Lord for he is good and his mercy endures forever.

Chap.
119

Blessed are those who walk in the ways of God. God has told us to obey his laws and I wish I could do this, then I would never be ashamed. I will keep trying, Lord, please don't forsake me.

How can a young fellow clean up his life? It's simple, just follow the word of God. Blessed are you, Lord, teach me your laws again and again. I really rejoice in your word, I meditate, and I will not forget your instructions.

Deal generously with me, Lord. Open my mind so that I can understand better your word. I need more information. I don't understand everything you do. People argue with me, but I still insist on advocating your way.

Help my understanding! I would like to be able to comprehend more of your ways so I could speak more fully in your behalf. Stay with me, Lord, even as I am staying with your regulations.

Give me a better understanding and it will be easier for me to keep your laws. I need to be influenced more to good and to enjoy good things more than I do. Protect me from conceit, and strengthen me in righteousness.

Be merciful to me, Lord, so that I may talk back to my enemies and demonstrate to them your support. I will enjoy your laws and I will tell other kings of you and your goodness.

My great comfort is the word of hope which you have given to me. I have been comforted by remembering your mighty acts of old, for I have plenty of enemies who talk constantly about how they despise me.

Have mercy on me, Lord. I have considered my plans and determined that I will follow your suggestions. The wicked have taken advantage of me, but I have clung to my faith. I try to associate with good people. I know that the whole earth is full of your mercy.

You have done well by me, Lord. Teach me more, though. I went astray, but I returned. You are good, and it was helpful to me to go bad and then reform. I would rather have possession of your law, O God, than to accumulate silver and gold.

I know your judgments are right. Let the proud be put to shame, but protect me from wandering from your law.

My soul sometimes begins to feel weak because your word seems scarce. I can't see clearly, and my mind becomes like a bottle of smoke. My problem is that I can't wait for you to punish my enemies.

Help me now, Lord. Show me your will clearly.

The faithfulness of God has been firmly established. This knowledge has pulled me through my troubles. I have seen that everything is perishable except your word.

I really enjoy your laws. I meditate on them all the time. Studying your commandments has made me wiser than my enemies, and I even know more now than most of the preachers. I even know more than the old-timers, for I am obeying the law of God.

How comforting are your words and they taste better than honey.

Your word is a lamp to my feet and a flashlight on my path. Please accept the praises of my lips. I am determined to obey your laws all my life.

I have grown to hate evil and to love good. Your word, Lord, is like a shield for me, or a hiding place. The Lord plans to put away all the wicked as if they were litter. It scares me to think of the power of God.

It is time to get with the program, though, Lord, for the wicked are getting mighty active and prosperous.

I love to read your word. It is hopeful, it gives light, it directs and teaches. I sometimes sit and cry because of all the wickedness that I see.

My enemies are getting right important, and I seem small and unimportant, but I still cling to your word.

I cried with my whole heart to God for help. I was so miserable and prayed so long that morning seemed as if it had been postponed. Hear my cry. The wicked are at work. Control them promptly, please.

My enemies are numerous. I know your mercy is great, O Lord, and I surely need some of it now. I know your word is true, and it really hurts to see these monkey heads making fun of you.

Great peace comes to those that love the Lord and observe his word. I keep such things fresh in my mind by having my devotionals seven times a day. Hear me now, Lord, and lend me a helping hand. I know I went astray, but I am back now in the fold.

In my trouble I called on the Lord and he heard me. Protect me now from the damage done by the lying lips of gossipmongers, help me. I am a man of peace, and yet all my advisers want me to declare war.

I lift up my eyes to the hills. From where does help come? My help comes from the Lord, who made heaven and earth.

He will not let you be knocked off balance, for He is a keeper that neither slumbers nor sleeps. God protects you, so that in the day the sun does not get you, nor will you get in trouble on a moonlight night,[1] but the Lord is able to preserve you, God will watch your going out and your coming in, from now on, and forever more.

I was delighted when they said it was time to go to church, particularly in Jerusalem. Jerusalem is a well built city and here the tribes of the Lord gather to give thanks to God. It is here that the thrones of Israel have been established.

Pray for the peace of Jerusalem. I pray that peace and prosperity may be found in Jerusalem, for the sake of the people, and because the great house of the Lord is in Jerusalem.

As the eyes of a servant looking toward the master, as a player to a coach,[2] as a girl to her hairdresser; so we look to God for instruction and help.

Have mercy on us, Lord, for we are fed up with seeing the proud, fat cats live at ease and scorn God.

If it had not been that the Lord was on our side, our enemies would have swallowed us. We would be desolate if it were not for the Lord. Blessed be the Lord who has enabled our souls to be free as a flying bird, for our help is in the name of the Lord, who made all things.

Those persons that trust in the Lord will become as stable as a mountain. The Lord surrounds those that trust him just as the hills surround and protect Jerusalem. God will prevent the good from being in the position of being forced into wickedness.

The Lord will guide those who turn aside from evil and peace shall finally come to Israel.

When the Lord freed us from captivity we became a people full of laughter and singing. We sang of the great deliverance and we praised the Lord for saving us.

[1]It ain't easy all the time   [2]Such as Lombardi

109

We are a happy people, for we went forth in sorrow and returned in great joy.

Except the Lord approve, those that build even a house are doing so in vain, and unless the Lord is keeping a city the watchman is wasting his time.

It is silly for a man to be so restless that he arises early and stays up late, for the Lord expects a person to sleep and to be free of worry.

A man with a family of kids is fortunate, for he is busy, and his children join in standing by him in time of need.

Blessed is everyone that really worships the Lord. Things will go well with such a man, he will enjoy eating, his wife will be a help to him and will produce children. A good man enjoys seeing his children grow and he particularly delights in his grandchildren.

Things have often gone hard for me, but the Lord has pulled me through my problems.

I would like to see all those that hate the people of God consumed by fire as if they were dry grass, and may they never receive the normal blessing of 'peace be with you,' or the like.

Out of the depths have I cried to the Lord. Listen, God, to my case. I know you believe in forgiveness or there would be none of us left. My soul waits for reassurance from God, even more anxiously than those who watch for the sunrise.

I am confident that the Lord will redeem all of Israel.

Lord, I do not think too highly of myself, nor do I aspire to accomplish things beyond my abilities or my opportunities. I am becoming very sensible. Let all the people of God see hope in the Lord.

Lord, remember David. He is the one who took an oath not to sleep or rest until there was a proper place for the ark of the covenant to dwell, a place which the Lord might consider home.

Bless the ark of the covenant, the church, and those who minister there. Remember your promise, Lord, to keep the throne of David intact, as long as the people worship you and obey your commandments.

God has chosen his people and his church. Jerusalem is the center. God has promised to clothe the ministers and priests with joy and to bless the people of the fellowship in the Lord.

The enemies of David will come to shame, but David shall prosper.

How pleasant it is to be in a church where the people get along well together. It is like cool oil on hot, dry skin. It is refreshing as the morning dew on the mountain of the Lord.

Bless the Lord all those that serve him, particularly those that guard the Lord's house. May the Lord bless you in return.

Praise the Lord, for he is good. The Lord has chosen Jacob and Israel for his special attention and I know that the Lord is great and that he is the Lord of all.

When the Lord created the heavens and the earth, he did everything exactly as he wanted. God set up the clouds, the lightning, the rain, the wind and the fogs.

The mighty acts of God are historical facts. God smote the first-born in Egypt, he sent plagues, he smote many nations who opposed the advance of Israel.

The Lord will judge his people and will separate them from those that serve gods made of silver and gold, for these gods are useless, they have mouths and don't speak, eyes that don't see, and ears that don't hear.

Bless the Lord. Serve him all you who are descended from Aaron or Levi, or any who recognized and worshipped the Lord God of hosts. Praise ye the Lord.

Give thanks to the Lord, for he is good, his mercy endures forever. It was the wisdom of God that caused the waters to be divided, that made the great lights of heaven, that delivered Israel, that opened the Red Sea, that overthrew Pharoah and overcame many kings.

God remembered us when we were down and out, he redeemed us from our enemies, and he fed us.[1]

We sat down and cried by the rivers of Babylon, we hung our guitars on hickory limbs, for we had been carried away captives, and they made fun of us, daring us to sing our favorite hymns in a heathen land.

How can we sing the songs of home in a strange land? It's easy! It would be easier to forget that I had a right hand than to forget the good ole days.

If I ever forget the joys of Jerusalem I hope my tongue clings to the roof of my mouth.

Be sure and remember, O Lord, what the Gestapo[2] did to our families in Jerusalem, and so bless the man who wipes out the Gestapo and kills them dead.

---

[1] The Israelites were greatly interested in eating   [2] Edomites

I will praise the Lord with my whole heart. I will face the temple in Jerusalem and praise the loving-kindness of the Lord. All the kings of the earth shall finally praise the Lord.

Great is the glory of God, and even though the Lord is high and lifted up, yet he is greatly concerned with the lowly, and God spearates himself from the haughty.

Though I walk in the middle of trouble, the Lord will be with me, he will strike my enemies. Continue to do your mighty acts, O Lord, for you are a God of mercy.

O Lord, you have had a good look at me. You know when I get up and when I lie down. There is not a word I speak that you don't hear. You are everywhere.

Just to think this way is really too much for my feeble mind. Surely though there is no way for me to be apart from God.

If I ascend to the clouds, you are there, if I go into the depths of the earth, you are there, if I take the wings of the Continental[1] and dwell on some island, you are there to guide me, and if I think I can hide at night from you I am wrong, for you make light out of darkness.

I will praise the Lord, for I am intricately made. It is appalling to consider the human body.

Yet you knew all about the body before it was made, you had it on the drawing board before man came into being.

How impressive it is to think thoughts, yet they come so much that they cannot be numbered.

One thing again, Lord. Surely you are going to get rid of the wicked. I want you to know that I'm against anybody that is against you.

Search me, Lord, try me, examine my thoughts and see if there is any wickedness in me at all,[2] then lead me in the way everlasting.

O Lord, deliver me from evil and violent people. There are too many people with sharp tongues who are always trying to stir up some strife, particularly against me.

I have publicly declared the Lord to be my God, strengthen me then in my time of need and protect me in the day of battle.

As for my enemies, it will suit me fine if their heads become exposed, if you send burning stones to whack them, let some of them be thrown in the fire and others in deep pits.[3] Surely the Lord will support the righteous and stand behind the afflicted.

Lord, hear my prayer. Protect me from saying some of the bad

---

[1] Golden-tailed bird   [2] I'm not quite as ready as David for this
[3] David disapproved of violence?

things I think. Don't let me be influenced by evil thoughts, and don't let me fall for the sins of the flesh.

If anybody is to correct me, let it be a righteous man who corrects with graciousness and is not offensive.

Constantly I look to the Lord for help, please save me from the daily snares of the wicked. Let the wicked fall in their own nets and let me escape.

Chap.
142

I cried to the Lord and I complained about my troubles. In the first place, I am deserted. No one seems to care for me. I have no men rallying to my cause. Naturally I cried to the Lord for the Lord is my refuge.

I am really down and my spirit is at a low ebb. Encourage me, Lord, bring my feelings out of the prison-like despair I feel, and then I can enthusiastically praise the Lord.

Chap.
143

Hear my prayer, O Lord. My enemies have laid me low. I am depressed and deserted.

I remember the good ole days, and I think back on the times of your mighty acts. Stimulate me, Lord, so that I will no longer think I am dying.

Reveal to me a new attitude so that I may start the day with freshness and vigor.

Destroy my enemies and raise my spirits for I am your servant, Lord.

Chap.
144

I will praise the name of the Lord every day forever and forever. Great is the Lord and greatly to be praised.

One generation shall pass along the information to the next generation concerning the mighty acts of God.

Really, what is man that you should pay any attention to him? Certainly he is just like a shadow that passes.

Get with the action again, Lord. Cause earthquakes, volcanoes, or floods and deal harshly with the wicked.

Then I will originate a new ballad and it will be like a hymn to be sung to the glory of God, for the Lord is good and his tender mercies endure forever.

Chap.
145

All the works of the Lord testify to his glory and his saints add their praises, for they tell of the power of God's kingdom, they speak of the mighty acts of God, and they proclaim that your kingdom is an everlasting kingdom and that it will endure through all generations.

The Lord supports the weak and looks out for the disabled. The Lord is righteous and opens his hand to make all the provisions of the world.

The Lord is near to all those that call upon his name and the Lord makes the life of the believer a full life.

The Lord will save those that love him and he will destroy those that don't.

My mouth will always praise the Lord, and may all people bless his holy name.

Put not your trust in leaders[1] for they are not dependable, they are also short-lived as other people are; so trust God. In trusting the Lord there is happiness.

The Lord is the creator of all things, he controls all things, he releases the prisoner, and provides food for the hungry. God is a great humanitarian.

The Lord shall reign forever and forever. Praise ye the Lord.

It is good as well as pleasant to sing praises to the Lord. God has gathered together the outcasts of Israel, he has healed the broken-hearted, he has relieved the wounded.

Great is the Lord. God even knows the names of the stars,[2] his power is great; so sing to the Lord.

Be thankful to the Lord for he is the one in charge of the rain,[3] he also causes the grass to grow on the hillsides, he feeds the birds and the animals.

God, however, is not particularly interested in track meets.[4] Praise ye the Lord.

Praise the Lord, for he is a strength to his people, he is a peacemaker, he issues orders to man and nature, he sends snow, and he sends freezing, icy days, and then he eases all this in the spring, and the snows melt and the waters flow.

God has revealed his truth to his people, and only to those that seek him. Praise ye the Lord.

Praise the Lord. Praise him all the angels, praise him all the people, let the whole earth praise the Lord.

Fire, hail, snow, dragons, golfers, winds, mountains, valleys, beasts, cattle, birds, kings of the earth, disc jockeys, anchor men, pretty girls, let them all praise the Lord for his name is excellent and his glory above heaven and earth. Praise ye the Lord.

Let all Israel rejoice. Let all those that worship God rejoice. Sing to the Lord.

Let the people dance[5] and sing before the Lord, praise God

---

[1] You can say that again   [2] Even the ones in Hollywood
[3] El Paso, Las Vegas, Oklahoma City
[4] That's what the Bible says!   [5] You mean in church?

with musical instruments,[1] and understand that God enjoys his people.

Let the believers rejoice and sing, even on cold, dark nights, for the Lord will punish the enemies of God, their kings shall be cast down, and the saints will be honored.[2] Praise ye the Lord.

Praise ye the Lord. Praise him in the church, praise him in the great outdoors, praise him for his mighty acts, praise him with the trumpet, with the guitar, with castanets, with dancing, praise him with great orchestras, let everything that has breath praise the Lord. Praise ye the Lord!

[1]Even the saxophone?   [2]Maybe some day in New Orleans

PROVERBS

Solomon, the son of David and the wise king of Israel, composed and collected a series of proverbs or thoughts for the day and even a few bumper sticker sayings. Here they are.

To become truly wise, so that even justice is clear, to adhere to fairness, to treat all men with equity, to be wise enough to teach young people, to be open-minded, to be able to distinguish between good and poor advice, and to clearly understand wise comment, a person must first stand in awe of the Almighty God. Fools disregard this.

Young people, listen to your fathers and mothers, for much of what they have to tell you is good.

Don't let evil doers snare you into joining them. If they tell you that they know any easy way to get a few fast bucks by taking advantage of someone, do not join them. Leave them entirely alone.

These types are always ready to shed blood, they are greedy, and finally the very net they spread catches them.

Wisdom and good sense often have no listeners and good words are often lost in street sounds.

God has offered wisdom, and those who refuse to take it will call in vain upon the Lord when calamity comes. It will be real terror to finally call on the Lord and hear nothing. Do not refuse to worship God and respect Him, or you will be left to yourself when trouble comes.

The work of fools and of evil men is self-defeating, but those who seek the Lord and call on his name shall find a real security.

People, if you will listen to God's word and meditate on his commandments, and truly seek to learn that which is right, so that you seek goodness as if you were searching for silver or gold, then you will begin to understand God and find a comfortable place in his presence.

The Lord grants real wisdom to those who seek him. God gives these people a very genuine type of protection.

As a person grows in wisdom, then understanding becomes pleasant, and discretion enters into a person's life, and a person begins to learn how to refrain from evil associations.

The judgments of the person seeking righteousness will cause him to depart from evil associations, to be leery of wild women, particularly one that flirts and flatters. Following such is a sure path to death.

Eventually the righteous will gradually begin to prosper and evil persons will be deprived of eternal life, and their pleasures will only be short-lived and transient.

Observe the law. This will result in a full life, and not one full of miserable worries.

Let mercy and truth be a definite part of your character, and you will be respected by both man and God.

Trust in the Lord. Do not let your own judgment oppose the law of God.

Do not think of yourself as being wise, but acknowledge that wisdom is of God.

Be generous and honor the Lord with your willingness to give, giving from whatever you first earn, not waiting to merely give what is left over. The Lord will look out for you.

Don't get upset when God teaches you by means of trouble. This just means that God is interested in you.

Happiness is really only finding wisdom through complete trust in God. This is a better possession than silver and gold, it is more precious than rubies, and more to be desired than anything.

Wisdom found in trusting the Lord means peace and happiness, a sense of fullness of life.

It was the wisdom of God that founded the earth. God in his wisdom created the heavens, the clouds, the dew. Don't forget that.

The only safe way to walk in this life is in the full trusting of God.

When you have a chance to do good, don't hold back or wait. Don't tell a neighbor that you'll help him later when it is more convenient.

Don't be quarrelsome.

Don't envy bullies, even though they may seem successful. The blessing of God is with the righteous, and God's curse is with the wicked.

God has no use for snobs, but he blesses the humble; God gives eventual glory to those who praise the Lord but shame shall come to the fools.

Chap. 4

Now listen to the good advice of an experienced father. I will tell it to you like it is. I learned these things from my father and my mother, and they were successful people.

Seek to understand life. Learn the truth of life, stick with the truth and the truth will stick with you.

Understanding is the key. Get wisdom, of course, but with it get understanding, a knowledge of how to apply wisdom.

If you observe the above, you will find life to be full and honorable.

Walk the straight and narrow. Continue to learn, never stop pursuing knowledge. Don't run around with goof-offs. All they do is live on trouble and they will involve you in it.

The path of the righteous is clear and bright, but the wicked are always stumbling around in the dark.

Don't fall for every pretty face. Avoid carefully the company of girls that kiss anybody anytime. Don't be a constant girl watcher. Keep your eyes on the road, particularly when you're driving.

In the search for wisdom you will find discretion. Stay clear of wild women. They look good and talk mighty cozy, but an evil woman will lead you to death and hell.

Listen, young people, don't gravitate to scoundrels. They merely seem attractive. If you defile yourself with wicked companions you will wind up sick and you will begin to degenerate.

Drink your own water that you know is safe. Don't have children by other women, but be faithful to your chosen wife. Why do you think you need to go to some woman other than your wife? The Lord keeps up with you, anyway. Those who wander from God's ways will be punished.

Don't go around endorsing just anybody's note. Be responsible for your own credit. Look at the ant. There's a good example. Each ant does its own work and is responsible for its own share of the common load.

Do you think you can get somewhere just sitting on your can? Get to work!

Have you noticed what a wicked man is like? He lies all the time, he uses signals in playing bridge, he cheats at poker, he starts arguments, and he will suddenly come apart all at once.

There are seven things that the Lord doesn't want to see. A man who is a snob, or a liar, a murderer, a crook who plans his sneaky crimes, a fellow who enjoys doing bad things, or a perjurer, or one who is always creating discord.

Son, follow the teachings of your father and mother and you will find these teachings a great comfort and a helpful companion.

The commandments of God are a lamp, and the law of God sheds light.

I seem to be harping on this, but please, son, stay away from prostitutes and loose women. There is nothing but trouble here.[1]

Actually a whore will just gradually get all your money and if you are cheating with another man's wife you just might get killed. It isn't worth it!

People will be right understanding of a thief who steals to keep from starving, but even in this case the fine is usually enough to bring starvation.

The man who commits adultery is really a fool. When the husband learns and seeks vengeance there will be no way of paying

---

[1] Solomon had 1,000 wives and concubines so he was speaking from experience, I guess.

him off.[1]

Study the commandments. Learn them so well that they are constantly at your fingertips. Think of righteousness as your sister. Be daily acquainted with her.

Let me tell you about something I saw. I was looking out the window and I saw a fine young man, full of life, walking down the sidewalk. It was just about dark and I saw a pretty woman move toward him. She was dressed with a low neck blouse and a split-skirt. The man should have run!

The woman smiled and said, "How fortunate! I am delighted to find you."

"Thank you, Ma'm," he said.

"I am celebrating, and I'm so glad you are here," she said as she pressed against him and kissed him.

"Come to my house," she continued. "My husband has left town with a bundle of money and I know he won't be back for a few days. I need a man very much, and you are just the one."

"I don't know if I should do that," said the fellow.

"Come on. I have put on clean sheets, and even perfumed the room. It will be an experience you can't forget! We can spend the whole night in great pleasure."

As a result, the man went with her, just as a steer heads for the butcher, or a bird to a snare.

Please, kids, don't fall for that way of life. It just isn't the fun it sounds to be. Lots of good, strong men have been reduced to nothing this very same way. If you want to find hell on earth, then that woman's house is the door to it.

Wisdom, which is really righteousness, is to be seen everywhere if you would look for it. Actually, it is just commonsense.

Listen to the truth. Wickedness just doesn't make sense. Learn the truth. It is better than getting silver or gold, in fact there is nothing to be compared to wisdom.

Wisdom encompasses good judgment. One way of showing wisdom is to stand in awe of God and to hate evil. Wisdom gives strength to kings and enables judges to make fair decisions. An interesting thing about righteousness is that those that seek righteousness find her.

A search for righteousness makes one rich in a sound and enduring fashion, as wisdom enables a person to grow in stability and strength.

Wisdom was in the beginning a part of God. Before fountains or mountains, before the earth existed, wisdom was present. Wisdom

---

[1] Solomon really must have had plenty of girl trouble.

was there when God laid out the plans for heaven and earth, when God established the clouds, defined the sea, and when God created the earth. Wisdom joined in the pleasure of the creation of man.

Blessed are those who follow the words of wisdom. Blessed is the man who hears God's word and observes the teachings. The person who finds wisdom and righteousness finds God, and God blesses them, but those that despise the word and hate God shall only find death.

Wisdom is a well established fact. Wisdom has its own attraction, it has its banquet scene, its delights, it has some good girls working for it. They call to the uninformed and invite them to become righteous, the good girls would have men set aside their foolishness.

There are some interesting observations in life. If you explain something to a phony, he gets irritated, but a wise man will thank you for the instruction. This is how a wise man becomes wiser.

Respect of God is the beginning of wisdom and the appreciation of holy matters is the start of understanding.

Wisdom is self rewarding and if you make light of wisdom or disdain it, then it is your loss.

It is not hard to tell a bad girl. She is usually loud and pushy, she approaches men, some of whom are busy attending to business. She says such things as "stolen fruits taste sweeter, or stolen drinks are more enjoyable." Then she entices the men to follow her. What she fails to tell them is that those who have previously heeded her are already halfway to hell, at least on earth.

A righteous son brings great happiness to his parents, but a wicked son is a heavy burden to bear.

The treasures of the wicked disappear at death, but the righteous take their treasures with them.

The Lord will always be concerned with the righteous, but the wicked can't count on his help.

A lazy man gets a poor return for he doesn't work, but a hard working man gains in life.

A wise man is alert to his opportunities and is not a victim of procrastination.

A just person is generally respected but a wicked man is very apt to get socked in the teeth.

The memory of a just man is very lasting, but the wicked are forgotten in short order.

A wise man will listen, while a fool prattles all the time.

An upright person can walk with confidence, but the wicked are always looking around nervously.

It is worthwhile listening to a righteous man, but it is a waste of time to listen to the wicked.

Hate causes trouble, while love smooths over anything.

A righteous man begins to accumulate wisdom, while a wicked person just gets lashes on the back or his credit card destroyed.

Sometimes the only thing a rich man has is his wealth, and sometimes riches is the only thing a poor man lacks.

A righteous working man has a full life, while all the wicked can do is pile up their sins.

A man is a fool who tries to deceive people and to hide his true feelings.

Beware of talking too much. With a lot of talk you are bound to say some of the wrong things.

The words of a good man are really worthwhile, but the words of the foolish are cheap and easy to come by.

God's blessing is a rich thing to receive and he doesn't add a penalty either.

Mischief is funny to a fool, but a wise man doesn't participate.

Fear usually catches up with a wicked man, while the righteous man usually has his hopes fulfilled.

The wicked will disappear as if blown away by the wind, but the righteous have eternal life.

A man who employs a loafer feels just as if he took a swig of vinegar and put his teeth on edge, or as if he got smoke in his eyes.

Respect for God gives life fullness, but the wicked are always running out of time.

The righteous man can look forward hopefully and gladly, while the wicked must know that only death awaits them.

The Lord will support the upright, but not the wicked. Eventually, the righteous shall prevail, and the wicked shall no longer have the use of the earth.

The word of the just is permanent, but wicked sayings will eventually all perish.

The upright man speaks good things, but the wicked are all negative and only criticize.

Chap.
11

Lack of fairness is greatly irritating to the Lord. God expects a person to give full value for what is received.

A man who begins to think he is self made or a great personal achiever is headed for trouble. The Lord blesses those who are humble.

The integrity of the honest man is a safe road to travel but cheaters have a pitfall awaiting them.

When the day of judgment comes it will be righteousness, not material possessions, that will be the pay load.

Righteousness provides a plain path but the wicked have to travel at great risk.

When a wicked man dies, he's a goner, but the righteous man continues to live.

A hypocrite attempts to destroy with his mouth, but the just man can survive underserved criticism.

A community enjoys two things, the success of a good man and the death of a bad one.

A fellow who doesn't know about life jumps to conclusions about his neighbors, but a smart fellow does not form snap opinions.

A good man keeps a secret, but a talebearer can't stop running off at the mouth.

A community that has no one living there to advise people is in bad shape. In fact, the counsel of many good men is better than the counsel of one.

A man who endorses notes for people he doesn't know is nutty, and he will suffer for it.

A gracious woman is honored and so is a man who knows how to handle financial matters.

A man full of mercy is always improving but a cruel man gets worse, and finally hurts himself.

Wicked men practice deceit, but righteousness brings its own reward.

The Lord doesn't care for a brassy person, but God delights in the upright citizen.

Even though the wicked organize into the Mafia, they will still be punished, but even the children of the righteous will receive a blessing.

A beautiful woman who is well behaved is like a precious gem.

Righteous people have good intentions, but the wicked are always planning trouble.

It is possible to be a giver and be better off after being generous; while a money grubber becomes poor because he thinks of himself as being poor.

People appreciate the person who makes his crops and goods available at a fair price, but the people learn to despise those that hold their goods for a price rise.[1]

A diligent person that looks for the good finds it, but the mischief maker gets caught in his own mischief.

A foolish man is always rationalizing in his own behalf, but a person who listens and learns becomes wise.

A fool blows his top while a wise man keeps his cool.

A wise person speaks and brings comfort while a fool injures with his big mouth.

Joy is the reward of the peace maker, but deceit accompanies the mischief minded.

[1]Pretty modern talk

A foolish man vainly displays his foolishness, but a wise man does not try to make a show of his knowledge.

A lazy man has to depend on someone else for his food, but not so with the diligent person.

There is no death along the road of righteousness, for it leads to eternal life.

Chap. 13

It is smart to listen to the advice of those of experience.

Control of the tongue is a mighty accomplishment.

A good man has no use for falsehoods, but the fool doesn't care.

It is possible to be rich in worldly goods and have nothing, and it is possible to be broke and have plenty.

A poor man never has to worry much about being kidnapped.

False pride creates controversy.

Wealth acquired improperly usually disappears, but riches secured by hard work will stick with a person.

Life rewards those who observe the commandments of God, and the respect for such laws is refreshing.

A sensible man plans ahead while a fool admits he doesn't care.

A reliable messenger is of great value for clear communciation is a real problem.[1]

A person that isn't interested in learning is headed for poverty and shame.

Everyone enjoys seeing plans work, but a fool continues with his plans even when it is obvious they are no good.

A wise man finds wise companions while a bunch of fools are usually seen heading for destruction together.

Righteous people are blessed, while wicked men are cursed.

Grandchildren profit from the inheritance of a righteous man, but the government usually takes all that a sinner leaves.

Injustice often prevents the poor from making a good living.

If a man loves his son he will correct him and not spoil him rotten.

A fool seems to live just to eat, while a wise man eats to live.

Chap. 14

A wise woman tries to make a home, while a foolish one is indifferent.

It is easy to keep an empty stable clean, but if you have no cattle you're a poor rancher.

A good witness tells the truth and a poor one lies.

An interested learner has no problem while the smart alec finds wisdom elusive.

[1]You certainly can't count on tapes

There is not much point in hanging around a foolish and deceitful person.

Fools make light of sin, but the wise think this is a serious matter.

Joy and sorrow can only be measured by the person concerned.

There are some things that seem pretty good to a person, but the end result is disaster.

You can cover sorrow or disappointment with laughter, but the sorrow is still there when the laughing ends.

The careless man becomes bored, but the righteous man sees a purpose in life.

A wise man doesn't believe everything he reads or sees.

A bright person is truly afraid of evil, but a nut thinks he can cover evil with rage and cursing.

A person with a short fuse is always getting into trouble.

Foolish people are called goofy while a wise man is respected.

People are more inclined to be friendly to the rich than to the poor, but blessings on those who do try to help the poor.

Mercy and truth are the companions of good people.

Work is a good thing, but just talking about it won't help.

Standing in awe of God creates strength and God offers protection to such persons and to their children.

A king measures his success by the number of people he rules.

It is wise to be slow to anger but a hasty temper invites trouble.

Envy will get you nowhere.

To the wicked the trip to the cemetery is the last ride, but to the righteous it is a road to a new life.

Righteousness is elevating to a nation, but sin drags a country downhill.[1]

A person who takes advantage of the poor is attacking God, so we should support those who show mercy and concern.

A ruler appreciates good help and doesn't care for lazy people.

A calm answer cools wrath, but a haughty spirit makes things worse.

A wise person knows when to speak and what to say, while a fool is a pop-off.

God is always watching!

A righteous man is rich in peace while a wicked man accumulates trouble.

The Lord despises the attempts of the wicked to buy him off, but the Lord appreciates the worshipful gifts of the good people.

A person who will not accept constructive criticism is doomed.

God knows all about heaven and hell, how can you think he

---

[1]Our crisis is not energy, but sin

doesn't know what goes on inside of you?

You can always spot a scornful person as he thinks he knows it all.

A happy person has his happiness reflected in his face.

It is better to be poor and love God than to be rich and headed for hell.

It is better to eat squash with a heart full of love than to eat sirloin steak with a mind full of hate.

A wise son makes his parents happy but a foolish one is a source of sadness.

An indifferent person has a thorny life while an upright man walks in a plain path.

Silly things are fun to a silly person.

It is wise to listen to the advice of more than one person.

How helpful it is to say the right thing at the right time.

The anti-godly are in trouble with God, but a righteous widow has a real good thing going for her.

Greed brings trouble.

A wise man thinks before he speaks, but the fool never waits.

The fool hasn't much chance in prayer for he is wicked, but the righteous are in communication with God instantly.

Everybody enjoys seeing beauty and hearing nice things.

The first step toward wisdom is respect for God, and humility is the first step toward success.

God is responsible for the outcome of everything, even though we may do the planning.

Most people can justify anything they do, but the Lord decides on the basis of intent; therefore a person should commit his life to God.

God is in charge of everything and everybody.

It won't do the wicked any good to get organized against God.

The best way to avoid evil is to think constantly of God.

When God is pleased with a person, the Lord even causes his enemies to think well of him.

When we make plans we should ask for God's guidance, and rulers would do well to do this particularly, for a ruler can only be fair with God's help.

A ruler can get good help from truthful aides.

A wise man will help calm down a king, for a king can cause a whole lot of trouble.[1]

It is better to become wise than rich.

You are better off to be sweating it out with the poor than sitting around dividing profits with evil rich people.

---

[1] Somebody needed to calm down Henry VIII for sure

Righteousness is like a fresh water fountain in a man's life, but evil makes a man stagnant.

An ungodly man is always digging up trouble and starting dissension, spreading gossip, taking advantage of his neighbor. Such a man sits around thinking up bad things to do.

A good, honest old man with white hair is worth much — listen to him.

If a person has learned to control himself he is more successful than a man who has control of a government.

Man can take all the chances he wants, but God is in charge of everything and doesn't leave anything to chance.

It is better to have a poor meal in peace than a seven course dinner during a big argument.

A wise servant should take advantage of his bosses' sons if the sons are no good.

You can purify silver and gold with fire but only God can purify the heart.

Wicked people and liars enjoy dirty jokes and malicious gossip.

God punishes those who laugh at other people's misfortunes.

A father glories in his children but the grandfather enjoys them the most.[1]

It is not proper for a leader of men to be untruthful and so you rarely find a fool talking straight.

A bribe often works, but it is a shame.

Nobody likes to be nagged.

Correcting a wise man once is better than whipping a fool a hundred times.

An evil plotter is always stirring up rebellion, and eventually it gets stirred up against him.

You are better off encountering a mad she bear with cubs than a fool on a binge.

A person who repays kindness with malice gets to keep the malice for a long time.

Starting trouble is like opening a watergate; so be careful when you start.[2]

The Lord has no use for those who justify the wicked or condemn the innocent.[3]

It is a waste for a student to pay to go to school who has no intention of learning.[4]

A good friend will stand by you anytime and a brother is usually ready to help in time of trouble.

[1] I thought I was the only one who knew this
[2] Once is enough   [3] Watch out, lawyers!
[4] I was never much on compulsory education

A troublemaker is usually boastful and looking for trouble.

The father of a fool has a hard life.

A joyful attitude is real good medicine, while a gloomy spirit makes your bones ache.

It is bad to offer bribes.

A fool is always seeking some weird and far away goal while the sensible man has a good purpose in life.

It is not good to punish the just, and it is wrong for those in authority to ask for kick-backs.

A knowledgeable man rarely runs loose at the mouth and so often a fool with his mouth shut is mistaken for the wise.

Chap.
18

A self-centered person twists everything around to suit himself.

Along with wickedness you will find indecency and contempt as companions.

The words of a man's mouth usually reflect the depth of his thinking.

A fool is always arguing, and if he is a golfer he always wants you to give him strokes.

The words of a gossip are malicious and deeply harmful.

A goof-off and a spendthrift are closely kin.

A righteous man receives strength in the safety and sureness of the name of the Lord.

Often a rich man uses his wealth to separate him from life and to build conceit.

There is no use talking to a man who has a closed mind.

When a man loses his courage he is reduced to nothing.

Proper use of a man's talent will often bring him into important circles.

Hearing only one side of a story is not enough, for one must hear both sides to be fair.

Often a touchy argument can be settled by the toss of a coin.

When you offend someone in your own family the damage is extremely hard to repair.

Being able to give good advice is as much fun as eating.

The tongue can really get you in trouble, especially when you say the wrong thing at the wrong time.

Finding a good wife is a real blessing.

Often when the poor seek help the well-to-do offend them and refuse.

There is no one any better for a person than a real good friend.

Chap.
19

It is better to be poor but honest, than to be affluent and a fool.

Being intentionally stupid is not an asset. It is also wrong to blame everything on God.

Wealth brings easy friends, while the poor aren't so popular.

Fasle witnesses and liars get theirs some day!

A ruler or a rich man are always being approached for favors or money. The poor man is neglected, even by his own friends.

If a person searches for the good it will be found.

It strikes me as being a shame when I see a fool as a ruler or an incompetent person head of a business.

A good man overlooks a lot of other people's faults.

When the king is angry he can cause terrible trouble, but when he likes a person he can make life easy for that one.

A foolish son and a nagging wife is about the worst thing that can happen to a man.

A man might inherit a house and a rich business, but if he gets a good wife he can thank the Lord.

Laziness is a real drag.

Keeping the commandments is the same as preserving one's soul.

When a person gives to the poor he is giving to the Lord.

Correct your son while he is young enough to be impressed.

A fellow with a hot temper is going to have a hectic life.

There are all kinds of thoughts in the mind of man, but attempt to discover which is of God.

Kindness should be instilled in everyone. Respect God and live.

A real lazy person is one that won't even feed himself.

A son who teases his mother and wastes his daddy's money is no good.

An ungodly witness doesn't care at all about justice.

Fools and scoffers are either criticized or given a beating.

Chap.
20

Wine and liquor lead to false courage and brawls and it is nutty to be mastered by strong drink.

It doesn't pay to make a king mad.

It is honorable to avoid strife.

A lazy man won't plow when it's cold and so he will go hungry.

It is unusual to find a truly faithful man, though there are plenty that say they are.

A good man is an asset and his children are fortunate.

A judge should consider all the evidence before rendering a decision.

No person can claim to be sinless.

The Lord doesn't care for any type of unfairness.

Even a child knows right from wrong and should be held accountable.

God made the ears and the eyes; so listen and look for the good things of God.

Don't sleep your life away. Get with it, boy!

A buyer acts as if he were getting gyped then brags to his friends about his bargain.

The words of wisdom are more precious than rubies and fine gems.

Again, don't make loans to strangers.

Deceiving a person may be fun at the time, but it won't work for happiness.

Don't declare war just on your own opinion.[1]

Be careful not to associate with a gossip.

Persons who turn against their parents will live in a dark world.

Inheriting a batch of money is no good unless you go to work with it.

Let the Lord punish the wicked, don't take it into your own hands.

A good ruler works against the wicked.

God's spirit is like a flashlight in a man, illuminating the reality of his life.[2]

A fair and merciful ruler is apt to last a long time.

Young men enjoy the strength of youth and old men have to be content with gray hair.

Effective punishment will often get rid of evil.

Chap.
21

The Lord directs the thoughts of leaders just as easily as water is used for irrigation.

God would prefer that a man be just and merciful than that he just make a big pledge to the church.[3]

A conceited attitude is a sin.

Hard, steady work is more productive than overnight speculation.

Ill-gotten gains will finally make you sick.

Crooks robbing crooks is a laugh, as it goes unreported.

A man is better off living alone in a tiny closet than living in a mansion with a talkative woman.

A good man learns a lot from watching the wicked catch it in the neck.

A person who will not listen to the pleas of the poor will some day find his own requests unnoticed.

Nothing calms and pacifies like sending someone a nice gift.

The wicked like to destroy and the righteous enjoy building.

[1] At least ask Congress   [2] That's a conscience
[3] It's the ones who do neither that are irksome.

A man who loves only pleasure, wine, and sauna baths won't last very long.

A fellow is better off living in the desert alone than in a fine palace with a contentious and angry female.[1]

A wise man doesn't spend everything he has at once.

The pursuit of righteousness results in the finding of life and honor.

Wisdom conquers anything.

A false witness must perish.

There is nothing that works successfully against God. It doesn't matter how prepared a person may be, God is still in charge of everything.

Chap. 22

A good reputation is rather to be chosen than great riches, and loving friends are better than silver or gold.

The rich and the poor have one thing in common; God made them all.

A smart fellow sees evil coming and gets out of the way.

The combination of humility and respect for God results in a man being rich in every way.

Train a child properly and when he is grown he will remember it.

The rich rule over the poor and the lender over the borrowers.[2]

An evil person becomes vain, and then he gets it.

Giving bountifully is a wonderful blessing to a person.

Rulers are always seeking the support of upright men.

The pessimist thinks that every time a circus comes to town he will be eaten by a lion.

A fellow who falls for the enticement of a wicked woman has just jumped over a cliff.

Kids are at times very foolish, but wise use of the paddle will straighten these things pretty quick.

Trust in the Lord, that is the secret to life.

Don't take advantage of the poor or the handicapped, for the Lord is especially interested in them.

There is no point in joining an angry man for fear you too will get angry.

Don't loan your money foolishly.

Leave the historical markers alone.

Do you know a real hard-working, honest man? Watch him. You will find around him the best people.

Chap. 23

If a rich man invites you to a special dinner don't eat like fury

---

[1] I keep remembering that Solomon had 1,000 wives and concubines
[2] Sad, but true

or believe everything he tells you. Surely he wants something from you.

Don't work just to get rich. Riches can easily disappear. Don't set riches up as a goal in life.

If evil men will offer you opportunities, turn them down. It is all a snare.

A man is no better than he thinks in his heart.

Don't waste a lot of wise advice on a fool with his ears closed.

Don't take advantage of orphans or others who have no protection. God is back of these people as a father.

It won't hurt to whip a child as a correction. A little whipping won't kill them, and it might save them.

Try not to envy sinners. They aren't as happy as they try to appear.

Don't be a heavy drinker or a glutton.

Don't rob the poor, or demand money for your advice from people who can't pay.

Stay away from prostitutes. They just wait for one unfaithful husband after another. They take your money and your soul.

Do you know what happens when you drink a lot of intoxicants? Well, you get red eyes, a babbling mouth, you become depressed, and you think the world has turned agaisnt you. I tell you, intoxicants are just like a snake bite.

When you've been drinking you get the notion to chase women, and you finally find yourself worn out, with a hangover and sick at the stomach. Phooey on that!

Chap.
24

Don't be envious of the evil ones. They really have nothing, while a wise and righteous man grows in strength and honor.

People who are always working up something bad get the reputation of being mischief makers.

You are not very strong if you let little setbacks discourage you.

If you have a chance to stand up for the innocent, don't keep quiet. There are no excuses for holding back.

Wisdom does the same thing for your person that honey does for your body; it gives strength and sweetness.

Evil men are always causing trouble for the righteous, but the good men can take it and bounce back.

Don't be pleased with the misfortunes of anyone. Never say happily, "Well, I see he got his."

My son, respect God and the law, and don't be an obstacle to those who would encourage change. No one is wise enough to know everything.

It is wrong to whitewash the wicked, but rebuke sin openly. People like straigthforward statements.

One day I passed by the field of a lazy farmer and I saw the

131

weeds and the careless maintenance. I learned a lesson. If you sleep too much and work too little your possessions will begin to disintegrate.

Some of the graduate students in the days when Hez was king copied down some of the proberbs of Solomon. Here they are.

God can keep as many secrets as he wishes, but a ruler should keep the people informed. You can't possibly know all the king knows, either. Finding out things is the king's business.

If you can get rid of the defective men working close to the king you will do for the kingdom what is done for silver when the dross is burned away.

Don't force yourself on important people. Let them ask for you.

Don't jump into a controversy without full knowledge. After learning all about a matter you may be able to offer some helpful advice.

A wise advisor is like a golden ear ring to a good listener.

A faithful messenger who tells it like it is arrives as refreshing as a brief snow storm on some hot laborers in a wheat field.

A person who claims to be able to do something he can't do is like a cloud that doesn't produce rain.

If you find an enjoyable pleasure don't over-use it or it will finally be tiring and make you sick.

Don't pester your neighbor. He can easily get enough of you.

A man who tells lies about his neighbors is worse than a swordsman gone berserk.

Trusting a man who is not dependable is like eating peanut brittle on a broken tooth or trying to race with a leg out of joint.

Singing giddy songs to a person stricken with grief is wrong, it is worse than snatching an old man's coat in the winter or putting vinegar on vanilla ice cream.

If your enemy is hungry give him food and if he is thirsty give him something to drink, for this will get to him, and the Lord will in time reward you.[1]

A sharp reply is as sure to cause anger as a north wind drives away rain.

Good news to people living in seclusion in the country is better than fresh water.

When a good man joins an evil outfit it is like a clear stream getting muddy.

Living to obtain glory for yourself won't work.

A man who has not learned self-control is like a city that has no walls and a crooked city council.

[1]Christ quotes this

Fools are no more associated with honor than snow with summer or rain with winter.

There is a reason for everything, for the bird migrating, the swallow flying, and the salmon going upstream.

A whip for the horse, a bridle for the donkey, and a paddle for the fool's tail all have the same purpose.

There is no point in arguing with a butt-headed fool.

There is no profit in trying to send messages through a foolish messenger.

A parable is no more help to a fool than bad legs to a crippled man.

If you honor a fool, you are just loading his gun and he'll soon shoot somebody.

Explaining something to a fool through a parable is as useless as sticking a thorn in a man dead drunk.

God will handle all the rewards and punishments.

The only thing worse than a fool is a man wise in his own conceit.

A real lazy man doesn't even turn over in bed very fast and he hates to feed himself, and yet he thinks he knows it all.

It is as foolish to stick your nose in other people's business as it is to grab a strange dog by the ears.

A man caught in a lie who says he was just teasing is as dangerous as a fellow on the loose with knives and guns.

When there is no one around to gossip, strife ceases just as a fire goes out when the wood is gone.

Pretty words are able to cover a wicked heart just like porcelain on a jar.

Beware of the man who speaks with the forked tongue. He is two-faced.

People who are always trying to trap others will eventually get trapped, and a person who throws stones is surely going to get hit.

Flattery is a wicked device and helps make a phony world.

Don't boast about all you are going to do. Let someone else praise you, don't push yourself.

A rebel is harder to carry around than sand or stone and envy is as difficult to confront as wrath and anger.

Open rebuke is sometimes better than secret love.

It is better to be wounded by a well intentioned friend than praised by a devious thinking enemy.

The hungrier a man is the less choosy he is about what he wants to eat.

A wandering man is like a bird lost from the nest.

A good friend makes life sweet, just as perfume helps a room.

In time of trouble it is better to seek help that is close at hand from friends of your own or friends of the family, than try to go to a brother in a distant land.

Don't wake your neighbor at daybreak yelling "Good morning." He won't like it!

A contentious woman and a droopy, gloomy day are just alike. Stopping a complaining woman is like trying to pick up something with oily hands, or blowing back against the wind.

A good worker is rewarded and blesses his employer.

A man can look at his heart just as he can view his reflection in a mirror.

Man is always looking for something new.

A fool is hard to cure.

Keep up with what you have and use it. There is no telling how long you'll live or how long you'll own the ranch. If you are careful, you will have enough food to eat, clothing for your family, and a place to live. Just don't think this will necessarily always be the case.

Chap.
28

A wicked man jumps and runs at every sound, but a righteous man doesn't have to worry.

When there is moral rot in a nation, the government is insecure and is always changing and confused.[1]

When the poor turn against the poor it is like a short shower that runs off and doesn't do anybody any good.

Law-abiding people usually stick together and the crooks are always working to free each other.

Wisdom comes to those who seek the Lord.

A law-abiding son is a great delight, but one who runs with shameful men is a sadness to the father.

Men who take advantage of the poor and then get rich will eventually have all their possessions taken over by charities.

Woe to the ones who cause the innocent to fall.

A rich man is apt to become a self glorified person while a poor man begins to learn about the real life.

No one enjoys seeing the wicked prosper, but it is pleasant for everyone when a good man makes a killing.

A person who confesses his sins and errors and apologizes comes out fine.

Happy is the man who always stands in awe of God.

A good king is apt to have a long and happy reign, but a wicked ruler is always being investigated.

Do not protect a man who has committed a crime of violence.

A man who works at his job will be far more content than a fellow looking for easy money.

To become rich quick will usually cost a man his integrity, and

[1]We know it! We know it!

134

it is not worth it.

There is no place in life for prejudice.

It is better to tell a man the truth than to lie to him in flattery.

A person who steals from his father and mother and uses as an excuse the idea that some day the possession will be his, is a Grad A rogue.

When the wicked are ruling good men are hard to find, but when a righteous man arises then good men can flourish everywhere.

A man who resents correction is doomed.

A good king is helpful, but one who is involved in graft ruins a nation.

Righteous people are concerned with the poor, but the wicked act as if the poor didn't exist.

A man who flatters his neighbor is just spreading a net in which he himself will be caught.

Wise men are peacemakers while fools are always trying to start fights.

Violent men hate the upright, but the righteous seek to save the souls of all.

A corrupt ruler usually secures corrupt aides.

The Lord makes no distinction in sending daylight for the rich and the poor.

A righteous ruler has it made, for God is with him.

Correction is a good thing for a child, for if you leave a kid on his own you get real trouble.

The wicked may multiply and evil increase, but in time the righteous will see all this change.

Where there is no vision, the people perish.

Sometimes words are not enough, but you must instruct by penalty.

A person who has someone work for him all his life and treats him properly will find that he has a son.

A man who is partner to a thief becomes accustomed to evil and doesn't even notice cursing.

A really good man is sorely hated by the wicked.

There was a man and his name was Aggie[1] and he made a profession of his philosophy and a confession of his own faults.

"I am a stupid brute," said Aggie. "I have no secular knowledge or any holy knowledge. Who knows the heavens? Who created the earth and gave it shape? What is the name of the maker of everything?

"It is God. Everything connected with God is pure. God is a

---

[1] Agur

shield to all those who trust him.

"Let no one add anything to the words of God. Two things I ask of God. Removal of lies and vanity. Let me be neither rich nor poor. I'm afraid if I was real rich I might think I didn't need God. Yet if I was very poor, I might be tempted to steal.

"There are some generations that do not respect their parents, that think they know it all, they go around filthy, they take advantage of everyone.

"There are four things that are never satisfied; the grave, a barren womb, earth without water, and fire.

"Those that don't respect their parents will be punished.

"There are four things that I can't understand. They are too wonderful for me to grasp. One is the way the eagle soars so effortless in the air, another is the way a snake crawls across a rock, the way a ship rides on the surface of the sea, and the way of a man with a maid. I might add another thing I don't understand, how can a prostitute entice a married man and then say, "What's wrong with that?"

There are four things that are not tolerable on this earth. A worker who takes over without authority, a fat fool, an unfaithful wife, and a maid who runs off with the husband.

"There are four things on earth which are small but quite wise. The ants are small and not strong, but they work all summer preparing for the winter. Cliff badgers are another. They live in the rocks. I don't see how they do it. Locusts are another. They have no leader, yet they divide into groups and organize in a marvelous fashion. The spider is another. The spider goes even into the king's palace. I don't understand how they string their web.[1]

"There are four important animals, as I see it. The lion, the king of the beasts, a greyhound, unbelievably fast, and a goat. Add to this a human animal, a king who rules in peace.

"Finally, keep your big mouth shut as much as possible. Just like churning stirs up the milk and makes butter, or the twisting of a nose brings blood; so angry talk causes strife."

Chap. 31

Now we have the words of Lem, things taught to him by his mother.

Don't waste all your energy on women. A good king is better off without wine and strong drink for the drinking might bring a poor decision or a bad judgment of a case.

If anybody should drink, it should be someone burdened with sorrow or someone who is in great pain and who may die.

As king, help those who cannot help themselves. Take the side of the needy and the poor.

[1]I don't either, Aggie

It is hard to find a really virtuous woman. She is worth a lot more than riches. Her husband can trust her. He doesn't need to constantly give her gifts. She will do him good and not evil all the days of his life.

She sews. She searches for good food. She gets up before day[1] and fixes breakfast for the family. She may buy some property if she sees some that is real good. She doesn't mind working in the garden. She stays in shape.

She looks out for the poor. She doesn't worry about cold weather for she has already made warm clothes for the family. She decorates her home herself. Her husband is greatly respected for she even sews enough to sell some of her things for the family income.

Strength and honor are hers, and she will some day be rewarded. She speaks wisely and kindly, she does not gossip. She never loafs. Her children love her and her husband loves her, and they are all proud of her.

Many girls have made good, but none like the one I've described. Beauty can be deceiving and a charming personality misleading, but a woman who trusts God shall be praised.

Let her share in what she has done. She has a right to profit.[2]

[1] Daylight Saving Time
[2] There you are, Libs. It's in the book!

ECCLESIASTES

Editorial Comment: Solomon is the recognized writer of this book. Solomon had everything: money, power, wisdom, good health, and off and on he had a case of the Blahs. I think he wrote this book during some of his attacks. — A.E.

Chap.
1

There is nothing to life. It is all one round of vanity, seeking and finding, and to what purpose? One generation comes, then another, and life goes on, repeating itself. Why? The sun rises, the sun sets, then circles to be ready to do the same thing again, the wind goes south, then turns back and goes north, the rivers all run into the sea but the sea never gets full because of evaporation, clouds, and then back to the rivers.

Everything is always active. Man's eye never sees enough nor does his ear ever hear enough. History just keeps repeating itself. There is nothing new under the sun.[1] Anything man discovers he then learns has pre-existed in some form. Yet it doesn't seem to matter. No one even seems to care if it has happened or if it will happen again.

"Just look at me," said Solomon, "I am the king and also I am the preacher.[2] I set out to learn everything about everything. I have seen everything, I have nothing to which to look forward, I've got the Blahs.

"That which is crooked can't be corrected and that which doesn't exist cannot be numbered.[3] I looked at myself and realized that I was real smart, in fact smarter than anybody who has ever been to Jerusalem. I devoted my life to learning. I even tried to learn of madness and folly. I decided that the more you know the sadder you get.

Chap.
2

"So I said to myself that I would dispel my sorrow with glee. As a result, I kicked up my heels and made merry. I was soon tired of laughing and joking, it all seemed silly.

"I tried drinking. I thought this might teach me that there was something helpful in being a fool. It didn't work.

"The next thing I tried was super activity. I put on the greatest building program ever conceived. I built buildings and houses, I planted vineyards, I planted all kinds of fruit trees, I made swimming pools everywhere and used the water for irrigation also. I accumulated a tremendous number of servants, I bought cattle until I was the biggest baron of them all, I collected silver and gold,[4] I organized a men's chorus, an all-girl singing group, as well as an

---

[1] He should have lived to see the Brooklyn Dodgers
[2] Mixing Church and State is a no-no, Solomon
[3] You left some of us behind on this one, Solomon
[4] Solomon was also the IRS so this didn't hurt him

orchestra with multiple types of instruments.

"O.K.; so I was great. I never lost my understanding doing all this. Anything that I saw which I wanted I bought. I tried everything that sounded like fun and gave it a whirl, but after all was said and done I was back where I started, frustrated, nowhere to go, nothing to do. I felt blah!"

"Then I began to study by the comparison method. On this basis I concluded that it was much better to be wise than to be foolish, just as light is preferable to darkness. The wise man walks in light, the fool stumbles around in darkness. Yet they both wind up with arthritis; so what gives? The wise and the foolish both wind up in the same way — dead. History makes very little distinction between a prominent wise man and a prominent fool.

"Why then should I live? For what? I regretted all the fine work for which I was responsible because I would die and all the fine things would be used by people coming after me that I don't know, many of whom have not yet been born. How do I know if the person who takes my place in life will be a wise man or a fool? So I despaired again.

"What good does it do to work anyway? Life is full of sorrow and disappointment.

"From watching the handiwork of God I decided that a man should eat, drink, and enjoy his work, directing it for good. God blesses such a man with wisdom and joy. The sinner receives inner disturbance from God. But both of these situations come from God; so what difference does it make?

Chap.
3

"To everything there is a season and a time to every purpose; such as, a time to be born, a time to die, a time to plant, and a time to dig up what's planted,[1] a time to kill and a time to heal, a time to tear down and a time to build, a time to weep and a time to laugh, and a time to be mournful and a time to dance, a time to embrace and a time to refrain from embracing, a time to get and a time to give, a time to rip and a time to mend, a time to keep silent and a time to speak,[2] a time to love and a time to hate, a time for war and a time for peace.

"Wherein does hard work profit for a man? God has made such a beautiful world, but God limited man so that man cannot see the whole thing. I conclude then that a man should make the most of the time he has, eating, drinking,[3] enjoying himself and the results of his efforts. All things are made possible by God; so enjoy yourself, man, if you can.

"Whatever God does that is it. There is no change with God.

[1] I get this one mixed up sometimes
[2] This is a real toughy   [3] Orange juice?

139

God is in complete charge of the past, the present and the future.

"There is a lot of crookedness in the world, and injustice, there even being politics in the church courts, but God will judge all these matters. Nothing escapes the scrutiny of God.

"I have decided that God lets things go along like they do to try men out, and see if they are any better than plain animals. Men live, beasts live, men die, beasts die; all the bodies disintegrate. Does anyone really know that a man's soul departs his body and continues while not so with a beast?

"As a result, I advise men to work at something they enjoy and get something going for them in this life.

Chap.
4

"Well, I continued studying, this time turning my attention to the people who had real hardships. A galley slave has a tough life and no one to comfort him. The powerful ruler who works the slave doesn't have a comforter either. They would both be better off dead. In fact, I sometimes think the best thing to do is not to get born.[1]

"Then I observed that the motive for work was usually to simply outdo the fellow next door. To that I would say, so what? Yet a man is a fool to be lazy and work just enough to stay alive, thinking that since it is all going to end in death why should he work himself to death.

"I have observed some other rather odd conditions. One is the case of a man who has no dependents, no heirs, and yet he works tirelessly trying to accumulate riches. Why? There is no one to leave it to and he can't take it with him.[2]

"It is better for two people to be working together than one, for one might have a heart attack and the other could help him. It is also better to sleep with someone, rather than by yourself, for it is warmer with two.[3]

"In case of being attacked in Central Park it is better to have two together to resist and even better with three.[4]

"It is better to be a poor but wise teen-ager than to be an old and foolish king.[5] In fact, a poor but wise teen-ager might be born in a ghetto and get to be President.[6] Such a person attracts help and becomes an idol and everybody shouts his name, and then a couple of generations pass and he's forgotten. So it still makes life seem to me to be like chasing the wind.

Chap.
5

"When you go to church, keep your ears open and if possible your mouth shut. Be real careful if you do say anything in church,

---

[1] You've lost me again, Solomon
[2] It's true. I know of a test case.
[3] So he knew about the energy crisis, too

[4] I'd be willing to go to four
[5] Some of these were bumper stickers on Solomon's chariots
[6] Please hurry!

for it is God's house. You can usually tell a fool by his being a lip artist.

"If you make a promise to God get with it at once. Don't delay a minute in fulfilling a promise to God. You'd be better off not taking the pledge if you don't intend to keep it. You can't talk your way out of the same thing you talked your way into.

"A lot of dreaming and yakking will get you nowhere. Stand in awe of God. That's a good way to do in church!

"No doubt you will see many injustices in life, with the strong taking advantage of the weak, and the rich pushing around the poor. Don't let it panic you. God is watching and in his time there'll be a real judgment.

"The earth is for everyone and it is necessary. The king has to eat, so the field is essential to him. A strange thing in life is that a person who loves money never gets enough. That's why I say life is like chasing the wind.

"A hard worker enjoys his sleep at night, the employer always wants more money so he wakes the guy up early for work.[1]

"I've seen a lot of trouble. I've seen rich men go broke. A man suddenly set back where he started. Then he usually becomes a frustrated grouch.

"That's why I say a man should eat and drink, enjoy his activities as much as he can while he is alive, and use the gifts that God has given him and be grateful. Such a fellow doesn't have to look back and groan, for the joy of the Lord is in him.

Chap.
6

"There is a terrible thing that I have observed occasionally, and that is a man working hard, acquiring good wealth and position, and then he loses his health and is not able to enjoy the fruits of his labor. I think that's a shame!

"If a fellow lives a mean life, even if he leaves a hundred sons,[2] when he's dead and gone and left nothing constructive behind him, why was he born in the first place? He would have done better not to be born! Never having lived, never having had a name is better than living two thousand years in waste. What's the difference?

"Wise men and fools both scramble for a living, but the wise man enjoys the scramble.

"Just wishing for things will get you nothing, you must work for what you get. This, too, is chasing the wind.

"God has always known what was in store for each man. Why buck it? What point is there to all this? That is what bugs me. How does a man know what is best for now or what the future will bring?

[1]And this was before DST!   [2]Pretty mean, I'd say

141

"A good reputation is better to have than money and the day of your death is more to be celebrated than the day of your birth.[1] It is more satisfying to attend funerals than to go to banquets, for you should concern yourself with the problems of death more than the problems of life.[2]

"Sorrow is more productive than laughter, for a solemn face doesn't get wrinkles quick; so a wise man is serious and fools laugh all the time.

"A person is improved who listens to criticism from a wise man instead of listening to a stream of musical groups. Praise from a fool vanishes like tissue paper in the fire and there is no value remaining.

"Attempting to bribe a good man makes the man angry and disgusts him with life.

"Finishing is more satisfying than starting and patience is more valuable than pride. A quick temper is no good, and makes a fool out of a person.

"Don't always be harping on the good old days. Your memory has just gone caput.

"Observe nature. Work with the way things are, for wisdom is a good protection, and so is money, but wisdom is a lot the better of the two.

"You can't improve or change what God has done or planned; so be happy when things are going good and be thoughtful when things are in poor shape. Actually God has built into life a balance of good and bad.

"Don't overdo anything, certainly don't be too wise or too foolish or you'll just burden your life with misery. I've seen good men die young and bad persons live a long time. The key to life is to learn to stand in awe of God.

"No one is perfect, but try to be good, for a city is in better shape with a good, wise man in it than if it had ten mighty powerful fools.

"Another thing, don't go around listening to other people's conversation. You are bound to hear some unpleasant things about yourself and it will also cause you to say unkind things about others.

"I determined to be completely wise, but it is impossible. I wanted to know why about everything, particularly wickedness and foolishness.

"Avoid a conniving woman. She is all snares and trouble, and the man inclined to sin is sure to get caught. In all my searching I have found a good man occasionally, about one out of a thousand, but I have never found a good woman.[3] In my opinion God made

---

[1] Who does the celebrating?
[2] Solomon may have been having a touch of the flu with the blahs
[3] Imagine being rich enough to talk like this

man all right, but women are always trying to ruin what God did.[1]

"A man who has learned something about living has it reflected in his face. A person should be a law-abiding citizen. Do your duty even if it means getting drafted. You do have some obligations. There is power in government. A wise man recognizes law and order.

"There is a certain amount of time set aside for misery; so learn to accept it, but you can't anticipate it; so don't worry about it.

"No man has control of death. It is coming to the just and the unjust. The unjust die and it is soon forgotten about how bad they were. Just because God doesn't punish people promptly for their sins many begin to think that it doesn't matter whether you are good or bad.

"There is much I don't understand for I see good men suffering and undergoing hardship and I see the wicked often having it easy. Life really puzzles me.

"For this reason I advise people to eat, drink and enjoy their work and let the chips fall where they may.

"I assure you that there is no way of learning all there is to know about life. Even if you could search and inquire day and night, without sleep, you could never probe all the mysteries of God.

"I tried to work on the theory that God looks out for the good and the wise. It doesn't work that way. God provides the same for everybody, the sun, the earth, the whole thing is equally available to good and bad alike, to the cursing sinners and to the righteous saint. It just doesn't seem fair.[2]

"Stay alive. There is always hope for the living. A living dog is better off than a dead lion. Since we don't know what happens after death, I suggest we stay alive. As far as we know death takes away all feelings; so don't risk it. Live and enjoy it. Wear clean clothes, use after shave lotion, stick with your wife, and whatever you decide to do give it all you've got. There is no knowledge, work or skill in the grave; so use all you have while you're alive.

"Another thought I had was that everything is left to chance. The race is not always won by the swiftest, nor the battle by the strongest, nor do the wise and good always get rich. Man never knows how long he will live, anymore than a fish knows when he will get caught in a net.

"I observed something one time that impressed me. There was a tiny rural village with only a few men in it and a powerful king with a strong company of soldiers came and laid siege to it. In the little village was a poor but wise man who devised a clever trick to save the

---

[1] I imagine a lot of good ladies dodged Solomon
[2] Hint to Solomon — "My ways are not your ways, saith the Lord"

city.[1] A few years later nobody could remember the name of the man who saved the village.

"Obviously, wisdom proved to be better than strength, but the wise man may be shortly forgotten. Anyway you cut it, though, a quiet word of wisdom is better than a lot of foolish shouting, and wisdom is always superior to weapons. I admit that a bad man, though, can cause a lot of trouble.

"A dead fly can cause a stink in a bottle of sweet odor, just like a little evil can ruin the whole reputation of a good and wise man.

"A good man is always planning good things while an evil man is cooking up mischief. A mischief-maker gets where he can be identified by the way he walks around the town.

"If the man for whom you are working blows his top you keep your cool. This is good advice.

"I have seen a lot of things in life that just don't seem proper. I've seen people in authority misuse their power, I've seen nuts given great recognition while a man who has become rich by his own skill is snubbed, I've seen a hard-working man digging a well and then fall in and break his back, or a person loading a truck let the load fall on him. Life is tough. Sometimes a person working hard building a wall gets snake bit. Try to be smart in your work, such as sharpening your axe so you won't have to swing it so hard.

"Just as a snake bites without any reason so does a blabbermouth speak forth without cause. A wise man speaks graciously, but a fool shows himself to be a fool by starting out with trivia and ending with a bad suggestion. Just thinking about work bothers a fool.

"Pity the nation with a playful kid as its ruler and whose selected leaders are already drunk in the morning. Happy is the land that has an honest ruler and whose leaders eat and drink for strength to do the work of the nation.

"Laziness and indifference will cause a building to be poorly constructed.

"A party is lots of fun and wine makes a person merry, but if you are rich you can have these things anytime you desire.

"Don't always be criticising the people over you or the government, or complaining even privately about the rich people, for somehow word of what you are saying leaks out and you'll get in trouble.

"Just do good for goodness sake, and goodness finally finds its way back to you. Don't hesitate to be generous.

When the clouds get full they empty themselves with rain, when

---

[1] Probably posted a smallpox sign

a tree falls it falls, whatever will be, will be; so don't procrastinate, waiting all the time for everything to be just right. Just as it is difficult to understand the way God arranged for a child to grow in the mother's womb; so you don't know all about life. Get to work. Sow your seed, for you never know how much will grow or which seed will prosper.

"It is good to wake up in the morning and see the sun and know you are alive. Enjoy the good days, for there will inevitably be bad days. It's God's way.

"Enjoy being young, but don't forget that God is watching and you will be held accountable for your actions. Be as happy as you can, but remember, young man, that you may have many years ahead and there is plenty of grief and pain to come.

"As a young man think about God and store up treasures of truth for the day will come when the fun of the young will be gone. It will be too late to try to find God when you are old and blind, when your brain is addled and your body is miserable. Old age doesn't have much to offer. You may be able to hear a quail, but you won't be able to whistle, you can't climb a ladder, or even go to the top of a hill, small noises like a cricket makes or a faucet dripping will be very irritating and your sexual desires will be gone.

"Remember God while you are young and able, for soon everything snaps, you can't drink from a cup without spilling it, you can't draw water from the well or even wait on yourself, and then you die and return to the dust from which you came. Why? I just don't understand why, and I was the Preacher.

"I was a good preacher. I taught the people good things, I wrote out a lot of proverbs and thoughts for the day, I used words carefully to nail down important truths. Good students listened and learned.

"In conclusion, young man, let me tell you that there is no end to people writing books, and studying hard is a tiresome affair, but the whole business centers on one thing, stand in awe of God, keep his commandments, for this is the whole purpose of man, for God will bring every work into judgment, even the very secret matters,[1] and God will judge whether it be good or whether it be evil."

[1] even tapes

SONG OF SOLOMON

Editorial Comment: It is not for me to try to justify this book being in the Bible. It is written for a purpose, for some day and age. It doesn't do much for me, but at least try it — it might be just the thing for you. A.E.

This is a song written by Solomon or written for Solomon or sung for entertainment during his evening meals.

"Let Solomon kiss me, for his kisses are more stimulating than wine," sang the lady singer, "and he smells good; so that even the very young girls fall for him at once.

"It is good that King Solomon plans to take me into his bedroom and make love to me, for I will rejoice, and it will be a memorable time.

"I know I am very dark-skinned, not like the local girls, but I am beautiful and I have been touched by the sun, for my family made me do all the dirty work outside, laboring daily in the vineyards.

"Tell me, Solomon, what is your program today? Where are you going? Let me join you, I don't want to hang around the palace all day with the rest of your crowd.

"I tell you what you do," replied Solomon, "just pack a lunch and follow my sheep. You are some woman! You have impressed me more than a group of Pharoah's best horses. Your cheeks are like rubies and your neck is golden, and we will get you additional jewelry of silver and gold to go around you."

"The king as he eats lying on the dinner lounge is enchanted by my perfume, which I have coming from a sachet between my breasts," sang the siren.

"You are a beautiful girl," chanted Solomon, "you are pleasant, a pretty sight as you recline on green grass, in the shade of the cedar trees, and look at me with eyes of the dove."

"Call me the lily of the valley," sang the girl.

"You are like a lily among the thorns when I see you with other girls. You are like an apple tree among scrub oaks when I see you with young men," chimed in Solomon.

"How much is my delight in being close in the shadow of my king. Solomon lets me eat with him and sit close to him. I am really lovesick. What a thrill when he places his hand under my head and with the other hand holds me in an embrace. Then the king goes to sleep, so keep quiet or get out, all you serving girls, don't dare awaken the king."

"Sometimes I can hear my beloved king coming," sang the girl,[1]

[1] Same song, second verse

"and he seems to me to come leaping forward like a young deer, for I saw him looking for me out of the window, I could see him moving through the lattice work. Then he called to me and suggested that we get going, for it is a delightful day and the rain has stopped, spring is here, the birds are singing, and the voice of the turtle can be heard.[1] The fig tree is turning green, the grapevines are smelling good, come on, he cries, come let's get away to some private place.

"How nice everything is. The foxes are eating the grapes, my lover king is mine, all is in order. Come stay with me, my king, all the night, and act like a young buck.

"One night I awoke and Solomon was no longer by my side," sang the girl,[2] "and I went everywhere looking for him. I went into the city and searched the streets. I found the night patrol and asked them if they had seen my lover. Not long after this I found him myself. I took him to my own home. Be quiet, everyone, particularly giggly girls, for my king is asleep and is not to be disturbed."

Then the girl chorus came on the program singing, "What is the big show we see coming? Who is the person who smells so good, who comes on like a cloud of smoke. It is Solomon![3] There are sixty mighty men around him, the greatest bodyguards in Israel, they watch carefully over Solomon day and night,[4] they have mighty swords, and Solomon is riding in a special chariot made of the cedars of Lebanon, a real Mark IV, trimmed in silver and gold, painted purple. Come on, all the girls of Jerusalem, look at this tremendous sight, King Solomon, dressed in all his finery, wearing his jeweled crown, and in a good humor."

"How beautiful is a beautiful girl!" spoke Solomon.[5] "Sweetie, you have the eyes of a dove. Your hair is more desirable than mohair. Your teeth, when you smile, look like a hillside of white sheep, freshly clipped, your lips are like a scarlet thread, your speech is soft, your temples are made to appear as pure as split pomegranates, your neck is as stately as the tower of David, a classic fortress, and your breasts are matched like twin fawns. You are super beautiful and you make the night a sweet smell and I long to spend that time with you, you are perfect, there is no blemish on you.

"Let's take a trip to Lebanon together. Let us climb a mountain together and see the sights, watch the leopards and the lions, and wild beasts frolic. You have really stolen my heart. One look from you makes my heart spin, and a glance at a part of your neck

---

[1] Not for ordinary listeners   [2] She had lots of songs. The pay was good
[3] Solomon really liked to hear this kind of song
[4] He slipped away once we know
[5] This could have been a talk to his regular Sunday night supper group

exposed makes me thrill to my bones. I love you so much, you are better than wine, and your perfume smells better than food. Your lips are sweeter than honey, being close to you is stimulating. Your smell is as pronounced as the fresh cut cedar of Lebanon.

"You wonderful girl, you are like a private garden, a secret spring, your very gestures are beautiful and fill my every need. You are like an artesian well, like a bounteous table decorated with the tasty things of life. Let the wind blow me to you and let me take advantage of all the glorious joys that are available through you."

Chap. 5

"I tell you people," chanted Solomon, "I really enjoy being in my garden. It smells good. I enjoy eating fruit here, drinking wine or milk with chocolate chip cookies. Join me. I like having a bunch of girls around. Eat and drink all you want.

"One night I lay dreaming," sang the lead girl singer, "and I thought I heard the voice of my king, then a knocking at my door, and it was the king wanting to get in, saying that the dew was heavy and he didn't have on his raincoat.[1]

"I told the king I was undressed and had gone to bed, even that I had washed my feet, and my clothes were not handy. My lover tried to open the door but it was latched on the inside. I couldn't stand it any longer, I longed for him, so flipping on a little perfume as I went, I unlatched the door, but the king was gone. I called for him and searched for him, but he was gone. I went out into the streets of the city searching for my love, the cops pushed me around for I was a nuisance. O girls, you cuties with the Jerusalem chorus, if you see my loved one tell him that I am lovesick."

"Tell us, beautiful, sunburned girl," sang the chorus, "what is so exceptional about this one you love. Describe him to us."

"My loved one," sang the soloist, "is ruddy complexioned, he would be easily selected from a crowd of 10,000, his head is like solid gold,[2] he has black, bushy hair, black as a raven, his eyes are like the eyes of doves reflected in clear water, his cheeks are rosy, his lips as soft as lilies and dripping honey, his hands are covered with jeweled rings and he wears a fantastic belt of ivory studded with sapphires, his legs are solid marble, he wears golden shoes, he is as impressive as the cedars of Lebanon, and his mouth is enticing and lovely. That's the man, that's our King Solomon![3]

Chap. 6

"Where has your lover gone, O beautiful singer, where shall we look for him?" sang the chorus.

"He has gone to one of his gardens, or perhaps to feed his sheep, or maybe to pick some flowers. I am so in love and I know he

---

[1] or some such excuse   [2] She meant well
[3] Solomon enjoyed listening to his singers

loves me," warbled the soloist.

"You are a beautiful woman, my beloved one, more beautiful than Jerusalem and more impressive than an army parading with its banners," chanted Solomon. "Don't look at me, as I melt under your gaze, you with your better than mohair hair, you with the sheep white teeth, and your skin like peaches. There are 60 wives available to me, 80 concubines, and no telling how many willing young girls,[1] but my love is only for you. You are the only girl that has ever been born as far as I am concerned.

"Everyone loves and admires my beautiful one, even my wives do.[2] You wonderful creature, you are like the morning in brightness and brilliant as a Mardi Gras parade."

"I went wandering along the garden, among the flowers," sang the soloist, "and as I observed the fruit and petals I became homesick."

"Don't go away. Come back to us," sang the chorus of girls.

"What do you see in me, a poor little girl from Atmore, Alabama?"[3]

Chap.
7

"You dance so wonderfully," chanted the king. "Your feet are super. Your hips were made absolutely perfect, and your navel is as inviting as a full glass of wine. Your waist is as trim as a wheat field bordered by lilies and your breasts are matched as twin fawns. Your neck is like a tower of ivory, your eyes as clear as two fish pools, your nose is as straight as the tower on the gate of the city of Lebanon, your head sits straight like the top of Mount Carmel and your hair holds the king in captivity as if it were a purple robe.

"What a joy and delight you are, my love. You are beautifully built, tall and slim, with lovely breasts, stately like a palm tree, and I would greatly desire to hold that tree, to receive your kisses, which will bring new life to me, quicker than can be done with wine."

"I give myself to my beloved, and my lover comes to me, let us go away together, let us walk the fields and visit the nearby towns, let us go inspect the vineyards together early in the morning. We will make love in the vineyard and we will eat grapes and other fruit."

Chap.
8

"How I wish we could go about as brother and sister so people wouldn't gossip about us," continued the songstress. "Then I could kiss you, lover, anytime I wanted, and I would take you to Mama who would know how to fix your drink.

"You would put your left hand under my head and embrace my body with your right. He's asleep now, girls; so don't awaken the king."

"Who is this that we see coming from the distance, leaning on

---

[1] Solomon was still young and hadn't secured his 1,000 wives yet.
[2] This is slightly exaggerated   [3] Shumanite girl

her beloved?" sang the Jerusalem girls chorus.

"I have loved my lovely doll ever since she was born under the apple tree," chanted Solomon.

"Seal me in your heart, my king, just as you would bind something to your arm, for my love is as strong and sure as death, and jealousy is a deep emotion also, burning one inside like the fires of hell. Nothing can quench the fires of love, no flood can drown it, and it cannot be bought, even if a person sold everything to raise the price."

"What happens to a little girl that is unattractive? What shall we do if someone wants to marry her?"

"We will devise and use all types of cosmetics and equipment to help her,"[1] chanted Solomon.

"How fortunate I am. I am slim and tall and beautifully shaped," sang the sunburned lead girl. "How lucky I am. Solomon had lots of property and for most of his places he leased for $10,000 a year, while I received mine free and sub-leased it.

"How wonderful, great lover, that so many have the privilege of listening to your voice. Please let me hear it also. Then come quickly to me, my lover, like a young buck frolicking on the hillside," sang the tall and beautiful girl.

---

[1] Actually Solomon apparently recommends silver falsies

ISAIAH

My name is Isaiah and I have had a vision which has revealed to me the generalities as well as a few specifics in the past, present and future of Israel.

Animals such as the donkey and the ox show more recognition of the Creator than do the children of Israel. Israel is now a sinful nation, full of evil, and a nation that has forsaken God. I am even afraid that matters will get worse before they get better.

The whole land is in ruin. The people are taken into captivity and the remnant that remains are a disadvantaged minority.

Let me urge you, you people of Israel, to hear what God has to say. The Lord of Israel wants to know why you waste time and substance with occasional offerings of rams and fresh beef. The Lord doesn't need such sacrifices. In fact, God is not interested in such silly attempts to appease God and cover your sins. The Lord wants you to abandon your evil ways, to be concerned with helping the poor and the needy. This is the type of offering to bring to God.

When you begin to do these things God says that though your sins be as scarlet He will make them white as snow. If you will obey God, the Lord will restore your land, but if you continue in your evil ways you will be destroyed.

The leaders of Israel are selfish and seek their own interests and Jerusalem itself is a contaminated city. God will restore his people and provide good leadership, but first He will purge the land of the transgressors and those that have forsaken the Lord will be consumed by their own greed.

The revelation of God which has come to me always indicates that at some far away time God shall be exalted on the earth, and people from everywhere will desire to come to Jerusalem and gather around the lofty mountain of the Lord, to hear His instructions. International law shall come from a meeting of nations at Jerusalem and the Lord shall be responsible.

As a result of this gathering, there shall be the voluntary surrender of all armaments and men shall be determined to make farm implements and household gadgets out of the weapons of war, and peace will come on earth.

At the present time, however, the Lord is not supporting his chosen people for they have sinned and rebelled, the people of Israel have turned to fortune tellers and strangers for their guidance. The people of Israel have contaminated themselves with possessions, and the people are fascinated by their own inventions. A nation cannot survive this way and in time the people will throw away their possessions and hide in caves or storm cellars because God will terrify them with his power. Be certain that the time will come when the

Lord will assert his power.

You people had better believe that the Lord means to act. Jerusalem and the holdings of the tribe of Judah will disappear. God will not accept being ignored by the chosen people. The Lord disapproves of the way the leadership has taken advantage of the young and the poor and the Lord intends to punish the nation and take away its many possessions and leave its people scattered.

In fact, times will get so bad that women will be pursuing men shamelessly just in hopes of getting something to eat. Then there will come a purging of the people and when the people seek again sincerely the Lord, the Lord will bless the land and the Lord will bless the people.

The Lord considers Israel as if it were a vineyard which had been well planted and properly nourished, but a vineyard which began to bring forth wild grapes instead of the proper grapes for marketing. God insists that He did everything for His people, and yet they were unfaithful and wandered from His very plain path.

God warns people and declares that they are foolish to let the thirst for property cause them to build too many houses and develop too many businesses. The Lord further warns against drinking liquor all day, and the indulging in fruitless social gatherings full of wasted time. It is this very type of thing that has caused the children of Israel to go into captivity. This type of conduct and foolishness only increases the number of people who will reside in hell. Be sure, though, that in time the Lord will be exalted.

The Lord issues a warning for various types of people, to those that demand immediate action from God, to those that pass off evil for good, and good for evil, to those that consider themselves wise, to those that ruin their judgment with too much drinking, to those that complain all the time and criticize people trying to do good, such persons will not be able to stand before God. The anger of the Lord is aroused easily against such persons.

Yet God will always make himself available to those who will respond, to those who repent and seek him, and the people who turn to God shall find him, their steps will be certain and they will not stumble. These are the people who will truly inherit the earth.

The next vision that I had came to me the same year that King Uz died. In this vision I could see the Lord high and lifted up, and the whole scene left the impression of power and mystery, with smoke and odd figures of the type you see in dreams, and all of the visionary creatures worshipped God and called forth "Holy, holy, holy is the Lord of hosts, the whole earth is full of his glory!"

I said to myself, "Woe is me! I have had it! I realize that I am a man of unclean speech and I associate with people who are just like me, yet my eyes have seen the glory of the Lord, I'm certain I will be struck dead."

Then one of the flying creatures in the vision came to me with a live coal in his hand, which he had taken from the altar with tongs, and he placed the burning coal on my mouth and he said, "Now that this hot ember from the altar has touched your lips you are free of sin."

Then I heard what I am certain was the voice of God saying, "Who will be my representative? Who will go out and witness for me?"

Then I said, "I am here, and I am willing to go."

Then the voice said, "Go. Tell them all you know of me, but they will not hear you. This is all right. Let them ignore me, let them sin and get fat in corruption, for they have never been a people who would understand and learn except under great pressure."

"How long, O God," I asked, "will this condition continue?"

"It will last until the cities of Israel are captured, the people led away, and then there will be a tenth of the people left, a sound hard core minority, and in them will reside the strength of Israel."

The Lord then instructed Isaiah further saying, "Go to Ahaz and encourage him. Tell him that all the threats from Syria are at present not worth his worry. The plot to go against Judah will fail this time."

Later the Lord spoke again for the benefit of Ahaz and said, "Would you care for a sign, ask for anything from bottom to top, and I will exhibit my power."

"I'm not going to get caught in the matter of questioning the word of God. I don't need a sign," said Ahaz.

Isaiah then said, "There is no way of pleasing you people. As a result the Lord will give you a sign anyway for a virgin shall one day in Israel give birth to a son and his nickname shall be 'God with you.' From the very first the child shall know the difference between good and evil and he shall always choose good. This will not occur during the reign of any of the present kings.

"Before this great blessed event your land shall be laid waste. The Egyptians and the Syrians shall plunder unmercifully and the people of Israel shall be desolate."

The Lord then spoke to Isaiah again in another revelation and the Lord said, "Write this down, Isaiah. I am going to give you a son. You are to call him Victor."[1]

---

[1] Nahershalolhashbaz

Immediately I sent for two reliable witnesses and they saw me write this prophecy.

Then I summoned my wife and took her to bed and nine months later my son Victor was born.

The Lord informed me that before Victor was old enough to speak distinctly the conqueror from Syria would come and invade.

The Lord spoke to me, Isaiah, again and said, "Tell the people to beware of making all kinds of weird confederations and alliances. Tell the people to stand on their own and trust their Lord. Advise them not to turn to mediums, or radical leaders with fancy plans, but to trust God.

"It is a shame for these people to stand in awe of Syrians or Egyptians when they should stand in awe only of God."

Israel and Judah refused to trust God, however, and there will be great trouble for them, including persecution, separation of families, loss of homes."

"Isaiah," God said, "write all these things down and protect the manuscript, seeing that it is handed down from one worthy and God-fearing man to another on through generations to come in order that mankind may know the Lord and understand his ways.

"I know that the only hope is in the Lord. I wish all the people of Israel and Judah felt as I feel. The Lord has left us some names, the names of hope in the future, and the names are Victor[1] , and God Saves,[2] and God Cares[3] .

It seems strange that the people cannot see the bright prospects in the coming generations. It is so stupid to guess about the future and depend on man's mind and man's own limited ability."

"Just check the so-called wise sayings of man," said God, "against my word. If the word of a man is different from the word of God then you know that the man is wrong. It is just that simple! The result of this foolishness of following erratic leaders will be poverty, desolation, captivity, and trouble. Undoubtedly my people will be scattered everywhere because of their failure to observe my law and follow my statutes."

Chap.
9

"Nevertheless," said God, "this sad account is not permanent and the feeling of loneliness, despair, and darkness shall be broken. For the people that dwell in darkness shall see a great light, and even those under the shadow of captivity and oppression, the light will even shine upon them.

"The people of God shall be restored. Again they shall be a great people, broken from the chains of oppression, full of joy at harvest time, again operating as a great nation.

"Eventually there will be peace. There will be no need for

[1] Nahershalolhashbaz   [2] Isaiah   [3] Shearjashub

154

weapons of war, or bloody uniforms, or military funerals, or medals for killing.

"The reason for this peace will be started with a child who will be born to us. The one true government shall be on his shoulders. The years shall add to his titles and he will be called such names as Wonderful, Superstar, Mighty God, Everlasting Father, and Prince of Peace.

"The spirit of the Lord will see that the type of kingdom that he establishes shall increase and it shall gradually encompass the earth. This will be no secret king. Nations all over the earth shall begin to notice this kingdom.

"The people of Israel will not believe and follow in this kingdom at first. The leaders of Israel shall be poor leaders, and the people will be scattered and persecuted. The divisions among the Jews themselves will be their undoing, for in forsaking God the Jews lose their point of common worship and brotherhood. The strife between tribes will increase and families will be divided. These things are the normal consequence of corruption and greed. Always, however, God leaves an outstretched hand for his people!"

Isaiah reports that in his vision, which vision was a revelation from God, he saw the judgment of God placed on the offending people of Israel. The people had forsaken God and now they had no one to whom to turn in the days of stress and difficulty. God will continue his punishment of his people until they thoroughly repent.

God plans to send a heathen force from Assyria to act as a punishing instrument for God, to take spoil from the people, and to kill many of the people. Why shouldn't God act this way? God allowed West Texas[1] to be captured and also Las Vegas[2] because of the worship of idols; so why shouldn't God do the same to Jerusalem and its people who are now worshipping idols.

The forces of Assyria will also in time be punished even though the Lord allows them to be victorious for a while as God's means of punishment.

The time will also come when a remnant of the people shall repent and place their trust in God, the Almighty of Israel. The people of Israel must suffer under the power of the Assyrian army, but God will accept the pleas of repentance from his people and the Lord will strike the Assyrians as surely as he struck the Egyptians. The small remnant of the Jews that repent and call upon the Lord shall return to the Promised Land and the Lord will bless this action.

The Lord will exercise his control in the day of repentance and the mighty shall be humbled before him.

---

[1]Samaria   [2]Hamath

Another portion of one of the visions of Isaiah reveals the announcement of the coming of a new type of king, a descendant of the line of King David, and the very Spirit of the Lord shall be upon him. This new king will not be fooled by outward appearances, but he will be capable of looking into the heart of man.

This new leader shall judge the people fairly and he will seek to arrange for equality among men. The weapon which this king will use will be words and his own life shall be above reproach. As a result of his teaching, there shall gradually develop an attitude of peace, so that even the animal kingdom will cease to fight among themselves for food. The whole earth will then become full of the knowledge of God.

This descendant of the line of David shall provide a symbol for the people,[1] and the symbol shall be accepted by the Gentiles.

Again the Lord will provide for a return of the people of Israel and they shall come from all over the world to establish themselves in the land of Canaan. The whole earth shall begin to recognize the sign of the cross and even the tribes of Israel will set aside their jealousy one toward another and they shall work together under one government.

The Lord will also destroy the opening of the Nile[2] and it shall be split into a number of smaller streams and the mouth of the great river shall be spread so wide that a man can walk across it, for it shall be shallow.[3]

When all this occurs, the Israeli people will praise God and they will say, "Now that your anger against us no longer exists, we welcome your comfort. We will no longer fear, for God is our salvation. We will draw water from the wells of the understanding of God, we will shout praises to the Lord, we will sing to the Lord in praise for the wonderful things that he has done for us, and we will proclaim the Lord as the Holy One of Israel."

The plan of God ultimately calls for the destruction of the wicked. Babylon, symbol of evil and treachery, is doomed by the Lord. All these things were revealed to Isaiah in a vision, and other matters also.

There will definitely be a Day of the Lord and at that time the Lord will gather all his forces from the far ends of heaven and the purpose of the Almighty will be the destruction of evil. This will be a time of great fear and all people everywhere will be impressed and many will groan as a woman in labor and the power of the Lord will

[1]My guess is that this refers to the cross
[2]I consider the Nile the "tongue of the Egyptian Sea"
[3]This, apparently, is yet to happen

be reflected on the faces of the people and God will destroy all the sinners.

The stars at this time will refuse to shed light and the sun will not show itself nor will the moon reflect the light of the sun. On this occasion the proud will be humbled, the wicked punished, and the arrogant shall be brought low.

God plans to shake the earth at this time and the earth will lose its place and terror will be everywhere. This will be the Day of the Lord. People will witness horrible destruction and torment and evil armies shall pillage and kill without concern for women or children.

Babylon, now a great city of evil, will be in its time reduced to rubble and no one will be able to rebuild it. The city will be a dump, a heap of ruins and furnish shelter for wild animals, but Arab people will never again reside within its old walls. Shepherds will no longer bring their flocks to the great city, but owls shall abide in the ruins and all kinds of strange animals shall use the old city as a dwelling place.

Chap.
14

God will in time show mercy to the line of Jacob and the children of Israel shall grow to the point some day of ruling over those who had previously ruled over them. The Jewish people will be brought together in Israel from many strange lands and the Lord will bless their return and they will be free from hard bondage and great fears. There will be great rejoicing when this occurs.

On such an occasion, evil will be reduced to the grave, and the devil himself, who weakened many nations, will be tossed into a permanent grave. The devil and the evil that he represents has long bragged about the success of the wicked and has proclaimed himself to be superior to God and to the ideas of goodness. The devil will be reduced to nothing and cast into a hell of his own making. While other people will have a place in eternity, dwelling in God's kingdom, the devil and his followers will not even have a grave in which to reside.

Particularly will there be the destruction of Babylon, for there will be nothing left except rubble and some mud holes where the city once stood. God promises to destroy the evil ones that shackle and torment his people.

The destruction of the evil regime of Babylon is just a beginning, for there will be other evil people and evil nations to rise, but they too in time will recognize that God has laid a strong foundation upon which the righteous can build, and the poor and the needy will find help in the Lord.

Chap.
15

The time will come when those who do evil will be a target of the Lord, whether the people be in China, Mississippi, New Jersey, Siberia, or anywhere. The misery of these people will come primarily from such natural disasters as floods and drouth, as the whole world will suffer because of the evil that many men will do.

I, Isaiah, foresee that the day will finally come when the extortioners, the oppressors of the poor, the money mad, the perpetrators of evil shall have had it. The Lord plans to bring all such to a miserable doom.

All the shallow pleasures of the wicked shall be taken away, and the miserly people who have created so much trouble shall have to live without joy, or water, or good lands, and there shall be no singing for them. The evilly inclined shall even try to call upon such false gods as force or money, but to no avail. The land of Moab where so much is evil at present shall last only three years, but it is a symbol and an illustration for what is in store for wicked people and evil localities or nations.

Damascus is a good illustration. Because it is now a place of wickedness, of slave trading and idolatry, Damascus will in time be levelled to a dung heap. The same fate is in store for any city or nation that continually despises God and seeks its own salvation.

The Lord rules, even though a nation be as far away as Ethiopia. These people also are under the will of God and when they rise up to discomfort God's people and move toward the promised land, their fate is sealed. These people cannot succeed and finally, after many conflicts, even these people shall come to Jerusalem with gifts and with a request for peace.

The land of Egypt will not be spared from the wrath of the Lord. In Egypt there shall be continuous internal strife and civil war. Accompanying all this shall be drouth and famine and water shall be a crucial need.

As a result of all this, the people of Egypt will finally stand in terror of all Israel.

God has sent foolishness into the minds of the advisors of Pharoah and as a result the program of Egypt is as poorly designed as the path of a drunk. Egypt shall finally be a nation that is a weakling, afraid of every threat. Conditions will actually reach a point that many Egyptians shall begin to praise God and seek to worship Him.

The forces of Assyria shall overcome Egypt and lead a great number of its people away as captives. After all these things have occured, there will be a religious movement in Egypt and the people shall seek the one God. As a result, many will turn to Jehovah and God will heal the land and bless it. As a result, there shall be three great leading nations in the Middle East; Egypt, Palestine, and Assyria.

The Lord spoke to Isaiah and told him of the immediate difficulty facing Egypt. The Lord spoke through Isaiah saying, "The king of Assyria will lead away the people of Egypt and Ethiopia, just as Isaiah is going around preaching barefooted; so shall the captured people be when they have fallen to the Assyrians."

The Lord intends to destroy Babylon. Babylon has been a destroyer of others and so the Lord will destroy the destroyer, which is always the way.

It staggers my mind to see the vision of the terrible destruction of Babylon. It will be a sudden thing. One moment everyone will be eating and partaking of a big banquet, and then the next moment there will be destruction.

The Lord suggested that I place a watchman on the wall and this I did. The destruction of Babylon is a solemn message from God to the wicked.

"Watchman, what of the night? When will all this happen?"

"Judgment Day is every day with God. Turn to God now, before it is too late. Seek the Lord first, then come and ask your question again," said the watchman.

God also has a warning to the people of Arabia. God will scatter the people and leave only a few, for this is God's way and His will.

God has a message for Jerusalem. The Lord wants to know why everyone has gone looney. The people are in great tumult and distress, and well they should be for God is no longer protecting Jerusalem from the plague or from invading armies.

Your trouble is that you think you are self-sufficient. You have great plans for mending the walls and providing a reservoir of water, but you have not asked for God's help or for his blessing.

The Lord expected you to worship and to practice self-denial and self-control, but instead of that you celebrated with big feasts and ornate parties. Your philosophy is eat, drink, and be merry for tomorrow we die, and the Lord will not overlook this sacrilege.

Because of this the Lord will see to it that you are taken away into captivity. You will be scattered and discarded as if you were litter.

However, the Lord says that there shall be a savior of the people, one who comes from the line of David, and he shall be given all power so that he may open or close everything, at his own discretion. This savior shall be as a nail thrust into a sure place and all the glory of all time will hang upon him, and all other nails will become as nothing. God has ordered that it be done in this way.

The Lord has turned his eyes on Tyre and God is displeased. Tyre is a wicked city, a prosperous city, and its merchants and rulers are great leaders, but the city is a place of slavery and God is displeased. The sea itself does not care to continue to behold the wickedness of Tyre.

The Lord has commanded that Tyre be destroyed. At first it shall simply be forgotten for seventy years and neglected by the men of commerce. Tyre shall revive, but the revival itself will be a renewal of wickedness, and so God shall command that the city be totally destroyed.

The land of Judah will also suffer because of the sins of the people. The Lord will make the land desolate and scatter the people of Judah in far away places. There shall be no distinction made between clergy and laity, between men and women, master and servant, or mistress and maid, the seller will go as well as the buyer, the one who pays usury as well as the one who demands it, and so the land shall be laid to waste, for this is God's will and God's judgment.

The story will be the same in every city, but always there will be a remnant spared.

Finally, it will seem as if all the world has gone bad with treachery, and hate, and malice. The earth will shake itself as if it were drunk, and then shall come the punishment of the Lord. The wicked leaders will get it first. Then all that are left shall be assembled as if they were prisoners, and the moon and the sun shall in shame hide their lights. Then the Lord and his saints shall reign in glory.

As for me, O Lord, I am a prophet that praises God and I will continue to praise thy name for all the wonderful things which you have done.

I have observed your power, how simple it is to reduce a mighty city to complete ruin. The most important people on earth are bound to recognize your greatness for you are a champion of the poor, a strength to the needy, and you put the quietus on noisy strangers.

Some day Jerusalem will be the headquarters for peace and the Lord shall prepare a great dinner for the celebration. At this time fear and death shall be abolished, and God will wipe away all tears from the eyes of his people.

On this occasion the people shall say, "The Lord is our God. We have waited for him and he has come. We are unbelievably happy in his salvation."

The wicked shall at this time be punished and their pride in their accomplishments shall be a frustration to them, and every form of protection or rationalization for the wicked shall be destroyed.

In that final time of victory for the righteous there shall be fantastic rejoicing. Salvation and peace shall be as walls for the city. The gate will be open to all the righteous from everywhere, without distinction. There will be perfect peace for those who have completely trusted in God, for God is everlasting strength.

The proud, the vain, the oppressors of the poor and the needy, they shall be brought down from their lofty positions. This is a day and a time worth waiting for, and even though in times past man has followed strange and inadequate gods, at this time there will be no name mentioned but that of the Lord God of Hosts.

For the Lord has gradually blessed the righteous people of the earth so that as if they were a nation unto themselves they have gradually taken the name of the Lord across the whole earth.

The people of God have prayed in time of distress as a woman cries before the delivery of a child. We, the people of earth, have not been able to develop a perfect kingdom. As a result we must face trials and tribulations, but in the end the Lord will come forth and declare his power and his justice.

The Lord will destroy evil and all its ugly manifestations. The anger of the Lord toward Israel will cease and again the Lord will bless the vineyards of his people, and Israel will prosper.

Israel has been punished for its sins, but not as much as the enemies of Israel. At times as the people of God are scattered it will seem as if they are forsaken, but when the great day draws near the Lord shall return them, small numbers at a time, from all over the world, to the land of promise to be near the holy city Jerusalem.

There is trouble for Samaria as it has become a place for God's people to revel and seek to escape God. The armed forces of Assyria shall come down on the city and destroy it and the glorious beauty of the place shall be destroyed by a heathen horde.

As always there will be a few of the faithful and they shall receive strength from the Lord. The leadership of Jerusalem at this time, however, is weak and sinful, with drunken judges and priests.

The people shout at me, "Who do you think you are, Isaiah, to keep telling us such things over and over again. We heard you the first time."

"It is because you won't listen," I told them. They still did not listen and the only language which they are capable of hearing is punishment, and God will speak this way to a wayward people.

As anxious as the Lord is that his people turn to him, the Lord has spoken now against them.

"You think you have made a deal," says the Lord, "to save yourselves when the evil ones come. This is a foolish plan. Man cannot save himself. Your only hope is to build on the solid foundation which I have laid down in plain language for the people of God. I know that you will have to suffer, but finally the truth will dawn on many of you.

"You see, you have made a bed to lie on that is too short and the cover is inadequate. Don't make fun of these sayings or else the Lord might deal even harder with you than he plans.

Remember that the Lord is a great teacher. The Lord has taught the farmer to plant as well as plow, and to use different seed in different areas at different times. This is the wisdom of God and He is trying to teach you.

God has pronounced difficulty for Jerusalem in payment of the sins of the people. The Lord will allow the enemies of Jerusalem to sack it and strangers shall come and go in the streets.

This is not for always, for God will bless the remnant and the repentant and the righteous. Because of them, the enemies in time will be blown away as if they were chaff and the Lord will thunder upon them and shake them with earthquakes.

You are dumb not to believe the promises of God. You had just as well be a staggering drunk as to hear of these things and believe them not. It is a shame that you are so concerned with yourselves and selfish matters that you do not have time to consider these words of truth.

Of course you can't hide from God. There is no such thing as doing something in secret. Don't you realize that the potter knows everything there is to know about the jar he makes; so it is with God who has made you.

The day will come when the land of Israeli will be full of fruit and then shall the people begin to understand the truth of the blessing of God. The wicked shall begin at this time to taste of the defeat which will in time be forthcoming. This will be an occasion of repentance and renewal.

"What a shame," says the Lord, "that the people of God are not content to trust in the Lord. Rather than come to me for help or advice my people foolishly turn to worldly authorities, such as going to Egypt with vast sums to buy support.

"Egypt is not capable of delivering you nor are they willing to be of great service. The same is true of other powers. Why do you not trust in me?" asks God, "for I am willing and able to do anything."

"Now listen to this," says the Holy One, "Because you don't trust in God, but choose to trust in man, great calamity shall befall you. Because you close your ears to the prophets who speak my truth in my behalf, you shall be broken as a potter drops and breaks a vase.

"You do not have the necessary faith to calmly stand firm in the face of mounting difficulties. Still the Lord always stands ready to receive you when you return to him and call upon his name. Even though the Lord will place adversity on you because of your sins, there will always be teachers left among you to help restore your faith. These good men are guides for the Lord and will influence you so that eventually you will realize the difference between material values and spiritual values.

"Once the Lord begins to heal the repentant people and the repentant nation, there will be great natural blessings given in good harvests and productive weather.

"You must remember, though, that the Lord acts with great shaking of the earth and mighty thunder when he is angry. God also will sort out the wicked nations and pour his wrath on them, but the people of God will be able to rejoice, and a deep happiness shall fill his people.

"As the Lord has spoken against Assyria and as His voice declares the downfall of these people so also does His voice declare the end of war and those who pursue such things.

Chap.
31

"The Lord does not appreciate people seeking help from men, particularly ungodly men, when all the time the Lord is available," said Isaiah. There is no point in turning to the Egyptians, for instance, simply because they may have access to good military equipment. There is no deliverance in this type of arrangement as the Lord will in time destroy both those who help and those who unfaithfully seek help on a practical or material basis."

In a way, the Lord is similar to strong lions who don't care whether they are confronted by one shepherd or a dozen. The Lord plans to defend the holy city Jerusalem as skillfully and as easily as birds fly.[1]

"My advice to you is simple, turn to God, serve him, and worship and then you shall see the destruction of the Assyrian as well as any others whose ways come in conflict with the Lord."

Chap.
32

"You can safely look for better days for the Lord will in time bring a righteous ruler with some inspired helpers. The happening shall be similar to a safe cave for a man on a windy day, or as refreshing water in a desert area, or a shady place in the heat of the day. The lives of men will begin to change and understanding will come to men who were accustomed to being short-tempered.

"This new approach will begin to change values, so that no longer will the violent and the wicked be heroes, for their falseness and their phony front will be obvious. In that day shall the goodness

[1] Some scholars consider this a prophecy of air support for Jerusalem. Quien sabe?

of the generous be a blessing and a strength, and will not be considered a weakness.

"This change in values will also affect women. Look out, girls! No longer will you be allowed to sit around, as some of you do, lazy and pampered by men just because you are girls, for you will be expected to do your part. You, too, will be expected to do good works, and be busy at the Lord's request.

"The end of all these things shall see the arrival of justice and peace. Calmness will come with comfort, and the people of God will dwell in safety under the protection of the Lord of hosts, who will bless his people abundantly.

Chap.
33

"Let me again and again warn the sinners and the enemies of God. There is no way to defeat the Lord. As long as you are wicked you are doomed, but for those who live righteously and speak truthfully to help their fellow man, for them God has prepared blessings. Jerusalem shall some day symbolize the safety of the children of God, for it shall be a quiet place, a holy place, and completely stable.

The Lord shall be as a vast expanse of water around his people so that no enemy might attack or torment the righteous.

Chap.
34

Again let me remind you that the Lord is opposed to evil, and God is opposed to those nations who act with evil intentions. These nations shall enter pointless wars and there shall be much blood shed, and it is God's way of expressing his disapproval, for it will leave finally every thoroughly wicked nation destitute and barren.

Chap.
35

On the other hand, God shall abundantly bless the righteous in his way and in his own time. The blessing will be an obvious matter, and there will be a great flowering in the desert and the hearts of the sad shall be made glad, and the discouraged shall see a new hope.

Man once again will be free to walk the streets and the highways with no fear of being attacked, and the songs of the people shall be songs of joy and gladness.

Chap.
36

Now in the fourteenth year of the reign of Hez, Big Hun came from Assyria with a gigantic army and he began to capture all the cities in the whole area.

As his custom was, Big Hun[1] sent his mouth-piece, a man high in the diplomatic corps, to intimidate Hez and the people of Jerusalem.

Standing in front of the wall at Jerusalem, the spokesman for Big Hun yelled to the King and the people, "My boss thinks you all are fools to think that Egypt will come to your rescue. The Egyptians have never been dependable, and have always been inclined to stab you in the back. Why deal with them? You merely

[1]Sennacherib

invite disaster. Fooling with Egypt is similar to leaning on a sharp stick.

"Maybe, however, you people are those foolish types that 'trust in God.' This is a laugh. One of your own kings defied your God and worshipped idols. How does that grab you?

"Big Hun, my leader, is a sport, though, and a gambling man. In fact, he has authorized me to bet you that you don't have 2,000 men ready to ride. Big Hun says that if you'll furnish 2,000 riders that he will furnish 2,000 horses. Even then you couldn't make a dent in a small fraction of the army that we have assembled.

"Finally, as a matter of information to you, the Lord himself has commanded us to conquer you. Now how about that?"

Then Fulbright and Harriman and Mills said to the speaker, "Don't talk to us in Hebrew, but speak Aramic. We can understand Aramic and the people can't and we don't want our people to know what you are saying."

"That's tough," called out the mouth-piece, "for Big Hun wants all the people to hear what he has to say. He wants the people to know that if you don't surrender that we'll lay siege, cut off all water and food supplies, and let all of you die a miserable death.

"Now hear this you people on the walls of Jerusalem," shouted the speaker, "don't let ole Hez fool you. Don't listen to his promises that the Lord will deliver the city and save you. Make an agreement with me and we will have a peaceful settlement. You will be fully protected until we can move you to some other country to live where you will have a nice easy life. Don't let ole Hez talk you out of this agreement, for it is either that or a sure death for each of you.

"Look at the record," the speaker continued, "and read the papers. Don't you know how we have laid flat Rome[1] and Athens[2]? What about their gods. Where were they when this happened? Have any of the gods saved any of the cities? What makes you think that your God will save Jerusalem?"

The people listened but they said not a single word for they loved and respected Hez and he had told them to stay silent.

Chap. 37

The details of all of this were immediately reported to Hez and he went into meditation and was greatly troubled. Hez then sent Fulbright, Harriman and Mills, his foreign policy people, to Isaiah with a message saying, "This is a time of great trouble and distress as if the nation were a woman in labor and yet unable to give birth to the child. Pray for us, Isaiah. Perhaps God heard the blaspheming of the Assyrian. I'm sure if God heard him that he won't let him get away with such talk. Pray for us, Isaiah."

When Isaiah received the message he spoke saying, "Tell King

---

[1]Hamath   [2]Arpad

Hez that God says don't worry about the big boasting of the Assyrian lip-flapper. For one thing, a rumor will start in the camp that will cause Big Hun to head for home fast, and when he gets there he will be killed."

Now the big mouth ambassador returned to Big Hun and reported and then Big Hun put his threat in writing and had it delivered to Hez at Jerusalem.

The letter contained all the threats that had been made orally and so Hez took the letter and went into the house of prayer and spread the matter in the presence of the Lord.

Then he prayed to God saying, "O Lord, I know you are the God of all creation, open your eyes and hear our problem and listen to our difficulty. The Assyrians have wiped out other cities and other nations, and we are next.

The Assyrians have thrown the gods of the other peoples into the fire, for of course they were gods made by the hands of men. Now, O God, deliver us from this monster so that all men everywhere will know that you are the one true Lord of all."

Isaiah then sent word to Hez saying that God had heard the prayer and that God despised Big Hun. Furthermore, the Lord reported that He was aware of the success of Big Hun and how he had been successful against small cities and weak nations, but now he had defied God and would be punished.

It is the will of God, that Big Hun will not get to so much as shoot one arrow over the wall at Jerusalem but he shall return home as if he were turned around by a bridle like a horse. God says that he will defend Jerusalem for his own sake and for the sake of his servant David.

That night the angel of the Lord went forth and passed through the camp of the army of Big Hun and smote the army with a sickness and in the morning many were dead and many were too sick to move or march. As a result, Big Hun departed the area and began to journey toward home and he was killed en route by cousins who wished to rule in his stead.

Chap.
38

A few years after this Hez became sick and his minister, Isaiah, came to call on him.

"The Lord has suggested to me," said Isaiah, "that I advise you to get your affairs in order for you are about to die."

This did not do much for ole Hez; so he began to pray to the Lord saying, "Lord, please remember that I have been as faithful as I could and I have really tried to live properly, and I'd like a little longer time to live."

Not long after this the Lord inspired Isaiah to call on Hez again and tell him that the Lord had heard his prayers and would give him about 15 more years to live. The Lord also revealed to Isaiah that

God would defend the city against the Assyrians while Hez was alive. As a sign from God to validate this promise the Lord would cause the sun dial to lose six minutes by the Lord holding back the sun for this amount of time[1].

As a result of this experience Hez became a little poetic and composed some lines in celebration of the occasion that went something like this:

> Things looked mighty dark to me
> Facing death so early
> No more would my friends I see
> No wonder I am surly.
> Delirious I chattered as a bird
> Mourning also like a dove
> Praying, praying, yet not heard
> Knowing my boil came from above.
> But heal me, Lord, heal me quick!
> Thank you, Lord, I needed that
> I know you're wise to make me sick
> But now I'm well and getting fat!

Praise God — He heals — He healed me and I will praise him forever.

To assist with the healing let it also be made known that Isaiah had instructed the servants to put an open fig on the boil and it drew the poison out. Praise the Lord.

Chap. 39

When Cannon,[2] king of Babylon, heard that Hez was sick he sent him a get well card. Hez was greatly pleased to get the card which was delivered in person by a number of Cannon's helpers. As a result, Hez excorted the visitors around and showed them all his antiques and even took them into the vault and let them see his treasures.

Isaiah came over to visit Hez in a few days and inquired about the visitors that had been noticed.

"What were those fellows doing here, Hez?" asked Isaiah. "What did they say, and from where did they come?"

"They came from a far country," replied Hez.

"What did they get to see?" asked Isaiah.

"Everything. I showed them the works," said Hez.

"Now hear this, Hez. You have really blown it. These fellows will some day get organized and come here and take everything they saw back to Babylon. In fact, God has revealed to me that they will even take your sons into captivity," said Isaiah.

"All right. I made a mistake, but at least I won't be alive when this happens, and for this I am grateful," concluded Hez.

---

[1] Science reports some missing time and here's 6 minutes of it!
[2] Merodachbaladan

"God has some encouraging words for His people," said Isaiah. "The people have been amply punished and have suffered sufficiently."

"I seem to hear a voice," continued Isaiah, "shouting from the wilderness and saying 'Prepare for a manifestation of God. Make a straight road for the emissary of the Lord, for in the coming of the one God will send equality will be established, the crooked shall be made straight, and the full glory of the Lord will be revealed. Everyone will see this for the Lord has planned that this shall be the way."

A voice spoke to Isaiah and said, "Speak out!"

"What shall I say?" asked Isaiah.

"Tell the people that they are like grass and flowers. The flesh of man grows and blooms and then it withers and dies as the breath of God blows and His spirit wills. The word of God, however, is undamaged and it is permanent.

"Tell the people, however, that there is good news. God will come with a strong hand and His arm shall rule for Him. The hand of the Lord shall be capable of rewarding and shall also initiate a great work. When He comes He shall feed His people as a shepherd feeds his lambs. He shall protect them in his everlasting arms, and He shall lead His people gently.

"Have you ever considered the majesty of God, the Creator, who measured the waters of the earth, whole oceans, in the palm of his hand, the One who placed the mountains, and balanced them delicately with the hills? Do you think God had to consult engineers?

"Nations must seem to God as drops in a bucket or dust on a scale. How then can you describe God, for there is no way of comparison.

"It is ridiculous to attempt to reduce God to a skillful image of gold made by an artist. Don't you know anything? Haven't you heard, were you not always told, don't you know that from the very beginning of the foundations of existence that there is only One that sits on top of everything? The creator, who spread the heavens as easily as a woman spreads a sheet, and set the earth like a tent in which man could live.

"God rules. God makes and breaks princes and judges. To whom then can the Lord be compared? To no one, for there is none like Him.

"Wake up. Take a look at the majesty and power of God. Who dares to think that anything can be hidden from God.

"Have you not heard, have you not known that the Everlasting God, the Lord, the creator of the ends of the earth is never weary, nor depressed, nor is there any way of equalling His understanding.

"God sometimes chooses to grant strength to the weak. It is also noticeable that even the young people with their vigor and freshness become tired and lose their force, but the people, young and old, who serve God have an inner strength from the Lord, and they shall continually be refreshed by the Lord, they shall often have their spirits soar as if borne on the wings of an eagle. They shall run and not notice their weariness, and they shall walk and feel no faintness."

"Be quiet a minute," spoke Isaiah, "and listen to what God has to say."

"Who makes history?" asks God. "I make it. Often have I blessed a righteous man and led him to victory. I also planned the system of generations and placed within man the seeds of cooperation so that the carpenter would encourage the goldsmith, and the various skills of various people would work together in order that buildings might be constructed. This is part of the plan.

"Also remember," says God, "that I have chosen Israel as my servant and Israel is not to be afraid. In due time I will strengthen Israel and I will confuse those that strive against the servants of God.

"Do not fear. I am the Lord. I will give you strong support. I will make of you, the servants of God, more effective than a threshing machine and those who oppose you will be scattered like dust and disappear in the wind.

"I will also be helpful to the poor. Their cries will be heard and I will make new springs for them for their thirst, I will cause trees to be planted in desert places, and I will enable the people to secure irrigation and make orchards in the desert. These things I will do in order that the people may know that I am the Lord, the Holy One of Israel.

"What about some of the idols made by hands that you have worshipped? Can they tell what has happened in the past or can they look into the future? No, but I the Lord can do these things.

"What about Cyrus? Did I not tell you that one would come from the north at my bidding? None of you or your idols, or soothsayers knew of this.

"Was I not the first to tell Jerusalem that help was on the way? Don't you see that your idols and your various little hang-ups are foolishness and a waste of time?"

"What is more, I am sending to you my very special servant. I shall place my own spirit upon him and he will come for the benefit of all nations and shall reveal real justice.

"My chosen one shall not be a loud mouth, a ranter, nor a great warrior, but He will be gentle and careful, not a harmful person. He will open up the barrel of truth, He will be completely successful, never discouraged in spite of difficulties, and his law shall spread over the whole earth.

"I am the Lord, and I will bless my chosen one, and I will give him complete rigtheousness and I will present him to the people as part of my promise. The chosen one shall be a shining light for all the world, for he shall enable the blind to see, and he will liberate men from prisons that are real as well as imaginary. I am God, and I will not share my glory with idols. In fact, the idol bit has had it. There is a new program on the way.

"As I announce my chosen one also I announce new ways and new thoughts for men. Begin to sing a new song to God, even you sailors. Sing a joyful song. Let the mountain people sing with joy and the wilderness folk.

"Let everyone give glory to God. I have waited long enough," says God. "Now I will go forth as a mighty man. When necessary, I will destroy. Sometimes I will use drouth and make water scarce. I will do wonderful things, providing all kinds of things for the blind, and I will straighten out many crooked problems for my servants.

"Many who have blindly worshipped idols shall repent, and many who have not listened to my voice will begin to hear. Often the worst offenders are my own people who refuse to see and who will not listen.

"Man is responsible for his own troubles for he refuses to hear God, or to behold his majesty and he brings calamity on himself. When will you learn? Even these miseries that man brings on himself are merely my way of trying to teach man to repent," says the Lord.

Chap. 43

"Again I say to you, Israel," says the Lord, "You have no cause for fear, for I have redeemed you, and named you, and claimed you. I stand with you in times of trouble.

"Some day I will gather you when you have scattered, and I will reassemble you from all over the world. I will protect you because you are called by my name.

"No one can testify or witness about their meagre gods as you can witness about me, the One Lord. You know what I have done. You know as a matter of record how I destroyed the Egyptians in the waters of the sea and how you were delivered from the menace of the great horde from the north.

"Remember, you are my witness that there is no other God but me. I am your Holy One, the Creator of Israel. What is more, I have great plans for the future, involving the reclamation of desert lands. In spite of all this, you have not properly worshipped me. You do not bring a fair portion to the house of the Lord, and you have wearied me with your sins and your errors. Because of this, I have caused people to think poorly of your priests and your judges. Yet I am still the Redeemer, and I continue to blot out your transgressions for my name's sake."

"I have declared myself again and again," says the Lord. "I am the one Holy One, I am the first and the last, and there is no God beside me. You are to be witnesses to this fact.

"The people that make graven images, and worship material things, they are in for it. There will be no peace in their minds, their downfall is assured.

"You remember me, you servants of the most high God. You are to be my witnesses. I have blotted out your sins and forgiven your errors. Therefore you are to testify in my behalf to all the world.

"Remind people that I am the Lord God of hosts. I am capable of confusing the liars, disproving the soothsayers, and making the highly educated seem to be fools. I can do all things. I will dry up rivers when necessary, and will use men like Cyrus and cause him to decree that the temple of the Lord be built again in Jerusalem."

"The Lord has announced," reported Isaiah, "that He has chosen Cyrus, a man who does not know God, to carry out the wishes of the Lord. The Lord will tear down the gates of the cities that resist Cyrus, and Cyrus will obtain hidden treasures to finance his conquest.

"The Lord is using Cyrus in order that everyone under the sun will know there is but one God. The Lord will use Cyrus to subdue Egypt and Ethiopia and then Cyrus will release the captives of Israel and encourage them to return to Jerusalem and to rebuild the temple. The Lord plans all these things for his own glory.

"To His people Israel the Lord orders them to look to Him for salvation for the Lord is a great God and a just God. The Lord has also decreed that eventually every knee shall bow and every tongue confess the righteousness of God and the availability of His salvation.

"It is a laugh the way the idol gods of Babylon fall off carts and can't stand being moved from one place to another. If these gods can't even help themselves, how can they possibly help anybody else?

"Would you be interested in comparing the Lord God of Israel, the creator, with a god made by a craftsman? Ridiculous, for there is only one true God, the Lord. In fact, He expects to bring his salvation to Israel, and to personalize his salvation among his chosen people.

"Babylon, you've had it," says the Lord. "You will be uncovered and shown to be as corrupt as you truly are.

"I let my people come under your rule because of their sin, but you mistreated them and you'll pay for it. You have flaunted your success and considered yourself to be the Queen of the kingdoms, but you will be degraded. You will lose your following. The astrologers, the stargazers, the soothsayers, the magicians, none of these can save you. You will be destroyed as a kingdom and you will be crushed by too much advice and by wickedness itself.

Chap. 48

"In a way, you are lucky, you descendants of Jacob," says the Lord, "for I am going to deliver you for the sake of my own name and for my glory. I have long told you of creation and also of things planned in the future so you would not be tempted to attribute anything to some graven image which you devised overnight.

"Remember that I am the Lord of all. I control the Babylonians as well as the children of Israel. I have never been shy about declaring that I am God, who rules all the earth and all the people. I have redeemed Israel as simply as I caused the water to flow for the people in the wilderness. Furthermore, have decreed that there will be no peace for the wicked.

Chap. 49

"Listen to me," says the Lord, "for I am sending one called from birth to pronounce my words and declare my glory. It is sad that my own people, of whom my servant is one, will not receive him, but the Gentiles will and He shall be a light to them. Kings and princes shall in time come to worship my anointed one.

"I will send my representative at a proper time and he shall be similar to a covenant for the people, so that those in darkness may see some light, prisoners may be freed who are unjustly held, and the prince that I send will lead in a gentle manner.

"This shall be the beginning of great joy and a great time of singing for the Lord will show mercy on his people. Those who have been forsaken because of their sins will be restored. Freedom will again be your prized possession.

"In spite of how sad and desolate the area may seem to you now, it will some day be crowded with people and prosperous. You wonder how these things shall be? I will see to it that the gentiles restore you themselves, they will provide transportation for your descendants to return. The gentiles will be concerned with your welfare and the great leaders among them shall be considerate and will bring things to you as if they were your servants.

"What is more, I will be against anyone who turns against you. This should be a comfort and a challenge to you. In time, every living person shall know that I am the one true Lord of all.

Chap. 50

"Do you know what caused you to be led captive in the first place?" asked Isaiah. "Well, it wasn't the weakness of God, for He can do anything, but it was sin and disobedience. God is always capable of anything, for he can fill the desert with water or dry up the seas.

"The Lord has blessed me with the wisdom of words and the Lord reveals to me what I should say. I am dead set on this matter and no one will stop me from speaking what God has told me to say.

"The people who try to stop me become enemies of God and they disappear as completely as an old sweater gets eaten by the moths. Trust in the Lord, even if you are in deep despair, trust in God, for God delivers. Those who try to tough it out for themselves and attempt to live without God will be miserable and their sorrows will increase.

Chap.
51

"Listen to me, those of you who seek to live a righteous way," says the Lord, "recall that I have encouraged you from the start. You are descendants of Abraham and I blessed him and I will bless your land for in time it shall change from a barren country to one that is fruitful and yields abundance.

"Those who are my people and seek my righteousness do not need to worry about being few in number or encountering difficulties. The wicked and their evil ways are perishable, but my salvation is eternal. Be sure that the righteous shall have their day, their times of great joy, for this promise is mine, and I am the Keeper of the Promises.

"Why should a righteous person be afraid of any man, for are not all of them short-lived, and nothing they do can impede the will of God. I have declared you to be my people, rejoice in that announcement and obey my laws.

"You have suffered enough for the time being. You have deserved it, but I am planning to bring you great relief.

Chap.
52

"Now get with it. Get up and get to work. I am with you always. My people need to remember that I am God and that I care for my people.

"How beautiful upon the mountains are the feet of them that bring good news, that speak of peace, and announce salvation. There is no greater shout than the refreshing words 'God reigns!'

"This will be no secret, but everyone in all the world will know of God and his offer of salvation. You are going to be properly released from captivity and God shall be your guide.

"My very special representative shall appear among you and he shall astonish the lowly and the mighty, even kings shall be dumbfounded by his teaching. He shall be physically abused, but even then shall he be an astonishment, for he shall speak wonders and declare new ideas.

Chap.
53

"Who is this servant of the Most High God? Well, he will grow up like anyone else, a root out of the ground, a tender plant, and he shall have no great physical characteristic that shall set him apart from ordinary people.

"He will, of course, be despised and rejected by men, a man who knows sorrow and has felt grief, and many people will ignore him. Yet the sorrows that he shall bear are our sorrows, and many of us will just think he is a nutty teacher, even though he will be wounded for our sakes, and beaten because we have sinned, and still his very scars shall be signs for our healing.

"When he is oppressed he does not blow his top and he appears as innocent and harmless before his tormentors as a lamb before the shearer. We are the ones who have gone astray, not him. Yet the Lord allowed him to accept the iniquity of us all.

"He will be taken from prison to judgment, for the sake of all of us poor sinners, he will die with the wicked and be buried with the rich, yet he committed no violence himself and he had not deceived anyone. It was God's will that he must suffer, and he shall understand that he does this for a worthy cause."

Chap.
54

"Now is a time for celebration," said Isaiah, "for great things are beginning to happen. Jerusalem can rejoice at this opportunity, and the great messages entrusted to Israel shall be made available to the people of the world. All of this is because God is Lord of the whole earth, and not just a part of it.

"At times it seems as if God has momentarily forgotten his people, and in his anger over the way men do things God sometimes seems to hide his face, but God returns with great mercy. For God has said that though the mountains and the hills might disappear, the kindness and the love of God will never cease.

"Let all the children be taught about God and in this manner they may attain his peace. What is more, when people organize against the followers of God, they shall not be successful. Remember, I have created the ones who destroy as well as the ones who build and I assure you that no weapon ever formed by man can do away with my people against my will. This is what comes of being a follower of God!

Chap.
55

"Are you thirsty or hungry?" asks God. "Well, come to me and be refreshed. I am willing to make an agreement with you as I did with David, and he is an example of how I deal with my people. Nations and people will seek you because they too want to be under the Lord God of all.

"Seek the Lord at once. Call on God while you have the chance. Tell the wicked to quit his evil ways, and encourage the unrighteous ones to even do away with evil thoughts. God stands ready to receive the repentant.

"This is because God's ways are not similar to our ways and His thoughts are different from ours and are higher thoughts than the heavens are higher than the earth.

"The word of God is like the rain as it comes down to water the earth, and causes the earth to bring forth plants and flowers, that it may provide seed for the sower and bread to the eater. This is the way of God's word, it shall not return to God unproductive, but it shall accomplish his will, and it shall fulfil his purpose.

"Because of this you shall learn to go out with great joy, and live in peace, the mountains and hills shall seem to be full of the sound of music, and the rustling leaves shall sound like applause. Where you were accustomed to seeing thorns you will see a fir tree and where there were briars you will see a myrtle tree, and these are to be everlasting signs marking the glory of God, and nothing can change this plan.

Chap. 56

"In God's name, I plead with you to do justly, for the revelation of God is close at hand," said Isaiah. "Blessings on those who refrain from evil and who pay proper tribute to the Lord on his holy day.

"Non-Jews have no reason for alarm. The Lord is ready to receive strangers, eunuchs, deformed, retarded, for God has prepared a place for everyone that calls on His name. God's house is a house of prayer, and it is a house for people. The Lord will gather to him all those that seek Him.

"Not so with those whose lives are a succession of selfish pursuits. Greedy people, looking out only for themselves, and ruining their minds with strong drink.

Chap. 57

"Why is it that often good people die young and long before they are old? Let me assure you that God often takes them to deliver them from evil days that might lie ahead for them. Remember, the godly who die surely rest in peace.

"Those who forsake God, and seek gods of their own, who pursue their own pleasure, and build altars for themselves on lofty places, there is no help for them. Their whole program is self-defeating.

"God has placed a limit on the idol worshippers and self-seeking people. The High and Holy God has a place for the humble and the contrite, but no place for the arrogant. The wicked shall be like a choppy sea whose waters turn up dirt and mire and there is no peace for the wicked, but there is peace for the righteous, for God heals and God bestows his peace.

Chap. 58

"God has instructed me," said Isaiah, "to speak frankly to you. You enjoy coming to church on Sunday and making the appearance of devoutness, but you continue to hate and despise people, to quarrel, and to seek material things. God is not impressed.

175

"God says that if you want to impress Him you should be concerning yourself with feeding the hungry and clothing the naked. God would have you free people from oppression. When you do these things, your own life will change, and you will shine as a fresh morning star and the glory of the Lord will be an escort for you. Try it, you'll like it! The Lord will see that you are uplifted in spirit and His joy will abide in you."

Chap.
59

"The big trouble with you people," continued Isaiah, "is that your sins have built a wall between you and God. You have trusted in vanity and mischief, and you disregard justice. Your feet run to evil and you think nothing of shedding innocent blood. Your very wickedness stands in the way of your peace, you walk in darkness and keep yelling for a light. Anyone who tries righteousness is scorned.

"God saw your plight and so he is sending a Redeemer, one who has righteousness strong as an armor and salvation like a helmet. The Redeemer will lay down the law, he will cover the earth like a flood, and he shall bless those who believe in him. Those who recognize him shall be filled with the Holy Spirit of God and they shall learn to love good and to hate evil.

Chap.
60

"Rise and shine! The time is coming for the glory of God to be revealed. All the peoples of the earth shall seek the new light that comes among you.

"There is a great future in store for you. Presidents and kings shall help you, transportation shall be furnished you to bring your relatives from distant lands, and foreign aid shall see to the rebuilding of your cities. Jerusalem shall again become the Glorious City. Peace and righteousness shall again some day be restored and violence shall disappear from your land. Your key words shall be salvation and praise and the glory of the Lord will shine to such an extent that the sun and the moon will almost go unnoticed. Your people will become good people and greatly beloved, for the Lord himself shall arrange this."

Chap.
61

"The spirit of the Lord has come upon me," proclaimed Isaiah, "and I am inspired of God to preach good news, to heal the broken hearted, and to liberate those who are oppressed in body or mind. I am prepared to exchange beauty for ashes, soothing oil for mourning, and praise for the neglected, and to thereby change people into trees of righteousness.

"Those who are so touched by the spirit of God shall become priests and ministers, and workers of good deeds. The Lord will reward you for all your trouble, and everlasting joy shall be your innermost possession. The Lord will cause the earth to break forth in righteousness in a manner similar to the budding of flowers and the beginning of spring."

Chap.
62

"The Lord has told me" said Isaiah, "that for the sake of his people the cause of righteousness shall prevail and people of all races and nations will have the opportunity of knowing the righteousness of God and they shall accept a new name for all those who follow the revealed righteousness of God. [1]

"No longer will you be despised and a new holiness will come to Jerusalem. The Lord also has planned that there shall be an end of the world, a day of judgment, a time for the full glory to the righteous. The righteous shall then be truly called a holy people."

Chap.
63

"Who is this that I see now in my vision?" called forth Isaiah.

"It is I, the Lord. I am announcing salvation and declaring that I am come to save."

"Why are your clothes so red, O Lord?" asked Isaiah.

"It is the blood of the enemies of God. I will stamp out evil in my fury. I sometimes crush whole nations because of their evil. I am capable of executing all necessary judgments."

"I will tell your people, O Lord, of your loving kindness to those who understand and your great goodness to your people of Israel. Surely God has become a saviour. He has redeemed his people in love and because of his pity for those who are afflicted. Those who rebelled and rejected him, they had to be treated as enemies."

"Now, Lord, hear my prayer. Remember your promises to Moses, remember how you made a glorious name by leading your people through the wilderness. O Lord, you are still our deliverer, you are still our father. It is not Abraham or some earthly father, but you are our Father. We confess that our hearts have been hardened and we have sinned, but return to us. Restore to us our name and our place.

Chap.
64

"It would be great, O Lord, if you would open the heavens and come down and be with us. This would make a great impression on all the earth and man could see the mountains melt and the waters boil as a sign of your presence and your power.

"We need a revelation. No eye has seen nor ear heard the thing you have prepared for the righteous. In the meantime, we find ourselves a wicked people living in sin. Take us, Father, like the potter takes the clay, and make us worthwhile. Everything is in a mess. Come help our world, O Lord, please come. Amen."

Chap.
65

"People who never showed any interest in me are now calling

[1] I think this is a prophecy of the name Christian

177

on my name," says the Lord. "I am glad for them. My own people, however, continue to reject me, even though I have extended my arms and sought them. My people continually turn to material things and worship prices and such commercial matters. Yet these very people disdain from associating with those they consider inferior persons. This just makes me smell smoke! I will not accept this kind of thing, and punishment is sure to come.

"I will not destroy all my people because there are some who still worship me properly and who seek righteousness. For their sake I will bring forth a saviour who will make provision for them.

"As for those who have forsaken me, you have had it. I will cause you inner discomfort. Food will not satisfy your hunger, nor will drink satisfy your thirst. While my servants shall be full of joy, you will be perplexed and uncomfortable. Your name will fade and a new name will be assigned to my followers."

"In the final times I will create a new heaven and a new earth," said the Lord. "All former things shall be forgotten and a great and joyful newness shall be everywhere. There shall be no more young and old, but all shall be ageless. There shall be houses and vineyards, but these shall be ceaseless. No one will build and then others enjoy the building, for a man will continue to live. No work shall be in vain and there shall be such a sense of peace that the wolf and the lamb shall reside together and there shall be no hurt nor any harm in all the holy mountain of God where I, the Lord, will dwell eternally with my people."

"Now hear my final words," says the Lord. "Heaven is my throne and earth is my footstool. You can't match that with a temple. My love turns to the humble and contrite man, who acknowledges that I, the Lord, rule over everything.

"To those others, however, who reject me and make fun of me, I will send massive troubles to them. Let them make sport for awhile of you who are my followers, but not far off is the sound of their destruction, for I will destroy them myself. I will punish them and the world with fire.

"In the middle of all the tumult there will be missionaries throughout the world proclaiming my name and publishing the good news. These persons shall have great success and shall win many to the cause of righteousness. These carriers of the gospel shall be considered by me as my representatives.

"When the time comes for my new heaven and new earth, my people will have a new eternal name, all worship shall be a regular matter and my people will realize that I have punished all the wicked and the wicked will be a pitiful sight to see."

JEREMIAH

Jerry,[1] an ordained minister from El Dorado,[2] received a number of messages from God and these are recorded here.

"I have known you a long time, Jerry," said the Lord, "for I planned that you should be born for a mission and I prepared you to be a prophet."

"I am overwhelmed by this news, God. I really am surprised for I seem to be very ordinary and certainly no great speaker," replied Jerry.

"Don't think of yourself as being ordinary or like a child for I intend to be with you and I will inspire you when you speak. Don't get mike fright, either, for remember that I am sponsoring you and as always I am willing and capable of delivering you at any time," said the Lord God.

The Lord then touched the tongue of Jerry and put words into Jerry's mouth.

"Bear in mind," said God, "that I have put you over nations and kingdoms, to pull down in some places and to build in others, and in some places to merely plant ideas."

God then said, "What do you see in your mind now, Jerry?"

"I see a hickory switch."

"Good. That is simply a sign of my intent to punish the wicked. What else do you see?"

"I see a pot boiling and the front of the pot is facing north."

"That is accurate. I am preparing the armies of the heathen people of the north and they will come south and march against Jerusalem. This is being done as punishment to my people who have forgotten me and who have turned to false gods and gods made by the hand of man."

"Don't be afraid to tell the king and all the people about this. They won't like to hear it, but they will not harm you for I will be at your side and I will see to it that nothing happens to you."

"Listen, you people of Israel, hear what God has to say," spoke Jerry.

"I remember well your history, you Israelites," said God. "I remember how eager your ancestors were to serve me in the wilderness, and how excited the people were who viewed the miracles of those early days."

"Now you've blown it. You and your fathers have wandered into strange ways and adopted many of the customs of the people you have conquered. How stupid can you get? You have changed

[1]Jeremiah   [2]Anathoth

gods, when you were prospering under the only one true God.

"My words and my commandments were like containers full of living water and you have exchanged this for broken pitchers. You should be ashamed like a thief caught in the act. Incidentally, now that you see disaster coming from the north and the peril of invasion at hand, where are your icky little gods? Can they help you?

"It amazes me how you have forgotten me. A bride never forgets the wedding gown, but you have forgotten me. You have even shed innocent blood for profit. You even try to picture yourself as innocent and intimate that you were a victim of circumstance. Hog wash! You cannot deceive the Lord, your maker."

Chap.
3

"There is an old law," said Jerry, "that says that if a man divorces his wife and then she marries someone else, the wife cannot return to her first husband because she has been corrupted. God knows that Israel has forgotten the Lord, departed to other gods, and deserves no consideration, but the Lord is still willing to receive again a penitent Israel.

"Your wickedness and your pursuit of strange gods has caused the Lord to withhold the spring rains. The Lord has spoken to me about such things."

"Do you know what God said to me? He said, 'Have you observed the evil that is being done by backsliding Israel? It is unbelievable how wicked Israel has become.'

"God also spoke about your sister tribe, Judah. You would think that Judah would learn from the experience of Israel, but such was not the case. Judah built graven images as fast as she could find the stones, and it is a rocky area.

"God has asked me to plead with you, Israel, and beg you to return to God, to acknowledge him and to worship him. The Lord has told me to remind you that He is merciful and that He will not keep His anger forever.

"Salvation doesn't come down like water flowing from the mountains, but it comes from God. God assures all of you people that if you will repent and call upon His name that He will receive you again.

"God promises that He will send wise leaders for you, that you will prosper, that you will recover your land, and that all the people of Israel and Judah will be as me. All you have to do is call God your father and walk in His ways.

Chap.
4

"The opportunity is here," said Jerry to the men of Israel and Judah. "All you need to do is turn to God, to call upon the name of the Lord and declare the Lord God to be your true ruler. If you would only do this, God would make of you a blessing and a leader among the nations of the earth.

"But look out, you people of Jerusalem. If you can run you'd better get with it, for you have failed to repent and because of your sin a great army is forming in the north and it is coming down fast. It is still not too late to repent, but if you turn to God you must do so instantly, for your doom is on the way.

"It is a sad thing for me to behold the ruin of the people, but you asked for it. The Lord is going to allow the northern horde to destroy this land and make it a desolate place, but there will at least be a small remnant saved. This is the way and the will of God. In my vision," continued Jerry, "I can see the people in distress and I can hear their gasping cries of frustration and pain.

Chap.
5

"It would be great if you could point out to me one fine, honest, God-fearing leader of the people, then the Lord could work through him and God would be willing to save the people. Unfortunately, there is no such person at present.

"You people are bull-headed and stiffnecked beyond description," said Jerry. "The leaders in government are the same way. All are doomed. There is no peace for the wicked. The Lord has definitely declared his judgment.

"God cannot overlook such defiance. Many of the people go so far as to say that God would not dare punish His own people. Well, you'd better believe it, for the Lord is a jealous God, and the Lord plans to bring a nation from a long distance, a nation with a strange language, and this nation shall consume and destroy.

"Some of you are dumb enough to ask why the Lord allows such a thing as a foreign people to capture Jerusalem. Well, it is because of the sins of the chosen ones. The ministers are preaching their own ideas and the judges rule on a basis of their own ideas, and the people are content to let this occur."

Chap.
6

"Now listen to me, you people of the tribe of Benjamin," said Jerry, "you had better get ready to split, for the forces of the north are coming against you. You are in bad shape because of your sins. Actually you are as helpless as a young and delicate girl surrounded by a bunch of hot blooded shepherds."

"I wish you had sense enough to repent at once, but to whom can I speak? You people have put plugs in your ears, and you will not listen to the word of the Lord.

"Actually I am as steamed up as God is in connection with your sins. The whole city is consumed with graft and evil doings, included in the wrongdoers are most of the judges, educators, and priests. These crooked people call forth 'peace, peace,' when there is no peace. What is more, the people and their leaders are not ashamed.

"As a result God has planned to punish you all with many problems and great dismay shall come your way.

181

"A cruel people from the north will descend on you and you shall be terrified long before the north men arrive in armored array. You have sinned and not repented, and so the Lord has cast you aside as damaged silver, no longer fit for use."

Chap.
7

"I have also a word to the tribe of Judah," proclaimed Jerry, as he stood on the top steps of the temple. "Change your ways. Begin to deal fairly with each other and with strangers, take an interest in helping the sick and the elderly, care for the widow, and God will preserve your place here in this fair land.

"Yet you steal, murder, and commit adultery during the week and then on the Sabbath day you come into the temple, which is known as God's sanctuary. and disregard all the evil which you continually plan. You have made God's house a den of robbers. God will do to this house, which is called by God's name, even as he did to the Westminster Encampment,[1] simply because of the evil you do.

"Don't you know what goes on at Jerusalem? Haven't you seen whole families working together to gather an offering to some strange god? This is not only a way of stirring God's anger, but it is a cause of confusion among the people.

"God is angry. The people have contaminated the church. There is sure destruction in store for the people and there shall be a great slaughter with no proper burials involved.

Chap.
8

"The invaders who come will be a mean bunch. In fact, they will dig up the bones of the prophets and the king and spread them in the sun. Times will be so difficult that the people who survive will envy the dead. One would think you would know better. The stork knows when to travel, so does the turtle, the crow, and the swallow, and yet you don't seem to understand the judgment of God.

"There are some so-called modern teachers among you who do not know enough to obey God, and they will go down the drain for sure. They will lose their wives and their possessions. Yet these same teachers have often said that everything was all right, yet they could easily see the sin and injustice that existed all around them.

"Bad times are close ahead, and when you look for peace, you will not find it and when you seek health you will find only new ailments.

"You people have no idea how grieved I am. I know what is going to happen and how you could save all this with great repentance, but there is no way to ease my pain, for the Lord is angry and vengeance is on its way."

Chap.
9

"I wish I could tie my body onto an artesian well so that I could cry all day without running out of tears.[2] I even wish I had a

[1] Shiloh   [2] Jerry is really pouring it on here

182

little cabin in the back woods where I could get away from it all. The people around will bend their tongues and shoot lies as arrows, but they will not take a bow and arrow to defend their country. The people have wilfully separated themselves from God.

"One of the worst things that has happened to you people," continued Jerry, "is that you lie to each other and deceive each other so much that the whole nation is in decay.

"The Lord will not let this condition remain unpunished and so Jerusalem shall be reduced to ruins, predators shall have dens in the city, and the communities of Judah shall be left desolate and uninhabited.

"The punishment that I have planned for these people is harsh, but they deserve it. For one thing, bitterness and a complaining attitude shall be part of their existence, and the people will be scattered throughout the world in many nations and in strange and far away lands they will be mistreated.

"You might as well alert the best moaners and groaners among your loudest women, for there is going to be plenty cause for loud wailing. You might as well pick out a wall for it now and get with it. Your ladies might teach your daughters how to wail, too, because there is going to be enough trouble to spread over more than one generation.

"The Lord suggests that the intelligent person should not think that he can make it on his own brain, nor the mighty warrior survive by his own strength, nor the rich man buy his way free, but let everyone turn to the Lord, and glory in God's name, and recognize the righteousness, the loving kindness, and the judgment of the Lord. The Lord has definitely decided to punish the wicked, regardless of race, color, creed, or national extraction."

Chap. 10

The very essence of ignorance is to go into the forest, cut down a tree, bring it into town, decorate it with silver, nail it so it cannot move, and then worship it as a god. How stupid can you get, you who serve such man-made gods.

The Lord is a true God, a living God, one who causes the earth to tremble, and no nation can withstand the displeasure of the Lord. The Lord God is the one who made the earth and all existence, the Lord utters his voice and it rains, and lightnings and winds are at His command.

The Lord has decided to eject from the land the people who turned against him. The Lord is greatly disappointed that the people have misused his church, and God is disturbed that the ministers and leaders of the church have polluted the worship in the sanctuary.

"Please, Lord," prayed Jerry, "ease down a bit on me. Do not be too harsh on me, for already I am in great trouble. Pour some of your anger on the wicked invaders who are making a wasteland out of our country."

"Now listen, Jerry," said God, "and pass this word to the people. I made an agreement with the fathers and forefathers in all Israel, and the arrangement was that the children of Israel would obey my commandments and I would bless them, and be with them, and protect them.

"What happened is very simple. The people ceased to obey my commandments and they sought strange gods and pursued evil and now they will be punished. Now Jerry, there is no point in your praying to me in behalf of these people because the evil is done and the punishment is on the way. It is because of the wickedness of the people in worshipping Baal that I am bringing great trouble on the people."

The Lord then revealed to me that among other things the leaders of the Jews were planning to kill me, and I was being set up as a lamb for slaughter. The Lord enabled me to understand that the leaders were worried over my prophecies and my messages and planned to stop these by killing me.

When I learned all this, and that the group that planned to kill me was known as the Black Shadow[1] Gang, I encouraged the Lord to deal with them justly. As a result, the Lord promised to punish the gang, and to see that they died by the sword or by famine, and other punishments would come until there were no remnants of the group to carry on their evil ways.

"Now, Lord," prayed Jerry, "I know you are righteous and wise but there is one thing that really bugs me, and that is the prosperity of the wicked. It seems obvious to me that the hell raisers are all happy and I am always in trouble. I would like to suggest a change in strategy. Why don't you just line the wicked up and have them march into the slaughter pens.

"The wicked really are doing us no good. They pollute the land, kill off all the game without observing the game laws, and they pooh-pooh the idea that you will do anything about it."

"All right, Jerry, now listen carefully to what I'm saying," said the Lord. "If you can't stand running with men, such as watching a few evil men prosper, how will you do when you must race against horses? If you can't keep the faith in a place where there is peace and quiet, what will you do when the Jordan overflows or other disasters take place?

"You do have troubles, Jerry. Your own family tells lies about you. Just don't depend on them or believe what they say. You can trust me, though, Jerry. What you must first understand is that I have abandoned my people for the present because of their sins. My people have trod upon my name and defiled my house.

[1] Anathoth

"Because of this my sword of destruction is already determined. The whole land shall be scorched and violated by the enemy. I will also punish the pagan neighbors and they too shall be taken into captivity. On the other hand, when my people repent, and if they call upon my name, I will in time restore the people to their native land and I will bless them. Again I say, over the long haul, the wicked will perish and the righteous shall enjoy the land.

Chap.
13

"Let me give you an illustration," said the Lord to Jerry. "Go and buy yourself a new pair of underwear. Wear it for a few days and then go hide it in a rock."

Jerry did as God said. About a month later the Lord moved Jerry to go and get his dirty underwear which he had stuffed in the rock. Jerry retrieved the clothing and found that it was ruined with mildew and general dirt and decay.

"Now, Jerry," said the Lord, "that is a good illustration of what is in store for Judah and Jerusalem. The people who follow strange gods and neglect to worship the Lord will end up just like dirty, shredded, worn-out underwear."

Jerry then turned to the people of the land and said, "Every bottle shall be filled with wine."

"That doesn't make sense," they replied, "for everybody knows that. So what?"

"It is God's way of saying that all of you with your wicked leaders shall be full of wine and you will be smashed against each other like bottles and your destruction is near," spoke Jerry.

"Why don't you shape up?" continued Jerry. "Give glory to God before it is too late, and He encloses you in darkness and despair. Tell your king and queen to humble themselves. As things stand now, the government will be overthrown and Judah will be taken captive. What then about your beautiful herds and flocks? When this destruction comes you will no doubt wonder why it is happening to you. I am telling you now. Your own evil and neglect of God has brought this whole trouble down upon you. In fact, you have become so accustomed to doing evil that changing to good all of a sudden would be almost like asking a leopard to change his spots."

"Because you have forgotten me," said the Lord, "and trusted in falsehood and your own selfish ways, you are doomed. I have watched your meanness and your self-centered evil and as a result Jerusalem will be destroyed. I wonder how long it will take you to repent."

Chap.
14

The word of the Lord came to Jerry and told him that there would be a terrible drought and famine in the land. The time would come when the head of the household would send the young men for water and they would return ashamed with empty canteens. The farmers would be ruined and the ranchers would lose their cattle.

"O Lord," prayed Jerry, "There is no doubt about our being a sinful nation, but for your own sake and your own reputation don't let strangers see the terrible trouble which you have promised. We are your people and this is your land; so please cancel the drought and famine."

"The people have rejected me, Jerry," said the Lord, "so don't waste your breath praying for them. I have planned to see that they are punished by the famine and also by military aggression."

"There are a lot of preachers, Lord," said Jerry, "that are telling the people that everything is going to be fine."

"They are preaching lies, then," said the Lord, "and I have not instructed or inspired them to speak this way. In fact, I will see to it that the famine and the sword shall make an end to these phony preachers. Also the people who listen to them will be punished and they will die in the streets of Jerusalem, some from famine and some from the sword of the enemy.

"This ungodly outfit can let their tears flow, for they are going to have plenty about which to cry."

"We confess our wickedness and the wickedness of our fathers[1], and now we plead with you to remember us. Do not disgrace your record of saving us. Where else can we receive help? Is there some other god on whom we can depend for rain? We will serve you, O Lord, for we know that all things are in your hands and under your care.

Chap. 15

"I am sorry, Jerry, but even if Moses and ole Sam asked me I would not change my mind about socking it to these people," said the Lord.

"What is more," continued the Lord, "if her people ask you what to do you can tell them of their four choices, one is just drop dead, another is to get a sword and fight back, another choice is to starve to death, and the fourth is to be led away into captivity.

"My plan is to see that my people who have forsaken me are led away into captivity. I will continually create difficult problems for them. There will be widows by the hundreds and the mothers will cry bitterly for all their sons will be dead."

Then Jerry spoke to himself saying, "Woe is me. My own dear mother must be sad for she has brought into the world an unsuccessful sad sack. Everybody hates me, even though I owe no money and nobody owes me any. I have prayed to you in their behalf and the people still curse me."

"Trying to change these people is like trying to break iron bars," said the Lord, "and so I will deliver them and all their wealth

---

[1] This has always been easy

186

to their enemies."

"Now, Lord," prayed Jerry, "I would like to say a few kind words in my own behalf. I have suffered terribly because of my faithfulness. I have been living on your words and speaking constantly in your behalf. When the others made fun of you, O Lord, I sat alone in your defense. Your help to me has been very spotty, a little here and a little there, but no real deliverance from all the people that persecute me."

"Don't be so touchy now, Jerry," said the Lord. "Your job is to speak for me to the people. You are not to be overwhelmed by them, but you are to overwhelm them with your sure words which I give you in my name. The people won't like it and they will try all kinds of things against you, but I am with you and I will watch carefully over you, for I am proud of you, and I will in time save you."

The Lord continued to speak to Jerry and told him not to get married and have children for such would merely bring grief for the Lord was going to punish the Jews and there would be death and shame. The Lord reminded Jerry that the peace of the Lord was going to be withheld at this time from the Jews. All joyous sounds of the people, such as occasioned by a wedding feast, and all mirth and laughter would come to a halt, for God reminded Jerry that the punishment for the people who had turned their back on God was sure and terrible.

God told Jerry that when all this was told by him to the people that they would not believe it. In fact, with some indignation they shall say, "What have we done?"

"When this occurs, Jerry," said the Lord, "tell the people it is because their fathers have forsaken the Lord and followed other gods and that the present generation is even worse. Tell them again that I will have them driven out of this land and scattered. The conditions will be awful.

"However," continued the Lord, "the great day will come when the living Lord will again be honored and recognized, but this time it will be for bringing people back to the promised land.

"In the meantime, however, I will see that your enemies fish you out of watery hiding places, and hunters search you out of caves and canyons, and I will double your punishment for defiling my land."

"Lord, my strength and my fortress," prayed Jerry, "I am sure that people from everywhere will begin to say how foolish their fathers have been, knowing that it is silly to think that a man may make a god with his own hands."

"Then, Jerry," said the Lord, "when the people come to me with the right attitude I will demonstrate my power and let them see that I alone am the true God."

The people of Judah sin as if it were a law to follow, one that was written with an iron pen or the point of a diamond, and so the people of God shall be punished and forced to live on foreign soil.

The Lord has said, "Cursed is the man who trusts in mankind and disregards the Lord. Such a man will be like a desert traveler seeing mirages, and yet he shall continue to remain in a parched and barren land.

"Happy indeed is the man who trusts in God. Such a man is like a tree planted by everflowing waters, a tree whose leaves stay green and whose roots do not have to worry about periodic droughts.

"A man's heart is a deceitful thing. Only God can really search and see the heart. One way of seeing the heart of a man is to give him freedom and see how he does on his own. Some people secure riches, but those that secure riches improperly are eventually as unproductive as a quail that sits on a nest and never hatches anything. A man is a fool then to secure riches improperly."

Then Jerry spoke forth saying, "Lord, you are the only hope of Israel, and I know that everyone who forsakes you has had it. Heal me, though, Lord, then I know I will be well, save me, and then I know I will have security.

"Lord, did you know we have some smart alecs who say, 'Where is God's word? We don't see anything happening.' Thank goodness, that's not me. I do the best I can and I minister as well as I know how to do. Continue, Lord, to be my hope and not my terror. Pour it on those that persecute me, though. Don't let me be discouraged, but let my enemies be discouraged. In fact, give them the old double whammy."

The Lord then instructed Jerry to take a stand by the common gate to Jerusalem through which gate the kings and the people of Judah have historically come and gone.

Jerry then began to teach the people in accordance with his inspiration from the Lord.

"Mend your ways," said Jerry. "One thing you can start on is the proper observance of the Sabbath. You are not to be using the Sabbath for unnecessary manual labor, but the Sabbath is a time to rest from your labors and to worship God.

"Your fathers didn't do this," continued Jerry, "but they turned a deaf ear and became stubborn and self regulated. If you, however, will listen and will worship God properly and observe his day, then once again the kings and princes of Judah will come and go through these gates, riding in style. People from all the rural areas will then come to worship and bring their gifts to God, coming to the tabernacle in Jerusalem.

"If you don't respond to this plea, however," emphasized Jerry, "the Lord plans to bring ruin of the worst kind on you all."

Jerry then went down to watch the potter as he turned his wheel and made his pots, for Jerry was inspired of God to do this to learn a lesson.

While Jerry was watching the potter a fault developed in the vessel which the potter was making so he threw it down and made another vessel.

"Do you get the lesson, Jerry?" asked the Lord. "The people are as clay in my hands even as the clay is to the potter. I will deal with people and with nations as the potter deals with the clay.

"Now, Jerry, go tell the people everywhere about this. Tell the people I am planning to cast them aside. I tell you all that I will make the land a pitiful place and people will wonder what has happened to Israel. I will scatter the people and I will hide my face from them."

The people listened to all this and became angry with Jerry and the people began to criticize him behind his back and to agree not to listen to him any more.

Jerry then turned to God saying, "Do I receive evil in exchange for all the good I've tried to do for these people? I pleaded with you in their behalf, and now they turn around and want to hang me. All I can say now, Lord, is let them have it! Kill them in battle, let their children starve to death, don't forgive any of their sins, and deal with them when you are at the peak of your anger."

The Lord then led Jerry with his spirit and moved him to go to Watergate[1] and to take with him a vase and then having arrived at Watergate accompanied by a group of curious spectators and some members of the press, Jerry spoke to the people, being inspired by God to do so.

"Now hear this," said Jerry. "That word goes for the king as well as the people, rich and poor alike, the Lord is pronouncing doom on this nation because it has forsaken the God of truth and the Lord of honesty. In place of serving God, the people and their leaders have decided to serve such gods as power and wealth, and therefore instead of a refreshing sound, the name Watergate shall be a stench in the nose of the people.

"The Lord will not allow the leaders and responsible parties to prosper for long who cause such problems and obviously relegate the Lord to a secondary power. I will see to it that the offenders turn on one another and consume each other with their own bitterness."

Jerry then broke the vase which he was carrying and said, "Even as I have broken this vessel; so shall the Lord break this nation and destroy all those who have worshipped strange and man-made gods. The Lord has pronounced this judgement on those who consistently

[1]Tophet

189

refuse to do his will."

Now Pete[1] was Chief of Security for the city of Jerusalem and when he heard all that Jerry had said he had Jerry put in chains and exhibited on the court house lawn.

The next day Pete had Jerry brought to his office for questioning.

"Let me tell you a thing or two, Pete," said Jerry. "In the first place your name is no longer Pete, but your name is Mud.[2] The Lord is planning to make you a real terror to everybody around you and you will even begin to hate yourself.

"The king of Babylon will come and take this whole city and lead the people away captive. In addition, the invaders will steal everything in sight. You will be led into captivity yourself and you will die there, for the Lord will not allow you to escape."

Later that day Jerry prayed to the Lord in anguish saying, "Lord, you haven't helped me a dime's worth yet. I am hourly taunted, threatened, and accused. I spoke frankly to the people, telling them all the bad things in store for them, just exactly as you told me to do. I certainly can't keep quiet when your word is burning in my heart. The people are fed up with hearing me denounce them. I have not said a kind word to them yet, for you have given me none.

"In spite of everything, I am still sticking with you, Lord, and I guess some day things will get better. At least let me live to see some of your vengeance on these people. That will help some. Yet I still praise the Lord, for I know he will deliver the unfortunate in his day and in his way."

"At the same time, I wish I had never been born. I feel like cursing the man who brought word to my father that I was born.[3] In fact, curses on anyone who was standing around with a sword and didn't kill me while I was a baby. It would have been much better for me if I had been born dead. Since I've come into this world all I've seen is labor and sorrow.[4] All I do now is live in shame."

King Z,[5] who ruled over the area which included Jerusalem, had
been told that Bad Ned[6] was preparing to declare war and invade and so he asked the Chief of Security, ole Pete, to check with Jerry and find out if the Lord was going to deliver them from their prospective trouble.

Jerry turned to Pete and said, "You go and tell King Z that the Lord is going to be on the other side. In fact, the Lord is angry enough to fight against you himself and he will not help you in any

[1]Pashur
[2]Magormisabib
[3]Jerry is pretty depressed at this point
[4]Jerry is really feeling sorry for himself
[5]Zedekiah
[6]Nebuchadre

encounter against anybody.

"You can also tell King Z that he will be captured along with all his family and his servants. In fact, you have only two choices to offer to the people. One is to go out of the city and surrender and be led away into captivity and the other is to stay in Jerusalem and die by either famine or the sword.

"All of this, the Lord reminds you, is because you have forsaken God and neglected to obey his commandments."

Jerry was then inspired of the Lord to go to the house of the king of Judah. When Jerry arrived he spoke to the king and to others who were present and would listen.

Jerry said, "I have a message from God. The Lord says to begin to deal justly with everyone, to advocate righteous living, and perform all business in an honest manner. Be kind to the poor, deliver the unfortunate from his oppressor, and be fair in dealing with strangers. If you obey these words then prosperity and peace will return, but if you don't, God will cause the defeat of this nation."

"In fact, the Lord warns you all that people will pass through this country and marvel at its desolation and they shall comment to one another that this is the type of thing that happens when God's people are unfaithful.

"People who have built huge buildings and paid low wages or none for the building, just like the king did for his palace, these places shall be destroyed. Do you want to hear about King Jay Jay?[1] He doesn't have a chance because of his wickedness. No one will mourn for him when he is killed and dragged out of the city like a dead jackass.

"The Lord warned you plenty during all your affluent years, but you wouldn't listen. Well, Bad Ned is going to get you, each and everyone. The throne of Jerusalem has been contaminated and the Lord doesn't want a king in Jerusalem again."

"The Lord has said that the blame rests primarily on the unrighteous leadership," continued Jerry, "for the leaders have failed to teach the people and have not visited the people and instructed them. God will correct this some day and God has revealed that in time there will come from the line of David a righteous teacher, his name shall be Lord of Understanding, and in his name shall restoration begin and a new day started.

"God is presently sick at his stomach over the corruption in government, the flagrant violations of moral law, all this business of everyone doing as he pleases without regard to morality or the

---

[1]Jehoiakim

convenience and concern of his fellow man.

"The prophets are for the most part not speaking for the Lord. The prophets are pleasing their own selfish desires, walking in lies, committing adultery themselves, encouraging evil people. The Lord will destroy these people as simply as He did Sodom.

"These prophets have been so bold as to tell the people that wickedness is acceptable. That God is not a God of punishment. This is pure nonsense!

"God is aware of what the prophets have been doing. Claiming, for instance, that every dream one of them has is a revelation of God. These prophets can't tell the difference between a dream and a direct revelation of God.

"Because of all these things, for the wicked leadership and the encouragement of permissive sin, the Lord has turned against his people, and punishment is a sure thing. Consider yourselves as of now, separated from God.

Chap.
24

In order that there should be no misunderstanding on Jerry's part, the Lord told Jerry to observe a pile of figs, some being good figs and some being evil.

God then revealed to Jerry that the good fig represented the people who surrendered and were taken into captivity, for in time these people would return and be part of the restoration program in times to come. The bad figs represent those who continued to defy God and they are those that shall be scattered throughout many countries and they shall perish by pestilence, and by the sword, and by famine.

Chap.
25

"It has been thirteen years," spoke Jerry to the people, "since I first began to tell you of my messages from God. Other prophets through the years have also carried the same messages from God, but you have refused to listen to them either. The result is that the anger of the Lord is risen against you.

"The Lord is going to use a pagan king, Big Hun, and he will come with a mighty conquering army and he will represent the fury of the Lord. As a result there will only be gloom and sad cries of anguish and despair for the Jewish people. The people will be led away from Jerusalem and the surrounding area as captives and shall remain in captivity for 70 years.

"After the passage of the 70 years then the Lord will punish the pagans of Babylon and they shall suffer for their sins and for their mistreatment of the Jews. Actually the Lord will in time reward all the nations and all the people in accordance with their deeds.

"The Lord has commissioned me to go to the leaders of various nations, such as Babylon, Egypt, Alabama,[1] Mississippi,[2] the

[1]Assah   [2]Moab

Moscow Muggers,[1] and Massachusetts,[2] and tell them that they shall have to drink of the cup of the fury of the Lord, and so will the English,[3] the Americans,[4] the Japanese,[5] and any nation that at any time shows great prejudice and is wishy-washy in the acknowledging of God as the Lord of all nations. There is no way for a nation to successfully renounce the Lord or fail to grant Him the rightful place of honor among all nations.

"The Lord will use natural forces such as storms and fires and there shall be great trouble throughout all the earth, and it will all be the manifestation of the fury of God because of man's disobedience."

Chap.
26

Once again Jerry came to the temple of the Lord and for his sermon on Sunday morning he spoke in a straightforward manner, with emphasis on the errors of the people, and Jerry told them that if they did not repent at once they would be destroyed.

The people became indignant that Jerry would use the pulpit to denounce them in such a forceful manner and immediately they began to mumble among themselves and soon they decided that the simplest answer to the problem was to execute Jerry.

The other members of the ministerial alliance were greatly alarmed and disturbed and they added their influence to the movement to execute Jerry.

Jerry then spoke again to the unruly assembly and said, "The Lord sent me to tell you the things that I have told. It is not my doing. Again I remind you that you can repent and mend your ways and return to an orthodox worship of God. As far as I am concerned, of course, you can kill me or do with me as you wish, but I warn you that you will be shedding innocent blood and you will bring even worse things upon yourselves, for I am a representative of the Lord God of Hosts."

A great argument arose then among the people. Some members of the ministerial alliance defended Jerry on a basis of his speaking forth for God and that it was asking for it to punish a man for speaking for God. Others did not agree and one man began to tell of the time years before when a prophet predicted the fall of Jerusalem and the king sent all the way to Egypt for him just to have him executed. However, the protection offered by Cardinal Cushing[6] was enough to save Jerry from the angry mob.

Chap.
27

Not long after this another message came to Jerry from God and as a result he made some miniature yokes, of the type that tie oxen to a cart, with the thongs, and he sent a set of these to each of the leaders of Alabama, Mississippi, Massachusetts, and a few selected

[1]Philistines   [2]Ekron   [3]Dedan   [4]Tema   [5]Buz   [6]Ahikam

others, and he wrote to each a note saying, "The Lord has arranged for Big Hun, the leader of Babylon, to take over the Hebrew nation, and the Lord has instructed me to tell you to submit to the rule of Big Hun, because the Lord is with him at present and there is no way you can successfully resist. If your prophets tell you otherwise, they are grossly misinformed. In fact, the Lord will punish any nation that will not submit to the yoke of Big Hun.

"If you agree to the demands of Big Hun and submit to Babylon, the Lord will see to it that you retain your homeland. It would be foolish not to submit, for the Lord will destroy with pestilence, famine, and the sword, the nation that does not submit.

"The message from God also says that the valuable altar ornaments, and precious vessels for communion shall not be hidden, but should be taken into Babylon along with the captured people. The Lord himself shall see that after the captivity the sacred vessels will be returned to Jerusalem."

Chap. 28

There came into prominence then a modern, loud talking prophet named Hank Guru[1] and in a public demonstration he broke the wooden, symbolic yoke which Jerry was wearing and the new prophet told the people that things were going to get better, that the Lord was going to allow the captivity to exist for no more than two years, and that the power of Big Hun would soon be crushed.

Following this big meeting, Jerry departed and the Lord spoke again to Jerry. The Lord told Jerry to go to Hank Guru and tell him that the breaking of the wooden yoke was child's play, for the yoke which the Lord had provided was made of iron. The Lord reminded Jerry that the Lord had placed a yoke of iron on the faulty nations and that such was not easily broken.

As a result, Jerry went to Hank Guru and said, "The Lord did not send you. You are a fake and a liar, and you are simply trying to please the people, and to win friends. The Lord has decided that because you have done this terrible thing and misrepresented matters to the people, you shall die this year, as punishment for your rebellion against God."

Seven months later Hank Guru died.

Chap. 29

Now by this time Big Hun had captured the Hebrew nation and had taken many captives[2] into Babylon. Jerry wrote a letter to these captives and it was xeroxed and distributed among them.

Dear Captives:

The Lord has instructed me to write you a letter and tell you how to conduct yourselves while you are in captivity. Get to work! Build houses, plant gardens, start fruit orchards, get married, build

[1]Hananiah   [2]All who surrendered

families, and cooperate with the authorities in the city where you dwell. If you live in peace with those around you, then peace will come to you.

Don't let your prophets or your rabble rousers disturb you. The Lord has decided that you are to remain in captivity for 70 years, so any rebellion at present will just simply get you killed.

The Lord has great plans for you and God will consider your case after the 70 years of punishment is terminated. Serve your term well and the Lord will then listen to your prayer in regard to returning to Jerusalem.

After you have served your time, and repented, then the Lord will lead you out of captivity and he will bring his people from all the various areas to which they have been scattered. Your punishment is deserved and you absolutely must fulfill your time in captivity.

The wicked leaders among you, the dishonest prophets and judges, the immoral politicians, all these will the Lord punish in His way and in His good time.

Yours truly,
Jerry

There was another man whose name was Cosell[1] and he decided to get into the communication business. As a result, he wrote a circular letter to all the people in captivity and proclaimed to them that he was the authorized representative of God and that all his pronouncements were accurate, and that anything he said superseded anything that Jerry had to say.

The people then began to call Cosell and write him letters saying that Jerry had told them to cool it for 70 years and they suggested Cosell get to work on Jerry.

Cosell then visited Jerry and read some of his fan mail to him.

The word of the Lord then came to Jerry and comforted him by assuring him that Cosell did not represent God and just to prove the point the Lord would see to it that Cosell had no male children and that he would not live to see the good days which the Lord had in store for his people.

Another message from God then came to Jerry, and this was a message of hope.

"The Lord has promised," spoke Jerry, "that the day shall come when the captivity of the people will be ended and the Jews will return to Palestine. Now the Jews live in strange countries, in fear and trembling, but the Lord will break the yoke and the Jews shall again serve the Lord and a new king will be born from the line of David.

---

[1] Shemaiah

"Just have patience, for God must do His thing. It is necessary that adequate punishment be given for the sins of the people. When the penalty has been paid, then the Lord will punish the people who are now punishing you.

"The Lord also has promised the rebuilding of Jerusalem and the restoration of the Promised Land. The Jews will prosper and will increase in numbers and in importance. Once again you will be the people of God. God's anger against the wicked will not fully be shown until near the end of the world."

Chap.
31

Jerry again spoke to the people and reminded them of the long time promise of God that Israel would be fully restored some day and that again it would become a great nation. The restoration of Israel, however, would always be conditioned on the people's acceptance of the Lord and their attitude toward His commandments and His statutes.

Jerry reported that the Lord had said, "I will bring the people from the north country, from the coasts, women and children, blind and lame, and they shall be joyful and there shall be singing again in the land of Israel."

"The Lord knows," continued Jerry, "that the weeping of his people could be heard in Berlin, in Moscow, and even occasionally at Miami Beach, and the weeping was the sobbing of Rachel as she cried for her children. All this will pass, and the Jews will be given their land again, for it is ordained of God that this be done.

"There will even be a new twist added as Israel will seek the Lord for a change. There will even be leadership from the women of Israel and they shall do their bit.

"The Lord has further declared that in time in Israel a man shall be accountable for his own actions and he shall no longer say that because his father ate sour grapes his own teeth are on edge.

"The time will come also, the Lord has said, when there will be a new agreement between God and man, and the law shall be written in the hearts of men and it will not be necessary to teach the young people about God, for they shall know the Lord first hand themselves.

"These promises come from the Lord who made the heavens, and set the course of the sun and moon, and hung the stars in their appropriate places. Great things are in store and even the boundaries of Jerusalem shall be extended."

Chap.
32

King Z became so furious at Jerry for telling the people that Big Hun would capture Jerusalem that he had Jerry put in jail. The Lord spoke to Jerry when he was in prison and prepared him for a visit from his cousin Burl.[1]

[1]Hananeel

Sure enough, Burl came to Jerry while Jerry was in jail and offered to sell him a piece of land.

"The land is cheap now, Jerry," said Burl, "because everybody has listened to your big talk about Big Hun capturing everything and everybody. The people are also dubious about your talk of the return of the Jew to the promised land and so I am willing to sell my land cheap and must, of course, offer it to my next of kin first."

"All right, Burl, I'll buy it and pay the fair market price. I want witnesses, and I want everything legal, for the Lord of Hosts has plainly stated that houses and fields shall be bought and sold again in the promised land."

Following this transaction Jerry then prayed to the Lord saying, "O God, I know you are in charge of everything and everybody, but getting me to buy land when the invading army is already storming the walls has got to be a shaky proposition."

"There is nothing too difficult or impossible with me, Jerry," said the Lord. "Big Hun and his army shall capture the city because of the sins of my people, for my people turned to Baal and to strange gods. Again, Jerry, I remind you, that though I provide destruction as a means of punishment, I also restore, and I do plan to restore Israel in future years. Just as I have brought hardships on my people because of their sins, when they return to me and repent then I will bring blessings more significant than the hardships."

Chap. 33

"It will be a great joy to me when the repentance of my people will enable me to restore them and to bless them. The cities of Israel shall again prosper and joyful sounds shall some day be forthcoming from all areas of Israel. This is my sure promise to my people," said the Lord.

Chap. 34

During the height of the siege of Jerusalem King Z had a conference with Jerry and again Jerry told him that disaster was ahead and that the king would be led away into captivity and that the king would die in peace and receive a decent burial.

Following this conference, King Z published a decree freeing all the Jews who were bonded or in slavery and the people obeyed the decree. This did not last long as very soon men began to secure slaves and servants again. This displeased the Lord greatly and again the Lord renewed his promise of punishment. Because of this and other sins the Lord renewed his promise of supporting Big Hun in his conquest.

Chap. 35

The word of the Lord then came to Jerry and Jerry was instructed to go to the Puritans[1] and to speak to the Puritans in the

---

[1] Rechabites

197

presence of some of the leaders at Jerusalem.

In accordance with the instructions of God, Jerry assembled a council of the Puritan leaders along with several of the rulers of Israel and Jerry placed an assortment of wine and strong drink before them, and he invited them to start drinking.

"We don't want to offend you, Jerry," said the Puritan spokesman, "but our grandfather and former leader, Miles Standish,[1] told us to beware of getting too civilized and he made us all take an oath not to drink, not to live in houses, not to be farmers, or ranchers, and so we live in tents,[2] we don't drink, and we just wander around and make out as best we can with our cruising herds.

"We wouldn't be here in Jerusalem now if it wasn't for Big Hun and his army. As soon as this cotton-picking war is over we are going to move our tents outside the city walls and start living again."

Then the Lord spoke to Jerry and told him to speak to the people of Israel and use the Puritans as an example.

"Tell the people," said God, "that although I sent prophets and messages, you disobeyed me and you will be conquered because of this, but the Puritans will be blessed for their faithfulness and as long as the earth lasts I will see to it that there is always a Puritan living and as such he shall have access to me very readily."

During the fourth year of the reign of Little Jay[3] as king of Judah, the Lord suggested to Jerry that he write down all the sayings of the Lord concerning the capture of the Jews by the army of Big Hun and specify what they must do to avert such a disaster.

As a result, Jerry wrote down the words of God, naming the sins of the people, and assuring everyone that under the present administration and with the failure of the people to observe the commandments of God there would be a time of captivity as punishment from God.

After Jerry had completed this document, he sent for Laughlin[4] and he asked Laughlin to take the document, saying to him, "Laughlin, you are the best reader in this area, and though I'm pretty good myself, I am also in jail and can't go to church. I want you to take this document to church Sunday and read it to the congregation for me."

Laughlin complied with Jerry's request and read the document.

Attending church that day was a man named Whisper,[5] and the first thing Monday morning Whisper went to the palace during the coffee break and told the leaders exactly what was said in church.[6]

The advisers to the king decided that it would be wise to secure

---

[1] Jonadab   [2] For some today this is reason enough to drink
[3] Jehoiakim   [4] Baruch   [5] Michaiah
[6] It has always been hard to get leaders in church in person

the sermon and have it read to the king so Laughlin was asked to appear and to read the word to the advisers. Laughlin did this and the certainty of the statement dealing with the fall of Jerusalem disturbed everyone. Laughlin was told to leave and hide and to keep his mouth shut about the sermon and to tell Jerry to do the same.

The advisers then hid the sermon, but the king learned of it[1] and sent for the word. By the time the king had heard the first few pages he was plenty mad and had the reader throw the whole thing into the fire.

The word of the Lord then came to Jerry and instructed him to write the sermon again and to add to it a few lines telling Little Jay that burning the Lord's word was dangerous and that as a result the Lord would punish Little Jay and everybody close around him.

Chap.
37

Now there was a local newsman named Earl Wilson[2] who had heard of the words and the prophecy of Jerry telling of the forthcoming captivity and of the invasion of Jerusalem and he made this information available to the cabinet members of the king.

The cabinet members then went to King Z and the spokesman said, "O King, this man Jerry is ruining us. He has stated that under the authority of God, he has declared the doom of your city and this has lowered the morale of the army.[3] What we would like to do is get rid of Jerry."

"It is out of my hands," said King Z, "and you can do with Jerry as you wish."

"As a result of this statement, the cabinet members had Jerry seized and they put him in a deep dungeon, without food or water.

Now Ears Black[4] kept the king informed on local matters and he reported to King Z that Jerry had been put in an old well, over 30 ft. deep, and that Jerry was stuck in the bottom of this old well. Ears explained to the king that Jerry would die of hunger or thirst[5] and Ears wanted the king to take action.

As a result, King Z gave Ears a rescue permit and Ears along with a few of his cronies tied a bunch of sheets together and lowered the sheet rope to Jerry and rescued him. Jerry was then smuggled into the king's private prison.

Later the king sent for Jerry and asked him for the real inside on what was going to happen.

"I will tell you what is going to happen if you promise not to have me executed," said Jerry.

"I will protect you, Jerry, but you must agree not to let the advisors to the king learn of my intentions," said King Z.[6]

---

[1] They had stool pigeons in those days also
[2] Shephatiah
[3] The old army morale problem again
[4] Ebedmelech
[5] Kings have never had time to think about such details
[6] King Z was a real sad sack

"O.K., King. Now here is the deal. If you resist the siege of Jerusalem the city will in time be captured and burned to the ground, but if you will surrender, you will have your life spared and you will be led away peaceably into captivity."

"I am afraid of what the Jews will do to me, Jerry, if they learn that I have been getting secret advice from you," said King Z.

"Don't worry. The Lord will see that you are kept intact," said Jerry.

"Well, just in case some of the cabinet members hear you are on the palace prison list and they begin to inquire about our relationship, don't tell them that we have been talking."

As a result of this arrangement Jerry stayed in the general confines of the palace prison until the Chaldeans captured Jerusalem.

Chap.
39

In a year or so the siege of Jerusalem by Big Hun became so intolerable that the army of the Jews in Jerusalem escaped from a door in the wall of Jerusalem during the night and so did King Z. The next day the patrols of Big Hun began to chase down those fleeing and one patrol captured King Z. Big Hun decided to spare his life and take him to Babylon as a captive, but he had his eyes put out and he had his sons executed in his presence before he was blinded.[1]

At the order of Big Hun, however, Jerry was freed, and was left in Jerusalem with a remnant of the Jews, consisting of the poor and the disadvantaged.

The word also came to Jerry that the Lord was going to save Ears Black because of his faithfulness and his kindness to Jerry.

Chap.
40

Now J. Edgar,[2] who was chief of security in charge of the prisoners for Big Hun, had taken Jerry along with the other captives to San Diego.[3]

J. Edgar sent for Jerry and said to him, "Now I know that the Lord has brought all these things to pass, and I know that you are the one who said that it would happen this way; so you are free. You can return with me to Babylon and be at ease there, or you can go back to the Jerusalem area and try to tough it out with the poor and the small remnant left there."

J. Edgar gave Jerry some food and spending money after Jerry had decided to return to Jerusalem. Jerry returned to Notre Dame[4] where a remnant of the refugees had gathered.

It so happened that Big Hun had appointed a man named Fast Katz[5] to represent him and to rule as a satellite prince over the people left in the promised land. When the people and their leaders came to Katz he encouraged them to learn to live under the Chaldean

[1] It didn't pay to lose a war then   [2] Nebuzaradan
[3] Ramah   [4] Mizpah   [5] Gedaliah

rule, to pay their taxes, and to adjust to controlled conditions. Katz explained that he planned to do as best he could and to work well under the Chaldeans.

Word of all this began to spread and many of the Jews who had hidden in the hills returned to start planting their vineyards again, for many had gone and hidden in the hills during the Chaldean invasion.

Some men came to Fast Katz and told him that there was a contract out on him and that one of the kings had employed Spear-Point[1] to kill Katz. Katz thought that this was a silly report as he could not think why anyone would be interested in killing him. In fact, one of the friends of Katz offered to kill Spear-Point before he could get to Katz, but Katz thought the whole thing sounded silly.

Chap.
41

Some months later, Spear-Point and his ten henchmen visited Katz and Katz invited them to dinner. After dinner, Spear-Point and his ten men attacked Katz and killed him, gangland style. Some of the servants of Katz came into the room, hearing the noise, and they were killed also.

About this time a small group of men came to the city to call on Fast Katz and Spear-Point and his men met them and invited them into the palace. When the men were inside, Spear-Point and his crew killed these men also.

Spear-Point had a big pit dug and threw the dead bodies in the pit, and then he took the people remaining who were alive and well and made captives of them. When word of this began to leak out, a warrior by the name of Sam Bass[2] gathered a small band of fighters and went to get Spear-Point and free the captives. The captives were freed, but during the fighting Spear-Point escaped and he made it safely across the border to Laredo.[3]

Sam Bass then led his small force and all the captives south toward Bethlehem in preparation for a flight into Egypt, for he expected more trouble than he could handle.

Chap.
42

Sam and a few of the top warriors then came to Jerry and asked him to pray to the Lord in their behalf as they were poorly armed and very short on food. Sam also wanted some advice on the next move.

"I'll do as you ask," said Jerry, "but remember, I will tell you exactly what the Lord advises and you may not like it."

"You tell it like it is and we will listen. We want the straight stuff," replied Sam.

Ten days later Jerry sent for Sam and his group and spoke to the whole gathering saying, "The Lord wants you to stay put here in this land. The Lord will bless you if you will try to tough it out. You

---

[1]Ishmael   [2]Johanan   [3]Land of Ammonites

are not to be afraid of Big Hun, for the Lord will protect you.

"However, if you say no to this and try to escape to Egypt, thinking there will be peace and security there, then you will have nothing but trouble. The war which you flee will catch you, and the famine that you fear will also find you in Egypt. All the men who make a move to Egypt shall die by the sword, or famine, or pestilence.

"The Lord says that as surely as His anger was turned on Jerusalem for the disobedience of the people, it will also be turned on you if you refuse to listen to this warning. Don't go into Egypt! That's exactly what God is saying. When you asked me to pray you promised to observe the answer, and now you have the answer, stay here and live under God's blessing, endure the hardships, or go to Egypt and die."

Chap.
43

Then one of the associates of Sam, a man named Sloppy Joe,[1] spoke forth saying, "You are not telling the truth. You have been bribed by Laughlin to get us to stay here and be captured and sent to Babylon as slaves. We are going to go to Egypt."

As a result, Sam Bass and all the gang gathered together the remnant of the Jews and left for Egypt. Jerry went with them.[2]

After arriving in Egypt, the Lord inspired Jerry to go and place some stones in a secret place near the entrance to Pharoah's house. The Jews were witnesses to this action and then Jerry spoke, "The Lord has decided to send Big Hun down here to conquer Egypt and he will build his royal pavilion over the top of these stones. When Big Hun comes he will kill some and capture some and he will burn houses and make a great destruction in Egypt, destroying many of the false gods."

Chap.
44

Then Jerry spoke to the Jews who had left Judah under Sam Bass and who were residing in Egypt saying, "You really blew it. God told you not to come to Egypt. You apparently did not learn anything from the example of your fathers who disobeyed God in Jerusalem. Now you are in Egypt and you are burning incense to the queen and you are worshipping strange gods.

"You are right, Jerry," one of their spokesmen replied. "We figure we have a better chance of surviving in Egypt by serving their gods and burning incense to their queen."

"God is going to punish you for this," said Jerry. "You will be killed, and die of famine or the sword. All of you who stay in Egypt shall perish. The Lord plans evil for you and not good, for you have forsaken the Lord. As a sign of the power of God, be certain that Pharoah will be conquered and you all shall be destroyed, that is all

[1] Azariah   [2] Where the congregation goes the preacher goes

of you who stay in Egypt."

Jerry then sent word to Laughlin reminding him that God was going to punish him also and that added to his grief and multiple troubles would be the destruction of buildings and the destroying of crops. Jerry wrote a denunciation of Laughlin, telling him that no matter how he sought to save himself, there was to be only misery and restlessness for him the rest of his days.

The word of the Lord then came to Jerry concerning the plight of Egypt. Jerry spoke forth in a public address and said, "Get your army in shape, O Egyptians. Sharpen your swords, brace your shields, call your best men into service, but none of this will do you any good. You are doomed.

"Assemble the best forces you can gather, even getting expert help from Ethiopia and Libya, but none of this will do any good. Get your entire strength together and go to meet the Big Hun from the north, but you will be defeated, for the Lord is going to punish Egypt and God is using the force of Big Hun to effect his decree.

"The only people to be delivered will be a small band of Jews who are faithful to God and we will seek to return to Jerusalem. The small remnant shall be blessed and restored in the Lord's time. God has promised that although many nations may be totally destroyed, the remnant of the Jews will be preserved and will be blessed."

The word of the Lord then came to Jerry and in God's name Jerry denounced the Moscow Muggers.

"You Moscow Muggers," said Jerry, "You will be destroyed by floods. The Lord will cause mighty waters to roar and there shall be great panic and distress. The wicked cities of Tyre and Sidon shall be cut off by floods for the Lord will spoil the land.

"The Lord will go forth with great destruction against the wicked and nature shall work at God's command."

The word of the Lord then came to Jerry and he was inspired to prophesy against Mississippi.[1]

"The land of Mississippi is doomed," said Jerry. "People will cease to speak well of Mississippi. It would be a good idea to leave Mississippi and go somewhere else to live.

"Mississippi has had it too easy for too long. Strangers will move into Mississippi and contaminate it. Shed some tears, for Mississippi is doomed. All kinds of miseries shall come upon the land, for it is no longer interested in God and there are too few unselfish people left.

[1]Moab

203

"You have never seen such sorrow as shall come to the land. This is God's way with any wicked area. Success seems so sure, but evil is self-destructive and the Lord in time punishes, and so Mississippi is a goner.

"There is no escape. If a man runs to avoid a pit he will be caught in a trap. The Lord has already arranged for the punishment of Mississippi. Still, in the latter days of the world, Mississippi will be restored and will again turn to the Lord."

Chap.
49

The Lord, according to Jerry, authorized him to speak and make pronouncements concerning some of the existing cities and nations.

"The Lord has decided to eliminate Laredo," said Jerry, "and to burn it to the ground. The town of Ai will be conquered also. Do you want to know about Edom? Well, they have grown stupid. The wander-curse of Esau will come upon them. The people will attempt to hide, but no one can hide from God.

"The Lord is arranging for some of the heathen nations to be God's instrument for punishing many of the wicked places. There is no way to escape from God. You cannot hide in caves or ascend like eagles, the Lord must in time be confronted. Edom is definitely doomed by the Lord's order, for He will cause the mighty men of Edom to become faint-hearted.

"Damascus is also in trouble. It will be a seething place, filled with internal disorders. Damascus shall be destroyed, for the Lord has so decided.

"Other areas, like Massachusetts,[1] that have failed to follow the Lord and to obey his commandments, these places are put on the expendable list. The Big Hun shall come and make a desolated place of this area.

"As for Hollywood[2] it shall be dismantled. It will finally reach a point where no one will agree to spend the night in the city. Other wicked places shall in turn receive similar treatment.

Chap
50

"The word of the Lord is also against Babylon," said Jerry. "The Lord used Babylon and the area people to punish the Jews, but in time the Lord will avenge himself on the Babylonians.

"Fierce people from the north, with unbending arrows, shall attack and they shall make Babylon a desolate place. The vengeance of the Lord shall cause the walls of Babylon to fall, the crops to fail, the people to be killed or captured.

"Through all these things, the Lord has not forgotten His promise to protect and preserve the faithful remnant of Israel. In the time of the restoration of Israel, there shall be a recovery of worship,

[1]Kedar   [2]Hazor

and the people will become faithful to the Lord and devout in their worship.

"The Lord has also planned the destruction of the neighboring allies of Babylon. Archers shall rain arrows on Babylon. The vengeance of the Lord will be thorough for Babylon shall be rewarded in accordance with her wicked works. Babylon has defied the Lord God of Israel, and the punishment of Babylon will be intense. The young and the old shall be slain in the streets, the proud shall stumble and fall, and fire will gut the city.

"The Lord God is the Redeemer, a strong and mighty ruler, and God will care for the faithful and confuse the wicked. The sword of the Lord is set against the rulers of Babylon, against its liars, against the treasures of the city, and the very waters of Babylon's existence shall be dried. Finally the wild beasts of the desert and the predators from the islands nearby will come to stay in Babylon, and the city will become similar to a haunted house with the owls making it their home. Babylon shall never be inhabited again as a testimony to the sureness of the acts of God. Babylon will exist no more, even as was the case with Sodom and Gomor.

"The destruction of Babylon shall arise from cruel people of the north who shall come with many horses and the warriors shall shout like mad. As the noise of the storming of Babylon is heard the king of Babylon shall know a deep fear, and all the nations of the earth shall hear of the cries and know that the Lord God of Israel is at work.

Chap. 51

If there is any chance to flee, be sure and get out of Babylon. Winds shall rip through the land, and many shall be slain by arrows and by spears. Be certain that this is a sign that Israel has not been forgotten by the Lord of Hosts.

"The Lord used Babylon and its prosperity in the manner that a golden cup full of wine is used to make men drunk; so Babylon has made nations drunk with power, but now she is doomed.

"Let everyone that would seek a righteous way of life flee to his own country and worship the Lord, recognizing that all of this history that is being made is of the Lord.

"It doesn't matter how well Babylon seems to be prepared, how adequate its watchmen may be or its defenses, for the Lord has proclaimed its doom. The enemies of Babylon will seem to be as thick and numerous as a migration of caterpillars.

"As punishment for all the evil that Babylon represents the Lord will act as a battle axe and will break into pieces nations, separate horse and rider, come between a man and his girl, scatter the flock and lose the shepherd, smash rulers and captains for such is the power of God.

"The Lord is against Babylon, and it will look like a black

mountain when God has finished with it, and there won't be enough stones left to start a new building. Every purpose of the Lord will be fulfilled; so already the men of the north are assembling, and the land is beginning to tremble in anticipation of the destruction.

"The men of Babylon shall turn chicken, they will burn their own homes, and doom shall be reported from one messenger to another, even before it happens. Babylon is similar to a threshing floor of ripe grain, the time is at hand for the threshing.

"Big Hun has defied God for the last time. The Lord plans to dry the springs and the wells, to remove the sea, and the desolation of Babylon is set. The city will be a place where people passing will make snide remarks and marvel that it no longer exists.

"The warriors of Babylon shall be full of wine and too drunk to fight back so that most of them will die without drawing a sword. A great storm from the sea shall in time come and wash away all that is left from the fire and from the pillage.

"Please let the captives of Israel who serve the Lord be impressed with this prophecy and let them make every effort to escape immediately. Think of Jerusalem and the power of God to restore the Jews. There is no way that Babylon can prevent her defeat or be delivered from her fate.

"The enemies of Babylon from the north shall come and find the leaders, the princes, the warriors, drunk and in no condition to fight. All last minute efforts shall fail, and fire and arrows shall begin the destruction."

Now all these sayings were written in a book by Jerry and he sent the book with a reader to Babylon to warn the Jews. The reader was also instructed that after reading the book to the people, a rock was to be bound to the book and it was to be cast into the sea. At this point the reader was to announce that the same thing was going to happen to Babylon that happened to the book.

Chap
52

Now King Z had never been a good king during his reign in Jerusalem and he did evil in the sight of the Lord. It was under King Z that Jerusalem revolted and it was under his reign when Big Hun conquered Jerusalem. King Z was captured as were most of the men of the army, all of whom had tried to flee from Jerusalem.

It was on this occasion that Big Hun became responsible for burning the house of the Lord in Jerusalem and most of the city as well as tearing down all the walls.

The tribe of Judah was carried away captive into Babylon, all except the poor and the indigent, who remained under the surveillance of J. Edgar. All of the brass vases and items of liturgical worship, and all the treasures of the house of the Lord were taken to Babylon. Many of the church leaders were condemned to death, but 3,023 Jews were spared and brought to Babylon as captives.

Over thirty years later the king of Babylon brought Little Jay out of prison and released him, giving him some authority in the land, feeding him well, and Little Jay ate his meals in his latter days with the king of Babylon.

How can I help but mourn when I see the condition of Jerusalem? A beautiful city teeming with people, now reduced to a grim reminder of the sins of the people of Judah. The people who really cared for Jerusalem have been taken into captivity and they dwell now in a heathen land.

The small remaining group of the people of God are sad for no one comes to church anymore, her family night suppers are dismal failures, and the ministers are greatly discouraged.

The enemies of God's people are a prosperous bunch, however, and this makes the affliction of the people seem to be even worse. About all that is left is the memory of the good old days, but they are gone, for enemies came and captured the city and its people and no one came to help.

Jerusalem became a sinful city and now she is paying for her excesses. The city seems barren and almost naked, the enemies have taken everything. The heathen have shown no respect for the church and they have contaminated all the things of God.

Jerusalem has really been discarded. There is no sorrow comparable to the sorrow of forsaken Jerusalem. The people that were taken into captivity are begging for bread and have already turned in most of their treasures to the pawnbrokers.

The Lord has done all this as punishment. The mighty men have been trampled under foot, the city and its people have been crushed as if they were placed in a winepress. No wonder there is this great sadness. There is apparently no comfort to be found, and Jerusalem has even reached the point of being of no use to her enemies.

Yet the city must cry out saying, "The Lord is righteous. The punishment which is received is justified. Behold, O Lord, our condition. We are desolate. Our enemies of the years have heard of our troubles and they are glad. How about giving our enemies a dose or two of the medicine we are receiving? We are distressed, our groans are real, our hearts are discouraged."

I am a prophet of the Lord, Jerry of El Dorado, and I have witnessed the collapse of Jerusalem. The Lord has certainly revealed his anger and let his wrath be as a cloud over Jerusalem, and the Lord has not even spared His church in His anger.

The Lord has done all these things. The Lord has destroyed the strongholds, corrupted the leaders of Judah, and the Lord did not contend with the enemies of Israel.

In fact, the Lord has treated Jerusalem as if it were an enemy, and the Lord destroyed all the beauty of the city. The Lord has broken down the churches, and ended all the pleasant assemblies of the people. The Lord has even allowed the heathen, the enemy, to come into the church and make all kinds of weird noises and strange sounds.

The elders of the city are grief stricken. They sit mournfully together with ashes on their heads and eyes staring into the ground. The young ladies are solemn and dejected and they are not bubbling with joy as they should be. The youngsters call for food and then they fall in weakness on their mothers sobbing, and the mothers have no help for them.

I wonder if there has ever been such sorrow as there is now in Jerusalem?

Most of the prophets have been selfish and misleading, they have lied to the people and failed to warn the people of the consequences of sin.

Everyone makes fun of Jerusalem. The great, beautiful, wonderful city is gone. The enemies of Jerusalem jeer at the city and remind everyone they see of how easy it was to swallow up Jerusalem.

All of this is simply the fulfilling of the will of God. The Lord has always told the people that the consequences of sin were dreadful.

The people have finally wept in the presence of the Lord. The tears of the people have created a wailing wall and it is in use day and night. I know the people need to repent, pray day and night, to lament before God in real sincerity.

The people need to cry to God and remind him that these suffering people are His people. Ministers are dying in the church and starvation is bringing the people almost to the point of cannibalism.

The dead lie in the streets. The young warriors were killed by the swords of heathen enemies, but all this was God's doing. The Lord has done a complete job of letting his anger fall on the sinful people.

Chap.
3

The Lord has really done it to me also. I have witnessed all of the destruction. The Lord led me into darkness and not into light. God is apparently against me also, for my bones ache and my skin is getting wrinkled,[1] my flashlight battery no longer works, and God has hemmed me in so that I cannot escape to do my own thing.

When I pray I don't seem to be getting through to God at all. The Lord has jumped on me as if He were a bear or a lion, and he has torn me to bits. The Lord caused me to be a source of derision among the people and small boys threw stones at me. The Lord has caused me to be bitter and the fillings have dropped out of my teeth. I can't even remember being prosperous and content. I will always be ashamed with bitter memories of tragic years.

There is only one small ray of hope. The Lord is basically

---

[1] It happens to everybody, Jerry.

compassionate and the Lord is good to those who serve him if they will be patient, for a man must hope and he must wait on the Lord.

It is very good for the young to learn about discipline, to sit quietly during adversity. It is a known thing that the Lord will not withhold his favor forever. Although the Lord causes grief, the Lord will also bring relief.

The Lord does not enjoy punishing his people nor inflicting on them all kinds of grief. It is not for man to question the judgment of God. Let us examine ourselves and let us return to the Lord. Let us lift up our hands and our voices to God.

We have sinned, but as yet God has not pardoned our sin. The Lord has had some of us tortured and others slain, and the Lord has apparently not been available for our prayers. Our enemies have overcome us, fear has come to us, desolation and destruction is everywhere, and our tears make streams of water.

I have personally even been put into a dungeon where I would not see the light of day. As I cried and lamented for the city and for the people of the city, then I called on the Lord out of my dungeon saying, "Lord, hear me. You told me once not to fear, you have always encouraged me, you have redeemed my life, but listen now to my case.

"You have seen all that has been done to me, you have heard all the denouncing of me. The people have criticized me so much that the words have been put to music.

"Take a whack at my enemies, O Lord, and reward them in accordance with all the bad things they have done. Give them the full treatment, Lord, and let your anger be strong against them."

Chap.
4

It is really pitiful to realize what has happened. Our most valuable possessions, even the gold trims from the altar in the temple, have been stolen or stomped in the dust. Our youth, our treasure for the future, they are starved, many of them are already dead without having had a chance to live.

Those accustomed to riches and fine food are in wretched condition. The Lord was kinder to Sodom, for He destroyed Sodom with one deadly blow, while we perish an inch at a time.

The lucky ones are the ones that were killed by the swords of the enemy in the street. It is much easier to die by the sword than to starve to death.

Some years back no one in the world would have believed that Jerusalem would be levelled to the present condition. Sinful prophets and sinful priests, they are part of the cause of the death in the streets. These same men are blindly wandering in the streets today, contaminating everything they touch. The Lord will not help these men for they persecuted the few prophets and priests who were faithful to God.

Those of us who are left are doomed. Our lives are in danger every hour. We had hoped for help from friendly nations, but it hasn't come and it is not likely to come. Actually our days are numbered. Our king was captured, and that meant another thin hope was gone. There was a time when we thought that under our king we could withstand all the nations of the earth.

As for the people who take advantage of our condition and who sponsored our defeat, you are doomed. Israel will one day be restored, but not the enemies of God. You have had it!

"O Lord," prayed Jerry, "remember all that has happened to us. Our homes, our nation, our city are full of strangers and we are apparently orphans in our own land. We have to buy water and we pay exorbitant prices for even the necessities of life. We are forced to work under painful conditions and we are constantly humiliated.

"We find ourselves begging for food, from Assyria to Egypt. Actually, it was the generation before ours that sinned, and yet we are getting the punishment.

"The people who formerly worked for us are now our rulers and we work for them. This hurts! Our skin shows how poorly we are doing.

"Our women aren't safe. It is no longer a crime to rape a Hebrew woman. Our princes are hung by the neck and our elders are treated as if they were little boys.

"There is no longer any music among our people. The teenagers don't even feel like playing a guitar. We are in deep distress, and we know it is the result of sin. The mountain of the Lord is so desolate that the foxes walk on it.

"Yet again we proclaim that thou, O Lord, are the everlasting God, thy throne from generation to generation. Please don't forget us for such a long time. Renew our spirit, O Lord, let us return to you, let us have the good old days back again. Yet it looks from here as if we have been utterly rejected and that you are still angry with us."

EZEKIEL

Among the many Jewish P.O.W.'s living as captives in the land of the Huns[1] was a man named Ezekiel, the son of a minister. This book is his testimony.

Ezekiel reports that when he was about 30 years old, living as a captive, he had a vision.

"The vision which I had," reported Ezekiel, "was too fantastic and impressive to adequately describe, what with the fire, the lightning, the shining brass, the retractable wheels, the roaring noises, the harmony of four wings with changing faces. The vision brought me to my knees."

The vision seemed almost to describe a UFO or a formation of four team flying jets. The wheels which had spokes were retractable and in the vision were sucked up by the four vehicles. The sound seemed to Ezekiel as the sound of roaring water and Ezekiel was certain that he was seeing a glimpse of the glory and majesty of God, and so he fell on his knees and listened for the words of the Lord.

"Son of man," came the voice from the glory of God, "stand on your feet and I will speak to you."

"The spirit of the Lord then entered me," reported Ezekiel, "and I stood on my feet and heard the message of God."

"Zeke,[2] I am sending you to the children of Israel," said the voice, "even though they are a rebellious nation, and even though their fathers have sinned and forsaken my way, and I realize that they are a stubborn outfit, but I want you to go to them and tell them that I sent you. Whether they will listen to you or not is not the point, but I want them to know that I am sufficiently interested to send them a prophet.

"Now Zeke," continued the voice, "don't be afraid or discouraged. I know it will be similar to living among thorns, but stick to your job. Disregard their verbal objections and their attempts to intimidate you. Speak my words to them, and whether they listen or not is not your problem.

"Now you are not to be rebellious as these people are, and I want you first to get a good dose of my word."

Zeke then looked and there was suddenly at hand a scroll and on it were the admonitions of God, his promises, his commandments, and his punishments.

The voice then said to me, "Take the scroll and eat it."[3]
I did as I was told and I absorbed the word of God which was

[1]Chaldeans   [2]Ezekiel
[3]Trying to play God we still say "I'll make you eat it!"

written on the scrolls and I began to feel better about things and a sweet taste came to me.

God then spoke to me and told me to go to the house of Israel that was in captivity and to speak to them about the word of God. The Lord reminded me that I was not a foreign missionary going to a strange land and encountering people of a different language, but that I was going to my own people and we had no barriers of language or custom between us.

The Lord reminded me, however, that I had a tough job for the captive people of Israel were stubborn, resentful, pig-headed, and hard-hearted. The Lord encouraged me somewhat by reminding me that I was made of the same stuff, and the Lord had made me as hard-headed as any of the Israelites.

The big thing, of course, was for me to learn the message of God for myself, to know His word, and to trust God completely before I began teaching all these things to others.

Again I was moved by the spirit and again I heard the noise of the mighty wings and the noise of wheels, and even though I moved reluctantly, I realized that the hand of God was upon me. The spirit moved me to Aspen[1] where a segment of our people were camping and in captivity.

After seven days here feeling as if I was in a trance, the word of the Lord came to me saying, "Zeke, I have decreed that you are to be as a watchman to Israel, and I want you to listen to me and then relay my word to the people.

"You really have quite a responsibility, Zeke. For instance, if I tell you to tell a wicked man that he shall surely die for his sins and you do not properly warn him to change his way, even though the wicked man shall die in sin, you will be held responsible.

"If, however, you warn the wicked as you should and the wicked men continue their wicked way, the wicked shall die, and you will be cleared of any responsibility.

"Let me give you another illustration. Suppose a righteous man ceases to be righteous and death comes to him, if you have failed to warn him, the responsibility is yours. If, however, you have properly preached to him, you are in the clear."

The spirit then moved me to the plains area and the glory of the Lord was there as surely as it had been at Aspen. The spirit then sent me into a house and there I remained confined by the Lord and realizing more certainly every hour how minutely I was under the guidance of God.

Chap. 4

"The next thing you are to do, Zeke," said the Lord, "is to take a large, flat piece of tile and begin to draw on it a picture of the siege

[1] Tel-a-bib

of Jerusalem. I want you to include all the details, with the battering rams and other siege devices. Encircle the entire model with a band of iron as a symbol to the house of Israel that the siege is total.

"In further preparation, in order that you might really impress the people, you will be paralyzed so that you will lie for about a year only on your left side. To prepare for this bake plenty of bread and arrange for water. You are to mix the bread dough carefully. You are to leave your right arm exposed as a symbol of attack and the days of your lying on your left side should represent the years of punishment to Israel. Then you will lie for a little over a month on your right side, and this shall represent the years of punishment to Judah.

"In making your bread dough, include ample vitamins by using wheat, barley, beans, millet and sage. Eat a small portion of meat regularly and drink water on a regular and measured basis.

"When you bake the bread use human dung as a covering, and this will be a sign to the children of Israel of the defilement of their bread because of the non-Jews who will be their conquerors."

"Wait a minute, please, Lord," said Zeke, "how about my using something besides human dung?[1] I wasn't raised on this kind of cooking."

"All right," said God, "you may use buffalo chips.[2] All this shall signify what is ahead for the people of Jerusalem, for there shall be such a shortage of food and water that rationing will be done in the most careful manner."

Chap.
5

The Lord then spoke to Zeke again and said, "Give the people of Jerusalem a prophecy and use visual aids in teaching. Take your hair and cut it off, and cleanly shave your beard, taking the hair from your head. You are to burn one third of it, destroy one third with a knife, and scatter a third to the winds, then the hair which has stuck to your robe you will destroy by burning your robe.

"Then you can tell the people of Jerusalem that all this is a picture of what is going to happen to them, for my people have disobeyed me, and have not walked in my statutes, but changed my laws to suit their own desires.

"Furthermore, my people have shown no restraint in controlling their population and have married any and everybody, and so I am against my people and I will punish my people in a worse manner than I have ever punished any nation.

"Suffering and famine will become so intense that strong family ties, such as between father and son, shall be completely disintegrated. Because my people have contaminated my church,"

[1] There was no foil then
[2] It is possible that the first chip throwing contest originated here.

continued the voice of God, "I will punish without pity. A third of the people will die of pestilence and famine, a third shall perish by the sword, and a third I will scatter to the four winds. I will pursue even these with violence, and then the people will know that I am the Lord God.

"As an additional stinger I will cause the nations of the world to feel unfriendly toward my people and it shall be generally known that I am angry with my people. You can expect famine and the sword, persecution and peril, evil beasts and blood diseases, for all these are part of the penalty.

Chap.
6

The word of the Lord then came to me[1] telling me that I should warn all the hill country people of Israel and tell them of God's anger. The hill country people have built graven images and placed them in beautiful groves in the hills, and the people have worshipped their own pleasures, and the Lord plans to destroy all this.

The people will be slain by the thousands and their images destroyed and treasuries stolen. The land shall be made desolate.

The Lord plans to leave a remnant of the people, but they shall be scattered, and carried away captives, and they can then testify in foreign lands as to the power of God. The people shall hate themselves for having forsaken me and they shall know again that I am the Lord God.

The Lord has instructed me to tell you these things forcibly, and that is why I stamp my foot and shake my fist, for the Lord has told me to preach in this manner.

When the hill country people see their men slain in their favorite pleasure haunts and their land made desolate then they will know for sure that the Lord is God of all.

Chap.
7

The word of the Lord continued to come to me and the Lord told me to announce to the land of Israel as to their fate and I spoke again saying, "You people of Israel, the time is short. The anger of the Lord is upon you and evil is about to come to you.

"The time is short as the coming of a morning, the day of trouble is very near, and the fury of the Lord is about to descend upon you.

"The trouble for Israel will make no distinction between buyer and seller, for no one will profit. Those that go forth with the sword shall perish with the sword, and those that remain behind shall be victims of pestilence and famine. There will be no relief. The people will try to buy off their enemies, but the Lord has prepared exceedingly wicked men to attack, and they shall kill and take

[1] Still Ole Zeke

215

everything as spoil, and money will be useless. Punishment will be given everyone from the king on down, and finally the people will know that the Lord is God."

Some time after this I was sitting in the presence of some of the elders of Judah and I went into a trance. I saw some weird images in my trance, and I seemed to be lifted up by a man of fire who held me by my hair[1] and in my trance I saw visions and had insights into the sins of the people of Jerusalem.

It was revealed to me the evil thoughts of men in church, and then I was taken in my fancy to a wall and told to dig, and I dug in the wall[2] and finally found a door. I opened the door and saw all the evil and wickedness of men in high places who thought they were concealed from the eyes of the world, and even from the Lord.

Then the man of fire led me to behold representatives of the women of the city and I saw that they were privately burning incense and worshipping a strange god of fertility. Finally, the man of fire showed me a group of men who had turned their backs on the church, and they worshipped only each day as it came into being and called forth to the sun as if to a god to give them prosperity.

The man of fire then said to me, "Now you have had a glimpse of what God sees, who can see into the hearts and minds of people. It is for these things that God is furious and there shall be no pity coming from God and the cries for mercy shall not be heard."

God then ordered me to summon the special seventy men that the Lord had provided for the city of Jerusalem. There were six of them and they came to me and one of them had writing material available. At the time, I was standing in the temple and the glory of the Lord filled the place and the spirit of the Lord was present.

"I want you to go through the city," said God to the warrior with the writing material, "and I want you to take a Gallup poll. Every person, man, woman, or young person, must be asked if he is sad because of the sins of the people, and those that are regretful are to be marked by you on their foreheads with the pen which you carry."

Then the Lord spoke to the remaining warriors and said, "Now you go through the city after the writer has had a chance to mark the people, and you are to slay with the sword all men, women, or young people who are not marked on the forehead. You are to begin with the church staff."

The warriors killed some who worked in the church and then many more throughout the city.

While this was happening, I fell down on my knees and prayed

[1] It had grown back by now
[2] Maybe a Watergate type of digging

saying, "Are you angry enough to destroy all of Israel?"

"The evil that has arisen in Israel and in Judah is great and the land is full of violence and injustice. The people think that the Lord has quit supervising the earth and I am reminding them that the earth is mine," replied the Lord.

It was not long before the warrior with the pen returned and stated that he had finished with his marking.

Chap. 10

Then as I stood at the entrance to the temple I beheld a strange vision, for a vehicle appeared out of the sky, and it had wheels, and it was capable of going in any direction. The strange contraption appeared to have eyes on each side, and as it landed the man clothed in linen, who I think was the writing material holder, walked under the shape and had in his hands a red flashlight.[1]

The vision was wondrous, and the sight of wheels within wheels[2] was amazing. The noise was the sound of mighty thunder and made me think that God was speaking. The whole scene was fantastic[3] and I was keenly aware of the presence of the glory of God.[4]

Chap. 11

As I stood in the temple then the spirit of the Lord led me to look toward the east, and there meeting in a corner were all the leading politicians, most of them prominent men, and the Lord spoke to me and said, "Zeke, do you see that bunch of fellows? They are selfish men, they seek to control everything, and they are telling the people that Jerusalem is as safe as Fort Knox and that now is the time to pass a big bond issue and rebuild the city. I want you to prophesy against them."

Then I went near to the men and spoke loudly, saying, "I know what you are thinking and plotting, and I know what you have done, for the Lord has revealed it to me. You have caused violence to be widespread in Jerusalem. You have been afraid of the sword that might come against you, and so God is going to arrange for such a sword to move against you.

"Some of you shall be taken into captivity and some shall die in battle, and these things will occur to remind you that God is the real ruler. God plans to judge you and there is no hiding from him.

"You have violated his law and failed to obey his commandments, and you have chosen to follow the customs of the wicked and godless people in your area."

When I said these things, one of the men, a fellow named W. Gate,[5] had a stroke and died on the spot.

---

[1] Burning coals, no doubt
[2] The first time he ever saw spokes
[5] Pelatiah

[3] Sounds similar to some UFO reports
[4] For better description read King James version

Then I prayed to the Lord earnestly for I wondered if all the people of Israel would be destroyed by God.

"Cool it a bit, Zeke," said God, "for the remnant that is still in Jerusalem have been saying that the exiles were the sinners and that the ones left behind in Jerusalem were saved by me. That is not so. Even though I arranged for the captivity of many of my people, yet I will constantly be available to them wherever they are. In time, I will reassemble my people, and bring them from the various countries to which they have been sent.

"When my people eventually return they will be a united people, and will no longer be divided into tribes, but will be a nation. There will be a new spirit in them, I will bless those that walk in my way and worship me sincerely. I will still be a means of punishment, however, for those who reject me."

Then the space ship, or what appeared to be a space ship, took me up and carried me to the people who were in captivity and I delivered God's message to them. Afterwards, I guess the space ship, which was used by the spirit of God, brought me back, for once again I was back in the city, ready to preach and teach again.

The spirit of the Lord then brought to my mind the sure knowledge that I was dealing with a stubborn and rebellious bunch of people and that even though the truth was spoken to them, they paid no attention. Then I was inspired to attract their attention and possibly teach them something by using the visual aid method.

Inspired by God with the idea, I then began to move my clothes and all my possessions out of my house in the daylight, so that all the people would notice and begin to wonder what the prophet was doing. Then I began to dig a small hole in the wall of Jerusalem, and then I took my baggage and all the belongings that I could carry and in late evening I went through the hole and disappeared from the city.

The next day I returned to the city and the people immediately began to ask me what in the world had I been doing, packing my things, digging a hole in the wall, and disappearing in the darkness.

"I'm glad you asked," Zeke replied. "I was simply demonstrating what is going to happen to you. Your top ruler shall dig a hole in the wall and escape in the night, covering his face so that he will not be identified. The Lord will see to it that he is captured by the Babylonians and he shall be blinded. The rest of you will be a big scramble, some being pursued by men with swords and some being captured and scattered through many lands, and then you may begin to know that God is the Lord of all. Of course, God will spare a few who shall be able to witness and testify to the power and majesty of God."

Another little touch of visual aid teaching came into being when I publicly began to eat bread with trembling hands and to ration water to myself. When the people asked why I was doing this, I replied, "God told me to do this to remind you that captivity means eating in fear, and living on rations."

Then the Lord spoke to me and expressed his great displeasure at the word that was being passed around Israel indicating that the prophets didn't know what they were saying, for the days kept going by and none of the predicted disasters had happened.

The Lord then spoke to me and full of his spirit I spoke to the people saying, "The Lord has decided to change your conversation. The new saying is 'The time is at hand.' There will be no more postponement of punishment and the last chance for repentance is now."

The Lord then reminded me that there were a lot of teachers and preachers trying to soothe the people and simply tell people what they like to hear.

As a result, I spoke to the General Assembly and said, "Pooh-pooh on you who speak from your own head and who do not speak from the inspiration of the spirit of God.

"O people of Israel, what a shame that you listened to these vain men. Listening to them is the same as expecting a fox to build a wall instead of burrowing under it. The Lord will fix these false preachers. They shall not be on the roll of the blessed.

"They have cried peace when there was no peace and they have given you nothing substantial but have constructed a wall and left out the mortar. Of course, all this will come tumbling down when adversity arrives and the storms of life begin to bring hail and wind. The Lord definitely intends to break down all the phony front that man devises. This is the fate of those who claim to see visions of peace, when there is no peace, and there is no vision."

"The Lord has instructed me also to denounce a bunch of women preachers, who are misleading the young, and who are offering to save souls by selling fancy arm bands, or pillows with sacred words sewn upon them. These people are profit makers, they are fakes. The Lord condemns these people, they shall finally fail, and God will deliver the innocent from them."

A committee then called upon me, all being elders in the realm, men of position, men who put up a false front, for they were wicked at heart. I really didn't want to meet with them, but God told me to tell it to them like it was.

"Now hear this," said Zeke, "for the Lord has instructed me to tell you that the Lord is going to make every phony answer directly to Him. Your only hope is to repent at once. You have come to God's prophet for some approval or to make a show of righteousness, but it won't work. Repent or you've had it. If you think I am wrong, then you are thinking God is wrong, for the Lord has told me to tell you these things.

"The Lord is doing these things and warning you in the hope that Israel will not go astray. Yet the Lord is prepared to punish the land with famine and with wild beasts. Even if Noah, Daniel, and Job were alive and living in Israel, the Lord would still punish, though these three would be spared.

"If the Lord uses a sword on the people of the land, even if Noah, Daniel, and Jonah were alive in Jerusalem, there would be great slaughter, though of course these three would be spared.

"The same with pestilence. If a plague began to spread through the land at God's order, not even Noah, Daniel, or Job could stop it, though if they were alive they would be spared.

"God is prepared to send the four judgments on Israel, famine, wild beasts, the sword, and the plague, and yet even after all these have taken their toll, a remnant will be left to testify to the power of God. There will be pleasure in the small remnant, for they shall rear their children in the knowledge and fear of the Lord, and they shall know that the destruction of the Lord was not done without good cause."

Chap.
15

The word of the Lord came to me again and revealed to me that the Lord likened Israel to the branch of the vine tree. The branch is not big enough for timber or strong enough to hang clothes on, and so it is used for fuel and is burned in the fire. The same with sinful Israel.

The Lord plans to throw Israel from one fire to another and this is being done to cause the people to return to God. The Lord will make the land desolate as a sign to the people that God is active.

Chap.
16

The history of Jerusalem is interesting. Actually there was no city of Jerusalem, but a stage coach stop for the changing of horses. Then the Lord adopted the city and blessed it. The Lord agreed to do wonderful things for the city and its people, and it was understood that the people were to worship God.

Jerusalem grew. The buildings of the city were beautifully designed, the people began to dress in high fashion, and jewelry was worn by everyone. The trouble was that shortly the people began to think that these things were the result of their own ingenuity and skill and they did not glorify God or worship him.

The marvelous food that was available and the good wine and honey, all these things were soon attributed to man's ability and no longer recognized as gifts of God. The people were willing to do anything for money, even using their own children to help produce greater profits. The people have completely forgotten how Jerusalem was before God became interested.

To make matters worse, the people began to substitute material concepts to worship instead of God. It is amazing what the business people of Jerusalem did just to make a profit. It didn't matter whether a person was a native or a stranger, the men of Jerusalem were out to cheat him.

Because of all this wickedness and the worship of material things, the Lord has pronounced a judgment. The people that have been cheated all these years are going to get together and revolt, and the Lord will help them destroy Jerusalem.

Sodom was a wicked city and the Lord destroyed it, but it wasn't as wicked as Jerusalem is today. Samaria was a land of sin, but not half the sinner that Jerusalem is, and God caused the Samaritans to be conquered. The Lord is terribly angry with Jerusalem and his wrath will soon be poured on the city.

The poor people of Sodom and the unfortunate of Samaria will receive help before the people of Jerusalem do. The Lord has promised to deal harshly with Jerusalem in accordance with what it deserves, nevertheless the day will come when Jerusalem will be ashamed and will repent. At this time, the Lord will establish a new covenant, it will be God's, not yours, and this shall come to pass when the Lord is pacified again concerning Israel and its people.

Chap.
17

The Lord then revealed a message to Zeke through an analogy in vision form. Zeke saw a huge eagle, with great long wings, and it flew to Lebanon and broke off the top branch of the biggest cedar on the highest mountain and carried it to the city. The eagle also transported some of the seed of the land and planted the seed in far places near great waters, and the seed grew and became great vines with many branches.

Zeke then saw another eagle and the vine reached forth toward the second eagle, but the vine couldn't do it, and the vine withered when the east wind blew upon it.

Being instructed of the Lord, Zeke then explained these visions to the people of Israel saying, "Do you know what those visions mean? Well, it means the king of Babylon is coming to capture the king of Israel, and the mighty men of Israel, and will transplant them in Babylon. The king of Israel, who violated the covenant with God, will die in Babylon.

"Furthermore, the attempt to arrange for the king of Egypt to help will fail. The followers of the king of Israel shall be caputred, and these things are done so that the people may know that God is the Lord.

"The Lord will take a tender cutting from a young cedar and place it on the highest mountain in Israel and there it shall grow and prosper and it shall be a witness to what the Lord has done to his people because of their sin."

Again inspired by God, Zeke taught the people saying, "There is an old saying that you use 'Our fathers have eaten sour grapes and our teeth are on edge." This is stupid. You cannot blame your troubles on the sins of your fathers. God is just, and has said that all souls are accountable. The father is responsible for his soul and the son for his. The soul that sins shall die.

"For example, if a man is just, lawful, and has not served alien gods, nor tampered with another man's wife, nor taken advantage of the poor, and one who has not been violent, but completely fair in his dealings with others, and tried to follow the commandments of God; such a man is just, and he shall surely live.

"If such a man has a son who is a robber, a violent man, an adulterer, an oppressor of the poor, such a son shall not be saved, he shall die, and it is his own fault.

"If there is a son who has a wicked father, and the son sees all the sins of the father, and decides to live justly himself, and he doesn't oppress the poor, or tamper with his neighbor's wife, such a son shall be saved, for the wickedness of his father is not the son's fault.

"Why is this? Well, the soul that sinneth, it shall die. The soul stands on its own, it does not take its associates along. If the wicked, however, decide to repent, and change from bad to good, forgiveness is available, and such a soul shall be saved. In fact, the past wickedness will not even be mentioned to such a repenter in the world to come.

"When a righteous person, however, turns wicked, he shall die for his wickedness and his past record won't help him. That doesn't sound fair? Well, you don't understand the justice of God. Be sure of this, people of Israel, each of you will be judged on his own merits. Repent now, and turn away from sin, and your sin will be forgotten. Throw away evil, and start a new way of life. Why do you choose to die? The Lord has no pleasure in your being lost. Repent and live is the plea of God."

I, Zeke, mourn the passing of Israel and lament that she is a goner. At one time Israel was like a wonderful lioness who raised some cubs. When one cub grew he became powerful, and began to destroy, and he was captured in a pit and taken to Egypt.

Then the lioness encouraged the second cub, and this cub also became powerful and exerted a great influence, and he too became destructive and violent. Finally, they put him in chains and took him to Babylon.

The mother Israel was also like a vine, growing, with many fine branches, but she was plucked up and transplanted, the east wind dried her, and she withered away. Now she is surviving in the desert, the fire and the enthusiasm has left her branches, and she is no longer a ruler. Woe is us! How sad, how sad.

A few months later, I had a committee of elders of Israel come to me and ask me about God and what I thought was in store for the people of Israel.

"Some nerve you have," I said, "putting on a show of turning to God. You know as well as I do what God has done and what God expects of his people. God realizes you boys are phonies.

"In God's name, though, let me remind you that God delivered the children of Israel from Egypt, out of the house of bondage, and God insisted then that the people worship the one true God and set aside the idols of the Egyptians.

"God gave the people statutes and commandments, declared for them a day of rest and worship. God punished the people in the wilderness for disobedience and prolonged their conquest of the promised land, and then again God re-asserted His commandments to the next generation and delivered them into the promised land.

"The same routine again occurred. The people sinned and God punished them. No nation can succeed for long without the blessing of God. Yet the Lord continually returns to plead with each new generation to turn to God and to obey His voice, and observe His statutes and His commandments.

"As for you fellows, God says to quit polluting His church with your phony righteousness. You have a choice, either turn to the foolishness of idol worship or sincerely turn to God and follow His commandments. No matter which choice you make, in time you will surely know that truly God is the one Lord.

"The Lord has also instructed me to tell you that the south area of Israel will be burned by the fire of God. When you see this, then you will know that the Lord He is God."

The Lord then instructed me to turn my attention to Jerusalem and to go about the city moaning and with bitter sighing. Naturally this made the people ask me what was wrong.

"I'll tell you what is wrong. It is the tidings that I receive from God. For God has drawn his sword against the city, against all of us, good or bad. Israel has sinned and punishment is near.

"The sword of the Lord is ready to be used. As I go about the city and occasionally stop and smite my hands together; so shall the sword of the Lord be. It will smite in all places in the city. The rich and important leaders will feel the sword, and so will the poor and ignorant, for all of Israel has sinned.

"The Lord has also revealed to me," spoke Zeke, "that trouble will come on two fronts. The army of Babylon will divide itself and one portion will attack the city and another will attack the countryside of Judah.

"The king will surely lose his crown for the anger of the Lord is sure, and the sword of the Lord will bring dire and dreadful punishment to Jerusalem and all the surrounding area. There is no escape.

"As for the Alabamians,[1] the Lord has sent his sword against them. Even though they were used of God to punish Israel, their lies and wicked ways will be punished. The sword of the Lord is against them, they shall be utterly destroyed and as a nation they shall be completely forgotten. This is the Lord's decree.

"Again I must speak against the city of Jerusalem," said Zeke. "The city has defiled itself with violence, with crime, and with the worship of material things. Because of this, the Lord will reduce the city to a mockery. It will become a shell of its former self.

"Let me remind you city people of some of your sins. You make light of marriage, you take advantage of visitors or strangers, you violate the Sabbath day, you are constantly plotting to make money, and you think nothing of shedding blood.

"There are all kinds of wicked practices being used. Many of you seem to think nothing of going to bed with your neighbor's wife, or even sometimes your daughter-in-law, you seem to think practicing of nudity is good sport, you make contract for people's lives, and you charge excessive interest rates if you think you can get by with them.

"God has had enough of your continuing to acquire dishonest gain. The Lord plans to have you captured, some of you city people will die by the sword and some will be taken into captivity. Hard and severe treatment by your conquerors will teach you a thing or two and you will know that the Lord reigns.

"God says that he will gather you people like the metal smiths get together gold, copper, iron and lead and toss them in the fire. You all will melt in the fire of the Lord. Just as silver is melted in a furnace.

"Furthermore, the Lord is aware of the false preaching that has been taking place. The ministers themselves have violated the holy laws. Many of these so-called leaders are just wolves in the barnyard, soothing the people, and rationalizing away their wicked ways. If there had been enough good men to influence the nation the people might have been saved, but there was no one to stand as a strong godly leader in the political leadership in Israel. As a result, God will bring on the people the very type of treatment that the people have used on the strangers and the unfortunate."

Inspired by the Lord, Zeke then attempted to teach the people by an allegorical treatment of their history and the consequences.

"Let me tell you the story of two sisters, Moll[2] and Doll.[3] The

---

[1] Ammonites   [2] Aholah   [3] Aholibah

224

two lived in Egypt and they were in the line of those whose God was the Lord. The two girls turned wild, however, disobeyed God and became as prostitutes, selling themselves in any way for profit.

"Moll primarily made herself available to the Assyrians, enticing them in every possible manner, impressed by their brashness and expensive tastes, and Moll deserted her God and became completely materialistic.

"As a result, the Babylonians took advantage of her, wore her down to nothing, discarded her, trampled her under their feet, and she was left a hopeless captive, and she had even separated herself from God.[1]

"The same thing applies to the case history of Doll. Like her sister, she was influenced by all the proferred delights of the heathen, and the opportunity for riches and great possessions swayed her and she also turned to prostitution. There was nothing that she would not do for a profit.

"As a result she also sold herself to the Babylonians and the Lord has decreed that the very people to whom she gravitated with great greed would be the ones who destroyed her.[2]

"The Lord has told me," continued Zeke, "to denounce you for your wickedness and for your greed for material possessions. For this, God plans to punish you and God will use the Assyrian hordes themselves to do this. God will punish and the land will be brought low and become destitute, and this will be so that you will know that the Lord is God."[3]

Almost a year later, the word of the Lord came to Zeke suggesting to him that at that very moment the king of Babylon was laying plans to conquer Samaria and Jerusalem.

"God has instructed me," Zeke said to the people, "to illustrate to you in Jerusalem what is in store for you."

As a result, Zeke took a dirty, rusty pot, filled it with water and built a fire under it. Then Zeke killed a lamb and put all the choice pieces of meat in the pot, along with all the bones, and he let the meat cook until it had fallen away from the bones. Then Zeke took the meat out and the bones and spread them upon nearby rocks and poured out the water, and the pot remained barren, dirty, and rusty. Even the scum remained in the pot.

"Now get the message, Jerusalem. You are a city of murder, violence, and money grubbing. You are like the pot. Even the good that is put in you does not change you. Even the heat of persecution and trouble does not cleanse you and you insist on sticking to your evil ways. The Lord wanted to cleanse you, but you refused and so

[1]He is speaking here of Samaria   [2]Referring to Jerusalem
[3]This chapter should be read by our Foreign Policy makers

225

you are doomed."

Then the Lord told Zeke that God was going to take Zeke's wife and spare her the tragedies ahead. The Lord also explained to Zeke that even this loss was to be used as a means of teaching.

"You are not to weep and wail at the grave," said God to Zeke. "You may sigh a bit but don't follow the custom of the times and don't even eat the food brought to you by friends."

The next day after Zeke's wife had died the people came to Zeke and inquired about him, wondering why he did not follow the normal customs of funerals and post grave activities.

"God has used my wife as a means of prophecy. Even as my beautiful wife has been taken from me so shall the beautiful temple of God in Jerusalem be destroyed. You will do as I have done. You will not get to wail aloud and eat bountifully. All these things are signs to you, and when they happen you will know then that the Lord is God."

God then comforted Zeke somewhat by telling him that when all these things came to pass the Lord would provide some eye witnesses to escape and come to Zeke and tell him of all things that they had witnessed.

The Lord then told Zeke that there was punishment coming to some of the hecklers in the stands who rejoiced over the plight of Israel.

God became very unhappy with some of the people on the Riviera[1] for they cheered when they heard of the destruction of God's temple in Jerusalem and they rejoiced when the news of the capture of the Jews was reported. Because of this, the Lord plans to have the Riviera gradually infiltrated by people from other places, many from up east, and they shall make many changes unpleasant to the natives. The Lord is doing this simply because many of the people clapped their hands and stamped their feet in joy when word arrived that Jerusalem had fallen to the wicked. When this happens, you all should know that God is the Lord.

The Lord has also some other plans for Mississippi[2] and Detroit[3]. This is being done because many of these people, when hearing of the troubles in Judah, said, "The whole outfit are a bunch of heathens." Because of this, the Lord plans some labor problems for Detroit, and the city of Memphis will be in Tennessee and not in Mississippi where it belongs.

The Lord has also said that punishment is due to France[4] and God will make many occasions of desolation there for they too were not sympathetic to God's people.

As for the Moscow Muggers,[5] the Lord will take vengeance on

[1] Ammonites   [2] Moab   [3] Seir   [4] Edom   [5] Philistines

226

them, for they continually took advantage of God's people. Over the years the Lord will wreak a terrible vengeance on these types of people and they shall finally know that the Lord is God.

The Lord is also unhappy with the city of Tyre. Tyre was jealous of Jerusalem and rejoiced over its destruction, for Tyre thought it would get all the business that had been going to Jerusalem.

The Lord does not plan things to work this way, for Tyre is a wicked city and every conceivable evil is there. Because of this, Tyre will be completely destroyed, and it will be scraped clean so that it will be left only as a place for the spreading of fish nets to dry in the sun.[1]

The Lord will cause the king of Babylon to fall upon Tyre and destroy it completely. In fact, the king of Babylon will tear down the walls and there will be so many horses stomping around that the city will be reduced to dust.

Finally the Lord has promised that the city will be left as a flat rock and it shall never be rebuilt.[2] There will be a lot of mourning for the good old days of Tyre, but it will never recover. The Lord plans to let Tyre be an example, a terror to remind man of the power of God. Often will attempts be made to rebuild Tyre, but none of the attempts will succeed.

The eulogy over the death of Tyre makes interesting reading. Tyre was a beautiful city, the builders constructed many magnificent edifices going down to the very edge of the sea. The ships of Tyre were the best in the world, being built with cedar from Lebanon and oak from California. The seats on the ships were made of ivory from Africa, and the upholstery was all of fine linen.

Tyre had secured the best seamen in the world for captains of its ships and trade was at its very best. The city itself was well protected by highly paid warriors all carefully selected from the best of the NFL teams,[3] and the sharpest merchants in the east lived in Tyre and aided its prosperity. Tyre had trade connections everywhere, with Damascus, Jerusalem, Rome, New York, Tokyo and Moscow. The Chinese traded here and also men from England, France, and Germany. It is truly amazing, the scope and influence of Tyre. All this will collapse, because Tyre decided to laugh at God. The moans for Tyre will be heard all over the world.

The Lord then encouraged Zeke to contact the leaders of Tyre

[1]This has happened! [2]Finally the sea has even cut off the old rock
[3]Persia, Lud, and Phut foundations from the mainland and today fishermen spread their nets on the rocks.

and to speak to them. Zeke did and he spoke to them saying, "God is angry with Tyre and the leaders there. You have become so important and so sure of yourself and your power that you think you are gods yourselves.

"You think you are wiser than Daniel, and that you have everything under control. You think you control all wealth, and all trade, and that you are protected by a highly paid army. Well, God has planned an invasion for your benefit. How will you feel when there is a strange sword at your throat? Will you think you are a god then? You will die, for God has decreed this.

"What about your king? He is spoiled rotten. He sits on a throne of beauty and power, and lives as if he was in the garden of Eden. Materialism has gotten the best of you. You have been overcome by prosperity, for prosperity has introduced violence and evil.

"The Lord will cause Tyre to be destroyed by fire and invasion. The destruction of Tyre will be a great astonishment and in time it will completely disappear and it will never be rebuilt.

"Zidon will get it also. It is not as important or as prosperous as Tyre, but it is wicked. God will destroy Zidon by disease and internal revolution, and there will be great trouble for Zidon. No longer will Zidon be a thorn in the flesh of Israel. Eventually, long after the people of God have been scattered over the whole earth, when they have eventually repented, and when God gathers them again to Jerusalem, then shall they build houses and vineyards, they shall live safely, and then they shall know that the Lord is their God.

Chap.
29

Then the word of the Lord came to Zeke and he was inspired to testify against Pharoah.

"Now Pharoah," said Zeke, "it is necessary for me to tell you that God is against you. You have decided for some strange reason that the Nile is yours, as if you had made it.

"When Israel called on you for help against the Babylonians, that was your chance, and you blew it. God is going to punish Egypt for this failure, and then you will know that God is the Lord.

"God plans to make Egypt desolate and a trouble spot as long as it thinks the Nile is its own. During one period of about 40 years Egypt will be practically deserted and worthless. This is just a sign from God.

"During this forty year period God will cause the Egyptians to be scattered all around the world, but eventually God will bring them back to Egypt. The importance of Egypt will be diminished and it will no longer be considered one of the most important or powerful nations in the world."

Not long after this, the word of the Lord came to Zeke telling him that God was using Big Ned[1] to conquer Tyre and effect the punishment of God and that therefore Big Ned would be rewarded by God in that God would allow him to also conquer Egypt.

God also told Zeke that eventually the glory of Israel would be restored and the people of Israel would again worship God, and know that God is the Lord.

Chap. 30

"The Lord was displeased when Egypt failed to aid the children of Israel, even though such was God's punishment. The Lord plans to bring long and monstrous trouble on Egypt," said Zeke.

"What is more," he continued, "all the piddling little countries that joined Egypt shall catch it in the neck also. God is quite certain that Egypt will eventually know that God is the Lord.

"The Lord plans to do most of this through Big Ned, who is very careless about lives and property. The Lord wants the people to know that all of these things are part of God's control of history.

"The Lord is plenty burned up with Pharoah and God will destroy his strongholds and embarrass his whole program. God will accomplish this by making Big Ned powerful and allowing him to conquer Egypt and to scatter the Egyptians. Big Ned will also destroy all the idols of the land."

Chap. 31

The Lord then spoke to Zeke during the eleventh year of the captivity and told Zeke to address himself to Pharoah.

"The Lord has a message for you, Pharoah," prophesied Zeke. "You and yours are going to get it. Actually, you have acted just like the Assyrians, and you have exalted yourself and you have indicated that your power and your importance is great. Well, your time is drawing near for punishment. The Lord is not going to permit you or any other nation to place itself above God or to attribute godly powers to its ruler.

"About all I can say is that the fall of Egypt will be big news. The Lord is going to bring you, Pharoah, and your followers to a point that is comparably as low as you have exalted yourself. Other nations shall see you all tumble and will say, 'What a pity for such a great nation to come apart at the seams.'"

Chap. 32

Almost a year later the Lord inspired Zeke to produce a funeral lamentation for Egypt, for the fall of Egypt was almost at hand.

"Woe, woe is Pharoah," cried out Zeke. "Pharoah is like a fish caught in a net and thrown out on the land to flop and die. That is what God is going to do to Pharoah and Egypt.

"As a fitting sign of what is happening to Egypt the Lord has arranged for an eclipse. The Lord has also arranged for the king of Babylon, the meanest man on earth[2], to devour Egypt. When the

[1] Nebuchadnezzar [2] An early day Don Rickles

terrible destruction of the Babylonians has levelled Egypt, then the people will know that God is the Lord."

"Pharoah will finally learn one thing though, and that is that the Lord in His own time plans to get around to all the baddies. The Babylonians will have a big time conquering Egypt, but they themselves will in time be destroyed.

"There shall arise new men of wickedness, and their days will also be numbered. It should slightly comfort Pharoah that he shares the darkness of the grave with some important has-beens[1]."

Still later, inspired by God, Zeke made another speech.

"Now hear this," said Zeke. "The situation is not completely hopeless. My preaching is like a warning trumpet blown by the watchman on the wall. The people who hear what I say and repent shall be saved. If the watchman doesn't blow his trumpet, the watchman is penalized, but I am telling everyone now, the terror of the Lord is close at hand!

"Again I speak to the house of Israel and implore them to repent. God doesn't enjoy getting rid of the wicked and punishing them. God's preference is that the wicked repent and the wanderer return to God.

"God has said that the wicked shall eternally die, but if the wicked repent, return anything that is stolen, and make what restitution they can of other sins, and then begin to walk uprightly in the statutes of God, then these wicked ones will not die but will live eternally.

"The people often criticize this system and accuse God of being unfair, as a wicked man who repents receives the same eternal reward as a righteous man who remained righteous. It is your warped sense of justice that is wrong."

The Lord then spoke to Zeke and reminded him what a tough job he had preaching. The people would come and listen and seem interested and nod their heads, but they would not change their lives.[2]

Then the word of the Lord came to Zeke and he was inspired to prophesy some more, this time to the leadership in Israel.

"You leaders of Israel are a miserable outfit," said Zeke. "You look out for yourselves real well, but you completely neglect the people. The Lord is plenty hot about this matter. You leaders were so busy with your own pleasures that you let the people go astray.

"God plans to look out for all the ones you have neglected. God will find the lost and to each will be given an opportunity for

[1] Hitler, Alexander the Great, the Kaiser, & Capt. Bligh
[2] How modern can you get?

230

restoration.

"God's plan is to provide one shepherd for the sheep, one leader for all of God's people throughout the whole earth. I will bless all the people who follow the shepherd that I send, the chosen one from the line of David.[1]

"The followers of this new leader will learn to feel safe in any land, for they shall know not to be afraid. They shall know that the Lord their God is with them and that they are His people."

Another message from God concerned the people that lived around Mount Seir. These people were strong and mighty warriors, and most people always said, "Yes, Seir" to them.

The Lord, however, took a dim view of the wicked way that these people treated others and the Lord felt that they were so bad that they should be discontinued as a people. The Lord would cause these people to be completely overwhelmed as a nation and their country would never be revived.[2]

The Lord again inspired Zeke to prophesy, this time a word of encouragement to the people of Israel.

"God would remind you, Israel," said Zeke, "that you are His first chosen people and that even though you have been scattered for your sins, you will be restored some day and your land will again be yours.

"God is always for his people, and in proper time there shall be an increase in the number of God's people, and the cities of Israel shall again be inhabited, and the waste areas will be reclaimed. Your situation will be better than it was when you first came to Canaan.

"These things will be done in order that God's name may be glorified, not because the people deserve this. The punishment which God sent, this was deserved. God had pity, though, on his people. Again God reminds you that the restoration of Israel is for the sake of God's Holy Name, and not a reward to the people.

"The Lord will gather Israel from all the nations and bring you again to your own land. God will put a new heart and a new spirit within you,[3] and you will choose to observe the laws of God and walk uprightly. At this time also God will multiply the success of those who plant grain and fruit orchards.

"People will be amazed at what happens in a land known for its desolation. These things God will do, for the sake of his Holy Name."

Not long after this Zeke had a strange experience. While walking

---

[1] Obvious prophecy of Christ   [2] There are no Seirs
[3] I think the Christian spirit

231

in the area where the dead were casually buried in open graves, Zeke began to think that he saw the dry bones move. Then Zeke saw the ankle bone begin to connect with the knee bone, and so forth. Then skin formed over the bones and all the dead of Israel seemed to rise as a great and mighty army. The wind had blown spirit and life into the whole cemetery area and Zeke was scared purple.[1]

God then cooled Zeke down by informing him that this was a vision and that it signified God's intent to restore Israel and to eventually see that the people of God were in control of the earth.

God then inspired Zeke to try a little visual aid in teaching the people. As a result, Zeke took two sticks. On one of them he wrote Joseph, and on one he wrote Judah. Zeke then joined the sticks together by grafting or splicing.

"Do you see what I have done?", asked Zeke. "Well, this symbolizes the joining of all of God's people everywhere some day, and they shall no longer consider themselves tribes, but shall all serve one master.[2] God will then make a new covenant of peace with his people, and they shall be a new outfit. The spirit of God will be with them and they shall be God's people. The wicked and idolatrous shall then know that God is the Lord."

Chap.
38

"Now God has a word for a bad bunch from the North.[3] The Lord knows that you have been a constant nuisance for centuries. Everytime you thought Israel was weak and her cities poorly fortified, you descended on Israel.

"One of these days, many, many years from now, you are going to do this once too often and you are going to find all of a sudden that the weak cities and desolate rural areas are defended by God, and it is strictly curtains for you when this time comes. This is God's way with the wicked. It is slow, but it is sure!"

Chap.
39

"God has told me to emphasize the fate of the North Birds. God says that knocking you Northers is going to be as swift as snatching a bow from an archer and throwing his arrows on the ground. It's coming, boys! God says then you fellows will know that the Lord is God!

"Just to give you a fearsome idea of how complete the destruction will be and how great the loss of life, the Lord says that it will take seven months to bury the dead.[4] In fact, tourist groups will assist in this burying.[5]

"The slaughter of these people is going to be so great that the Lord wants me to alert the buzzards as the land will need plenty of

[1] This should have caused a halt to his prophesying
[2] I think this is a reference to Christ as head of the church
[3] Not necessarily Yankees   [4] Well before burial insurance, of course
[5] "Everyone out of the bus now for burying detail!" yells travel agent

232

them.[1]

"All these things will witness to the power and glory of God, and the heathen shall be astonished. Again God reminds his people that when they have repented and returned to the Lord, when the new shepherd has come, then God will no longer hide his face, but will pour forth his spirit on the people and Israel shall come into being again."

Chap.
40

Fourteen years after Jerusalem had fallen Zeke had a vision, and in this vision he seemed to be transported to the top of a mountain and from there he could behold a great city. There was present in the vision a man who shone as if he were made of brass and he instructed Zeke to look carefully at what he saw and report it to the Israelites who were still in captivity.

The vision of the city was seemingly quite accurate, with specific measurements for vestibules, rooms, the temple, and other buildings. Primarily the measurements concerned the inner and outer portion of the temple.

Chap.
41

More minute measurements and details of the vision of the temple seen by Zeke.

Chap.
42

After all the careful examination of the temple, the brass man took Zeke toward the eastern part of the temple, and the glory of the Lord of Israel became manifest. The vision was the same as with the earlier vision of the vehicle with wheels and wings, and the glory of the Lord filled the entire temple.

Then God spoke to Zeke in this vision and said, "Zeke, here are my headquarters. I have come to stay. I will not allow my temple to be continually contaminated. Tell the people to put away their idols, for I the Lord have come to stay."

The Lord then in the vision told Zeke to describe all that he had seen, particularly the temple. "If the people repent, let them have all the tiny details," said God.[2]

Chap.
43

Then God made available the details.[3]

Chap.
44

In the vision, then God closed the east gate and decreed that no one should enter it, for here had passed the glory of God. Only the priest of God could be near, and he will sit near the gate and eat bread.

Then was Zeke transported to the north gate and here reminded that the children of Israel had sinned in allowing strangers and

[1] Ezekiel was a natural born buzzard alerter.   [3] Read Ezekiel 43: 13-27
[2] Somebody repented for Zeke has all the details

plunderers to pollute the temple of God. There must be a real housecleaning in the church. Even though the regularly ordained ministers were wrong and have sinned, yet they must return and run the sanctuary. These ministers must observe the statutes assigned to them.

There are some ministers who never strayed nor were persuaded to follow strange cults and tangents. Let these ministers know they are welcome again as keepers of the house of God.

These ministers must be properly and unobtrusively dressed, and they must be robed when conducting regular services. These men are not to let their hair grow long, nor are they to drink, and if they marry they must marry maidens and not widows, unless the woman be a widow of a minister.

The ministers shall teach the people the difference between the holy and the profane, and in cases of dispute, the minister must render judgment. The ministers shall obey the laws of God and see that the sabbath is observed.

The first portion of the gifts that the people bring to the church shall go to the minister.[1] The ministers must remember not to eat anything dead of itself; so don't bring sick sheep as part of your church pledge.

Chap.
45

The vision also outlined the need of setting aside a certain amount of land to be considered church property. This should include a place for the minister's house.[2]

The Lord also suggested that Zeke remind the rulers that justice was needed, and also fairness. A standard for weights and measurements was recommended and the rulers were urged to see that there was no cheating of the people by the merchants.[3]

The remainder of the chapter tells about paying your church pledge in livestock and only the principle is presently applicable. Giving to God is still emphasized as basic to worship!

Chap.
46

Ordinances are set forth here instructing the ministers on how to prepare a family night supper without blemish.

Chap.
47,

The brass man from God then let Zeke look out of the east gate again and there he showed him a river beginning with waters joining waters until a great stream was created and flowed forth into the mighty sea. The vision was explained to Zeke indicating that as the waters expanded the power and truth of God would also go forth. Each tribe and each nation would be assigned an area suitable to their habitation.

[1] We all know that the preacher has to be paid

[2] Small lots were often selected
[3] Keep trying!

The land was to be divided first among the tribes and the area with bounds for each tribe was described and is recorded in Chapter 48. There would be set aside an area for a great city and this great city shall be called The City of God.

DANIEL

When J.J.[1] had been king of Judah for only about 3 years, Big Ned[2] came and declared war against Jerusalem. The Lord, in accordance with His plan of punishment, gave Big Ned the victory and J.J. was carried away captive to Babylon. Also Big Ned confiscated quite a number of the antique vessels and beautiful altar pieces from the church and had these valuable symbols placed in the pagan church in Babylon.

Big Ned then ordered his executive vice president, Aggie[3], to select the outstanding teenagers from among the captured people and to enroll them in the Big Ned University. At the college, the students were to be taught the language of the Northers,[4] general science, some psychology, political science, and palace manners.

One feature of the college was the training table. All the youngsters were to learn to eat rich foods, such as caviar and cherry jubilee. Among the teenagers were four named Daniel, Slim,[5] Tommy,[6] and Pablo[7].

Daniel, somewhat of a rebel anyway, decided that he would not eat all the rich food at the training table. Daniel had already made friends with the Dean of Student Life[8] and was therefore free to talk and reason with him.

"Dean," said Daniel, "I'm just not going to stuff my gullet with all that high chloresterol food you serve."

"Now, Daniel," said the Dean, "it is not a simple matter. If I don't feed you what the king has ordered and you get thin, then the king will have me beheaded."[9]

"Well, give us a try. Slim, Tommy, Pablo and I have agreed that if you feed us steak, milk and potatoes for ten days and we are not healthier than those who eat souffle' and eels, we will go with your system," suggested Daniel.

"That's a fair deal," said the Dean.[10]

At the end of the ten days Daniel and his friends looked much better than most of their carousing compadres and so the Dean put them completely and permanently on steak, potatoes, and milk.

God particularly blessed these young men and they grew in wisdom and stature, and Daniel was given an extra ability in the area of visions and dreams.

When graduation time arrived, the Dean brought the four young men to the king as his top graduates. The king asked them some

---

[1]Jehoiakim   [2]Nebuchadnezzar   [3]Ashpenaz   [4]Chaldeans
[5]Shadrach   [6]Meshach   [7]Abednigo   [8]Melzar
[9]Almost like working for a school board
[10]Probably the first decent offer the Dean had had from the students

questions and they replied in exemplary fashion and the king decided that they were more intelligent than the consultants that the king had been paying.

Some months after this the king had a bad dream and he awoke in the middle of the night, tormented by his dream. To make matters worse, all he could remember was that he had been having a bad dream, though the details escaped him.

As a result, the king sent for his consultants and told them of his problem.

"Just tell us the dream, Sir King, and we will tell you what it means."

"The problem is," replied the king, "that I don't remember the dream. If you will tell me the dream and what it means then I will give each of you a big bonus, but if you don't, I'll have all the consultants in the county executed."

"Nobody can do that," wailed the head of the magician's union.

"You are just stalling for time," said the king. "I've long suspected you all are phonies, telling me only what I wish to hear. Come up with the answer, or it is death to all of you."

Daniel heard about this, as he was one of those considered a consultant, and knew his head would go also. In fact, Clothes-Line Sid,[1] who was in charge of head-hunting, came to Daniel and Daniel went to the king and asked for a little time to come up with an answer.

"If you can get the answer, fine," said the king, "and we will postpone the executions for a few days."

Then Daniel went back to the apartment and he told Tommy, Pablo, and Slim about the matter and they immediately formed a small prayer group.

As a result of their prayers to God, Daniel received a revelation concerning the dream of the king.

"Thank you, God" said Daniel. "Blessed is the name of the Lord, for the Lord is in charge of all the earth, God changes the seasons regularly, wisdom and power are all of God, and God controls history, putting kings in power and taking them away.

"God knows," continued Daniel, "what is in the darkness and God is responsible for all light. I thank God for the wisdom which the Lord has given to me, for I know it is God's wisdom. Amen."

Then Clothes-line Sid escorted Daniel into the presence of Big Ned and introduced him to the king.[2]

"Are you able, son, to tell me the dream that I have dreamed and also the interpretation of it?

"You better believe it! The consultants, the magicians, the astrologers are no help to you in this because only God knows and

[1] Arioch   [2] Big Ned couldn't remember names

237

only God can decide to reveal, for your dream tells of the future.

"First, the reason I know about the dream is simply because God has chosen to reveal it to me, and not because I am smarter than anyone else.

"In your dream you saw a great figure; it stood before you, shining with a terrible brightness. The head was of solid gold while the chest and arms were of silver, with the belly and thighs being of brass. The legs of the figure were of iron, and the feet were part iron and part clay.

"All of a sudden, the iron, clay, brass, silver, and gold were all busted into fine grain like dust and the wind blew it all away. The stone, which was just suddenly on the scene, and which had smashed all the figure to pieces, then became a great mountain and filled the whole earth. That was some dream you had, O King!"

"Now let me tell you what all that means," said Daniel. "You are a great and powerful king, for God has arranged it to be that way. God has put you in charge of the known world. You are represented in the dream by the head of gold."

"After you shall come an inferior kingdom, then a third kingdom, represented by the brass which is still more inferior, but it shall rule the earth. Then comes a strong kingdom, strong as iron. It shall break things in pieces and shall rule with ruthless power. The kingdom, however, shall become divided, as you saw the iron and clay mixed, so the kingdom will be partly strong and partly weak.

"At this point in time, God shall begin a new type of kingdom that shall never be destroyed. This new type kingdom shall gradually encompass the earth, not by action as a kingdom, but by different parts and different people gradually taking the word of the new kingdom throughout the earth.

"God has chosen to reveal to you this glimpse of the future." Daniel then sat down and mopped his brow.

The king was overcome with the speech. Immediately he ordered a new Mastercharge card for Daniel and a box of candy.

The king then said, "Surely, Daniel, your God is a God of gods, a Lord of kings, a revealer of secrets. Blessings on you, Daniel."

Then the king made Daniel a great man, gave him many gifts, and appointed him Governor of governors. At Daniel's request, the king then made Slim, Tommy, and Pablo assistants to the Governor of governors.

Chap.
3

Big Ned one day decided that he had had a great idea[1] and as a result he caused to be constructed a huge figure, covered with gold, that stood about 5 stories high. Upon the completion of this huge edifice there was, of course, a necessity to have a ribbon cutting and

---

[1] Actually it came from the suggestion box

dedication service.

All the government workers were invited to come through a memorandum from the king which made it clear that attendance was not optional. As a result, the princes, governors, sheriffs, judges, city managers, fire chiefs, chariot supervisors, consultants, and disc jockeys were all assembled on a set date for the big service.

One of the speakers at the dedication suggested that in honor of Big Ned a law be passed to the effect that when the palace orchestra began to blare forth on all the varied instruments of music, that this be a signal for everyone to bow down and face the new gold image, and worship this great creation of the king.[1] The penalty suggested for failure to obey this law was being thrown into a fiery furnace.

The law was passed by voice vote of the king and Big Ned gave the signal to the orchestra and all the local musicians blew it as best they could.

Some of the Chaldeans, however, noticed that some of the Jews didn't bow.[2] Two or three of these stool pigeons came to Big Ned and said, "It was a great ceremony, but we saw three guys who didn't bow, and it ruined the day for most of us."

"Ye gods and little fishes!" roared Big Ned, for he was terribly angry. "Go get the men and bring them here at once!"

This was done and the three turned out to be Tommy, Slim, and Pablo.

"Is it true that you kids failed to bow to the image and to worship as I had ordered?" asked Big Ned.

"It is true," they replied.

"Well, we'll give you another chance. I'll signal the orchestra again and this time bow or it's the fiery furnace for you all!" sternly said Big Ned.

"Mighty king, we can save you a few toots from the orchestra, for we are not going to serve or acknowledge any image, for we worship the true God. In fact, our God is able to deliver us,"[3] spoke Slim for the three.

At this point Big Ned had turned a deep purple and screamed at the furnace committee to throw another log on the fire. The king also ordered the security police to bind the hands of Slim, Tommy and Pablo, and to leave them in their clothes, even leaving their hats on their heads.

When the furnace had become seven times hotter than was normal for people throwing, Big Ned gave the order to the stokers to throw the men into the furnace.

---

[1] Actually he just paid for it with tax money
[2] I've always been puzzled by the ability of people with their heads bowed to see those that aren't.
[3] Of course, they realized God might decide not to deliver them

The flames were so intense that the stokers were burned to death getting close enough to throw the three in the fire.[1] Tommy, Slim, and Pablo then fell down with their hands tied into the flames.

Suddenly Big Ned rose in wonder and yelled, "Did we not throw three men into the furnace?"

"Yes, sir, that is right," replied the two nearest vice-presidents.

"But I see four men loose, walking in the flames, and they are not hurt, and the form of the fourth is like the Son of God," said Big Ned.

Then Big Ned came as close to the furnace as he dared and said, "Come on out, Slim. You, too, Tommy and Pablo."

The three came forth and all the many witnesses saw that they were unharmed, that not a single hair was singed, and there was not even the smell of smoke upon them.

Then Big Ned stood up and said, "I hereby make a decree, that anybody, in any nation, that ever says anything bad, in any language, about the God of Slim, Tommy, or Pablo, shall be cut to pieces and their home torn down, for there is no other god anywhere that can do the type of thing that I have seen today."

Following this, Slim, Tommy and Pablo were all promoted to sergeant.

Chap.
4

Then Big Ned went about his business as usual. Sometime later, however, he came out with another of his all-points bulletins, which were posted everywhere for everyone to see.

"Peace be unto you. I have decided that it is good to pass on to the people the things that the true God has made available to me through his wonderful signs. The kingdom of God is an everlasting kingdom and the dominion of God is from generation to generation.

"Now here is the way it happened. I, Big Ned, was at rest in my house and living it up, for things were going my way. Then I had a dream and I saw visions and I could not figure out the meaning. My consultants, magicians, and even my shrinks were of no use to me.

"However, Daniel, the smartest sidekick I ever had and one in whom God confides, came to me and offered to interpret my dreams.

"Well, Daniel, in my vision I saw a tree of great height in the middle of the earth, and the tree grew and finally it seemed to reach almost to heaven. The leaves were pretty and there was plenty of fruit for everybody, all the beasts of the field could reside in the shade and the birds of the air could perch on the limbs.

"Then a watchman came down from heaven and ordered me to chop down the tree, cut off the branches, shake off the leaves, scatter the beasts, and shoo away the birds. Yet I was supposed to

---

[1] It was difficult to recruit replacements also.

leave a stump, with the roots still firmly in the ground, surrounded by grass that would catch and hold the dew from heaven.

"Then I was told to transplant a beast's heart into the stump in place of a man's heart,[1] and then let there be time for adjustment to the new heart. The watchers were doing this so that the living might know that God reigns over man and gives rule to whomever God chooses. Now tell me, Daniel, what in the thunderation does all that mean?

"I want to report to the people," said Big Ned, "that Daniel went into shock for about an hour, but then he began to speak to me and he said, 'The dream applies to your enemies. The tree which reached to heaven, with the great shade and the mighty branches is you. You have become a great and powerful king and your greatness extends throughout the known world.[2] Unfortunately, however, the cutting down of the tree, the heart transplant and all this signifies what your enemies are going to do to you.

"Actually, they will drive you crazy and you will be a mental case, getting down on your hands and knees and eating grass with the oxen.[3] You will soon, however, acknowledge the power of God and as a result you will be permitted to retain your kingdom.

"My suggestion to you, Great King, is to reform at once, cease your life of sin and repent. Begin to show mercy to the poor and God may then lengthen your period of peace.'

"As King then I took the matter under advisement, but twelve months later I was still postponing reform.

"Then one day a voice from heaven was heard by me saying, "You've had it, Big Ned. You never took the advice. Your kingdom is a goner."

"That same hour I went nuts and was driven from the palace and went out in the fields and began to eat grass in competition with the oxen.

"Then I let my hair grow until it was as awful looking as Tiny Tim's and also I let my fingernails grow into claws.

"Sometime later I began to come to my senses and I lifted up my eyes to heaven, I blessed God, and acknowledged that the kingdom of God is the one kingdom that is forever, and that the dominion of God is forever. Then my recovery became complete.

"I returned to my palace and placed the kingdom back in operation, and now I, Big Ned, make this witness to the true God of heaven, all of whose works are truth, and be sure that those who walk in pride can be easily cut down to size by the true God.[4] "

---

[1] Just an ordinary heart transplant
[2] A PR man couldn't have done better
[3] A bad situation in an election year
[4] Not long after this Big Ned died

241

Sometime after this the son of Big Ned became king in his father's place and he mainly went into high social living. After a rather brief period of being king, Huey,[1] the new king, gave one of the biggest, most ornate banquets every staged. Huey even served the wine in the gold and silver vessels which had been taken from Solomon's temple in Jerusalem.

The whole crowd, consisting of princes, wives, go-go girls, and one or two party crashers all got to drinking expensive wine from the costly containers and they all became roaring drunk.

When the party was at its peak, suddenly the fingers of a man's hand appeared and wrote on the wall. The king saw the hand and the writing, and he turned pale, and his knees began to knock, for he was scared silly.

The king then howled for the magicians, the consultants, and even the local astrologers, and Huey spoke to them and said, "Read this writing. It is in a strange language. Whoever is able to translate this will get a new suit of clothes, two matching ties, and will be named third vice-president of L.S.U."

All the smarties looked on the wall, but none of them could translate the words. Huey then became greatly depressed and the party came to a screeching halt.

Now Ann Landers, the queen, had remained sober and she turned to Huey and said, "Don't be so down in the mouth. There is a man in town who can translate this. The man's name is Daniel and he was always bailing out your old man when he was stuck with a problem that the consultants or magicians could not handle. Just send for Daniel and let him do his thing."

Then was Daniel brought into the banquet hall and Huey spoke to him and asked, "Are you Daniel, the captive from Judah, who Daddy brought here?"

Daniel nodded.

"Well, I've heard of you," continued Huey, "and I understand that you have special insights and great wisdom. Well, my own staff of wise men have flunked out, and they cannot read the writing on the wall. If you can read the message you get two suits of clothes, two ties, and you'll be third vice-president of L.S.U."

"First, Huey, you can forget the gifts. Particularly the vice-president deal. I will, however, read the words to you," said Daniel.

"Almighty God gave your father glory and honor,[2] and because of this all nations and people trembled and were afraid of the power inherent in your father's rule. When your Dad thought somebody needed killing, he had them killed, or if someone needed to be

---

[1] Belshazzar

[2] Excuse Daniel for being a little eloquent, but he hadn't been on a program all year.

demoted, he also did that.

"In fact, your father became such a big shot that pride took the best of him, and God struck him down, so that he lost his glory, and he went nuts, getting out on the lawn and eating grass with the oxen. When he finally began to recognize God and call upon the name of the Lord, he was restored in power.

"You knew all this, yet you started out from the first with no humility, and you have lifted yourself even above God, stooping to use the priceless vessels taken from the temple at Jerusalem as a means of holding wine to get all the princes, the wives, the go-go girls, and the visitors all drunk.

"You have been toasting each other, and you have been toasting the gods of wood, or stone, or gold, or brass, or whatever. Yet you have not mentioned in any way the God of all, the one who furnishes life and breath.

"As a result, God has written you a note on the wall and the note says 'God has pulled the card on your kingdom, you are weighed yourself in the balances, and you don't measure correctly; so your kingdom is being given to the Medes and Persians."

Huey was greatly impressed, and immediately gave Daniel two suits of clothes and two neckties, and announced that Daniel was third vice-president of L.S.U. whether he liked it or not.

That night, Huey was killed and a young man named Darius claimed the kingdom. Darius was a Mede.

Chap.
6

Darius immediately re-organized the government.[1] First he appointed 120 princes, and over them he appointed a Board of Directors of three men, and Daniel was named one of these and then made Chairman of the Board. The new king figured that Daniel would then be able to run the kingdom and the king could spend more time at Camp David.

It developed that the other two board members and the princes didn't care for this as Daniel was honest and would not allow them to pad their expense accounts. In spite of employing a private investigator, the group could not come up with any dirt on Daniel.

The group was always meeting over the matter, however.

"I tell you what," said one of the board members, "we aren't going to find anything crooked about Daniel so we had better attack his religion."

As a result, a plan was devised. Representatives, including the two board members, called on Darius and said, "We have a law that we would like to pass," said the spokesman. "As an honor to you, we want the law to say that for 30 days no one shall petition or ask anything of any god or man except you, or be thrown in a den of

---

[1] I think this type of thing is still going on.

lions."

"Well, it appeals to me more than simply being made Jaycee Man of the Month," said Darius.

"Fine, mighty king. Now write out the law in accordance with the code of the Medes and the Persians, so that there can be no alteration or amendments," continued the spokesman.

Darius did as they suggested.

Daniel, of course, learned of this shortly and he merely went about his usual custom of kneeling in prayer to the Lord God of Israel as he faced Jerusalem. Daniel did this three times a day at an open window.

Needless to say, the men who designed the law arranged to catch Daniel. As soon as they had documented their case with eyewitnesses, the group came to the king and charged Daniel with breaking the law. They even mentioned that Daniel did this three times a day.

Now the king became very peeved with himself for he realized he had been had. At once Darius began to check if there was a legal way out of his jam and he worked all day on the problem, seeking a loophole in the law.

The group assembled again before the king the next day and said, "We hate to keep mentioning this, king, but there is no way of altering the law of the Medes and the Persians."

The king then ordered that Daniel be thrown into a den of lions. The king tried to console Daniel by saying, "Daniel, even though I can't do anything your God who you religiously serve will deliver you."

Then Daniel was put in the den with the lions and a stone was placed to seal the den, and the king's private lock was placed on the door to make sure there was no escape.

The king went to his palace and passed up the evening meal, even making the servants cut off the stereo. The king spent a sleepless night worrying about his friend Daniel.[1]

The first thing in the morning the king ran down to the lions' den and began to call, "Daniel, Daniel! Was your God able to deliver you from the lions?"

"You better believe it, King!" said Daniel. "My God shut the mouths of the lions and they have not hurt me. This was done because I am innocent of any wrong."

The king then was very happy and ordered the immediate release of Daniel. Just to make sure, Darius had one of his medics check Daniel, and there was no mark on him.

The king then decided to celebrate the safety of Daniel by arresting the originators of the law and throwing them into the lion's den. Since it was togetherness week, the families were thrown in with the men.[2]

[1] Daniel went to sleep probably after the lions did   [2] This law has been revised

Then King Darius published an all points bulletin which was released to all the media stating, "I make a decree that in every area of my kingdom men tremble and stand in awe of the God of Daniel; for He is a living God, and steadfast forever, and His kingdom that which shall not be destroyed and his rule shall be unto the end of time.

"The God of Daniel delivers and rescues, He works signs and wonders in heaven and on earth, He delivered Daniel from the power of the Lions."

Signed by hand
Darius, the King.

Chap.
7

The remainder of this book of Daniel consists of a record of prophetic dreams and visions which came to Daniel. The first of these occurred during the reign of Huey.

Daniel in reporting the vision stated that there appeared to him the impression of the four winds of heaven all blowing on the sea at once.[1] The commotion was so great that four sea monsters came to the top. The first monster looked like a lion with wings. All of a sudden the wings disappeared and the lion was forced to stand up like a man, and a man's heart was put into the beast.

The second beast appeared to be a big bear with somebody's ribs[2] in his mouth, and the bear was instructed to launch a big people eating program.

The third monster was like a leopard with four wings, and it also had four heads.[3]

The fourth monster was really hideous, very strong, with iron teeth, it was really mean, and it had ten horns, and suddenly there grew forth a little horn and it ate up three of the regular horns. The little horn had eyes like a man and it spoke like a politician.

The dream continued until all the thrones of the beastly rulers were destroyed and the Lord himself appeared on the throne of judgment. The throne of God looked like a flame itself and it had fiery wheels. All the people of all time stood in God's presence before the throne. I plainly saw the destruction of evil.

In the vision also there appeared the Son of man and he was in great glory before the throne of God. God gave him dominion and power over all the nations and all the kingdoms, and the kingdom given to him was the kingdom that cannot be destroyed.

Daniel, naturally, was a mite confused by all this, and so in his dream he stepped forward and asked one of the ones close to the throne to explain.

---

[1] As an old time sailor I promise you that made things tough
[2] The origin of spareribs
[3] Daniel was no doubt ready for Alka-Seltzer here

The answer was that the four monsters from the deep were four kings that would come to power, but that eventually the believers in the eternal kingdom would triumph.

When Daniel in his dream inquired further, asking in particular about the fourth monster, the informer explained that the fourth monster was different from and worse than the others. The establishment of this fourth kingdom shall be on a world-wide basis. Later ten kings shall arise from this mess, and then one small king shall arise and destroy three of the other kings. This upstart shall speak against God and shall give the saints a hard time. This evil king and his kingdom shall attempt to change all laws, even the matter of time,[1] and he shall be successful for awhile, but the judgment of God will get him and his kingdom, and the whole kingdom of the earth shall be given to the believers in God, and all people will serve under the head of the church of God.[2] Daniel awoke the next morning with a headache.

Chap.
8

A couple of years later Daniel had another weirdo of a dream. In the vision Daniel saw himself in a mansion overlooking Lake Susan.[3] There appeared on the edge of the lake a ram with two horns, and one horn was higher than the other, although it started growing last. The ram was taking charge of everything westward, northward, and southward.[4] The ram did as he pleased and became really the king of the mountain.

While Daniel observed this, an odd looking goat with one horn between his eyes came from the west and traveled without touching the ground.[5] The goat came to the ram and immediately attacked him. The goat whipped the ram thoroughly.

The goat then became king of the mountain and overlooked Lake Susan[6] with haughtiness. The goat grew stronger and his horn broke off, but in its place came forth four other horns. Out of one of the four horns then came a little horn which became very prominent and became interested in the land of the free.[7] This particular horn magnified itself tremendously and in spite of defying the hosts of heaven, the little horn prospered. The worship of God was outlawed and evil reigned.

Then there entered the dream two saints of old and one of them said, "How long do you think evil will be in control?"

"Two thousand and three hundred days," replied the other.

The dream seemed to fade and Daniel seemed to see in the

[1] There is that daylight saving deal!   [2] I believe this is a reference to Christ
[3] Ulai   [4] The Lake was probably eastward   [5] Amtrack?
[6] There have been some notable goats at Lake Susan
[7] America? Sicily? Monaco?

vision the appearance of a man.[1] Daniel then heard the man as he stood by Lake Susan speak to the angel Gabriel and say, "Gabriel, you are chairman of the End of Time Committee, tell this fellow Daniel what the dream means."

When Gabriel approached, Daniel trembled, even in his dream.[2]

"Try to understand what I am telling you, Daniel," said Gabriel, "for it has to do with your vision concerning the end of time."

At this point Daniel fainted.[3] Gabriel then held some smelling salts under Daniel's nose and stood Daniel on his feet.[4]

"I will tell you, Daniel," said Gabriel, "about the last days of trouble and struggle. The rams with the two horns are the kings of Media and Persia. The goat is the kingdom of Greece. Finally this empire breaks into four pieces of lesser importance and then a really, truly baddie comes along. The power of this guy is terrific[5] and he kills, conquers, deceives and makes a mess of everything and everybody, including God's people in Israel. God will handle him simply.[6]

"In your vision, Daniel, you heard about the 2300 days. That is an exact figure, but all this is so far off from your day that you might as well forget it. In fact, there is no point at present in your blabbing this all over town. Write it down for future scholars."[7]

When Daniel awoke the next morning he had a tummy ache. In fact, Daniel stayed sick for several days. The next week, however, Daniel was back on duty, advising the king, and entertaining everyone at the coffee breaks with his astonishing dreams.

Chap.
9

Another year passed, and Daniel in sincere prayer and meditation spoke to God and said, "Father, our people have sinned and fallen short of obeying the commandments. The people have been rebellious, have not been good about attending church, and when they did go they didn't listen.[8] Father, we are confused because we have wandered from the faith and have not found a proper way of life. We are sinners, and we have not repented, and we have turned to you, Father, as we should.

"All Israel is guilty. We know that evil has come to us because of our sins. We know that you, O Lord, directed the evil so that it would affect us, and hopefully bring us repentantly back to you.

"Father, take the heat off us now. We have sinned, we admit it. We have been punished; so ease up on us, and let your face shine upon us and listen to our pleas. We plead not on a basis of our

---

[1] This was another dream or the continuation of the present dream. So what?
[2] Daniel could no doubt see the trumpet   [3] I don't blame him one bit
[4] He couldn't steady his knees, though
[5] Alexander the Great? Antioches Epjphanes? Onassis?
[6] Alexander drank himself to death at 32   [7] So they can fuss, fuss, fuss
[8] The old, old story

247

righteousness, but on a basis of your mercies.

"Forgive us, O Lord. Remember Jerusalem, for it is called the city of God, and remember the Israelites, for we are called the children of God."

While Daniel was praying and in deep meditation, ole Gabriel arrived again.

"All right, Daniel," said Gabriel, "I have come to give you a little inside information. You are in real good standing with the Lord and God has permitted me to pass on to you some information.

"There will be 490 years more of trouble and disappointment, but at last the people will learn to serve God. At the end of this time the everlasting kingdom of God will begin to form on the earth. From the time the order is given to rebuild the temple until the first coming of the Messiah shall be 483 years.[1] The Messiah shall live only briefly, but he will die for the sake of others.

"After this there shall come a king with an army and he will destroy Jerusalem and defy God, even defiling the sanctuary of God.[2] God in the time and manner of His plan shall destroy this evil person, and God's judgment will be against him."

Daniel, having received visions and insights, appeared before Darius at various times and reported to him; so he could share in Daniel's glimpses of the future.

"Know something, Darius," said Daniel, "there will be three kings in Persia, then a fourth that will be greater than any of the three ahead of him. This king will even attack Greece, for the king will have great strength and great wealth.[3] This king will be overthrown and his kingdom divided, but not among his sons.[4]

"Sometime after this shall arise a king in the south with a great following, but he will lose out through internal problems. Some years later an Egyptian ruler will form an alliance with Syria by giving his daughter in marriage to the king of Syria. This didn't work, as the girl didn't make a good wife.[5]

"Later, however, when the girl's brother becomes head of Egypt, he will organize an army and declare war on Syria. The brother will be successful and will bring many captives to Egypt.

"First thing you know, though, the sons of the defeated king of Syria will grow to manhood and they will decide to seek vengeance on Egypt.[6] There shall be much fighting back and forth for years, many shall be killed, and nothing much solved. In fact, the marrying a king's daughter stunt will be tried again and it will fizzle.

---

[1] Good scholars can explain the apparent 7 years discrepancy
[2] Probably Titus in 70 A.D.   [3] Xerxes? Quien Sabe?
[4] Xerxes forgot to write out his will   [5] That's what the king said
[6] The Middle East still has a few problems

"Some of the kings get killed in battle and some die of ulcers. One king will try sending a tax collector into Israel to collect a surtax, but the collector and the king both will die mysteriously.[1]

"Also in times to come in the middle east turmoil there will arise a Robin Hood type of king, who will declare war on all the rich and divide their land and their money with the poor. This king also dies, and the city slickers get the land and money again like they are supposed to do.

"Often two kings will sit at the conference table and plot against each other even while they are sitting there.[2] All these things are under the plan of God. Wickedness, hate, deceit, all these continually plague the world, but such is life, and all still is under God's scrutiny.

"As these kings down through the years fight back and forth Jerusalem and Palestine catch it coming and going. All this is God's process of purifying and punishing. None of these God-defying kings last long, though, as they die like everybody else."[3]

Chap.
12

When the time comes for the consolidating of God's kingdom, Michael, the angel in charge of God's executive branch, shall attend to the deliverance of everyone recorded in the Lord's book of life.

Those who have already passed from this life shall be awakened, some to everlasting life, and some to everlasting shame and contempt.[4] Those who died in the Lord shall shine in great brightness and those who influenced others for good shall shine as bright as stars on a dark night.

"That's enough, Daniel," said Gabriel. "The book is closed. Don't add any more to it. There is going to be a lot of coming and going between now and the end of time."

About then in the vision Daniel saw two figures, one on each side of Lake Susan. One of the men turned to the other, who was actually already standing in the lake up to his ankles and said, "How long will it be before these things happen?"

Then the other man answered and said, "It shall be times, time, and a half. It will be after God has scattered the believers all over the world and all of God's plans are set."[5]

Daniel heard this, but he didn't understand it.[6]

Then Daniel asked, "What, O Lord, shall come about, and what will happen?"

"Sorry, Daniel, but it is none of your business. The information is top secret. You can be sure, though, that many will reform, that

[1] End of this plan   [2] How did Roosevelt & Stalin get in the scriptures?
[3] Alexander, Kaiser, Stalin, Hitler, Ptolemy, Antiochus — all dead! Good show!
[4] Surely Hitler is in this group   [5] Even less definite than a weather forecast
[6] I'm with you, Daniel

249

the wicked will continue to be wicked, and they won't understand. The searchers for God and his righteousness will understand what life is all about, though.

Anyway, from the time that the daily sacrifice is taken away[1] and the abomination that maketh desolate[2] is taken away, there shall be one thousand two hundred and thirty-five days.

"The people who are actually alive on the last day will really get to see a show, but you go on about your business for you won't live to see the day. You will be in your place, though, Daniel, at the end of the world."

[1] Whatever that is
[2] The Income Tax Law? The 55 mile speed limit? Alimony

HOSEA

The people of Israel had departed from the ways of the Lord and had become completely materialistic, doing anything for money. Now Hosea was inspired by God to attempt to learn about God and also to do something about the conditions.

Hosea felt that the Lord wanted him to learn by first marrying a girl who was a prostitute, and an example of the evil that was flagrant in the land. As a result, Hosea selected a girl named Marlene[1] who was beautiful and desirable, but who was a prostitute working for the church.[2]

The marriage went fine for awhile. First there was born a son and the Lord told Hosea to name the boy Victor[3] for he would be a conqueror someday to restore Israel and defeat Steve McQueen.[4]

Next there was born a daughter and the Lord said name the girl Miss Clean[5] for she will be a symbol of my cleaning up Israel, but I will deliver Judah and have mercy on this tribe for they are not as bad now as the others.

There was born then a third child, a son, and the Lord said he should be named Split[6], for I am separating myself from this ungodly outfit.

However, God, the Keeper of the Promises, also said that the numbers in Israel would become great as God had promised Abraham, and that when repentance came God would forgive and unite the tribes again. Hosea didn't understand this at the time.

Marlene began to stray again, however, and she started working part time as a prostitute for the temple.

Hosea then went to his kin people and even to his children and said "Some of you talk to Marlene. Plead with her to give up her wild ways and selling her body. In fact, if she doesn't reform, I plan to take all her clothes and possessions from her and place her naked in the street, and I will also desert the children for having been born to her."[7]

Hosea then began to plan to see if he could do something. In fact, he began trying to lock her in the room, then chain her to a fence post while he was away. If she gets on the loose I will pay fellows to block her path, he said to himself, until finally she will figure it a better deal at home with me, than the wild life whoredom was giving her. All this time, however, in spite of the threats, Hosea because of his love for Marlene paid her Temple percent and saw that

---

[1]Gomer   [3]Jezreel   [4]Jehu   [5]Loruhamah   [6]Loammi
[2]The Church or Temple in Israel was truly money mad at this time.
[7]At this point, Hosea was pretty angry.

she received corn, and wine, and the necessities of life.

At other times Hosea would become so frustrated that he would consider spying on her and catching her in the act with one of her lovers and then put her out of business with bodily harm if necessary and put an end to all her joy, and mirth, and celebrations. "What is more, I will steal all the profits of her prostitution," he mumbled to himself.

Hosea began to see that his feeling toward Marlene was the same as God's feeling toward the wayward people of Israel. For the Lord began to enlighten Hosea and to say that first He would speak quietly to his people to bring them back, and that through his word the Lord would persuade Israel to repent, and God will then destroy Baal and the false gods, and God will again bestow his love and mercy, for God is a forgiving God, for the Lord has promised mercy even to those who deserve no mercy, for the love of God is a forgiving love, it is a healing love, and boundless love, and God will plead continually with his people through his word to repent.

Chap
3

Hosea then began to understand why God had moved him to marry a whore. Through the experience of his relationship with Marlene, Hosea began to understand a new theology, the forgiving love of God.

As a result, Hosea said to Marlene "You are forgiven. You may return to my house and be my wife. You will be faithful to me and I will be to you. This is the way it will be with the children of Israel, who have strayed from God and wandered off in other pursuits. The children of Israel shall suffer and be separated from God, but Israel shall return and seek the Lord their God, and they shall be united under God through David their king, a servant of the Almighty God."

Chap.
4

Having learned this great lesson and filled with the wisdom of experience, Hosea began to preach and teach the wayward people of Israel.

In his first sermon Hosea said to the people "The Lord is unhappy with his people. There is no truth among you, there is no mercy, and there is no seeking to learn of God. Most of you are swearing and lying and killing and committing adultery, and bloody violence is in the land. As a result the land will become polluted and the fish of the sea shall die with a red tide, and even the innocent will have to suffer because of the sins of the many.[1]

God says that since you seem to have forgotten the law of God, the Lord will just forget you. The former glory of Israel shall turn to shame. The people will be punished and will be rewarded in

[1]Who said the Bible wasn't relevant today?

252

accordance with their evil deeds.

The people will eat, but will never seem to get enough. There shall be recipe books by the thousands, but the people will still not be satisfied.

Constantly chasing wild women, and drinking wine incessantly shall affect the people in every way. The people will be disatisfied with the stock market and shall ask the experts what is the matter with the economy, and the answer is simply that Israel has forsaken God.

Your daughters and your wives shall run off with strange men, but I will not punish them says God because you have driven them to it with your greedy way of life.

"Judah, praise God, is still reasonably faithful, but not so with some of the other tribes, and the Lord will blow the winds of storms on them and create for them many difficulties."

Chap.
5

After this Hosea was asked to come and speak as a guest lecturer at a gathering of ministers and priests.

"Part of this trouble must be laid at your feet. The Lord is determined to punish his people. Even Judah will suffer because it has tolerated the sins of the other tribes. You preachers have found excuses for yourselves and for your people, but there is no excuse. God will punish."

Chap.
6

"That is the bad news. Now the good news is that we can return to the Lord. What God has torn, God is willing to heal. After two days will he revive us, and the third day shall he arise in our sight.[1] Then shall we know the Lord in a new way and it shall be as refreshing as the gentle rain."

"The trouble is that the goodness of so many is like the morning dew, it shortly fades away, or an early morning cloud that the first wind blows away. The people have the idea that as long as they drop a decent sum in the collection plate and learn the 23rd Psalm that God is pleased, but God wants to see action in the form of mercy, not just liturgy. I lay a lot of this blame on you priests and preachers. You have not laid it down tough enough to the people. Take Southern California,[2] the greed and sin, the Lord will now and then shake the earth under such, and other places."

Chap.
7

The Lord stands ready to heal. It is never too late for anyone. The Lord forgives. I, of all people, understand this at last. But the people do not hear. They do not listen to reason. They are like the baker who leaves his oven on all night and worries not, though in the

[1] A prophecy of Christ and the resurrection. I doubt if Hosea really understood the significance.　　　　　　　　　　　　　　　　　　[2] Gilead and Ephraim

morning his bakery will be burned to the ground.

"So many of the people do not even learn anything as they grow older. They refuse to see the grey hairs, they do not see the signs of decay of the nation and that they need to turn to God.

The Lord is angry over this. The Lord will spread his net and it matters not whether you fly to Egypt or Switzerland,[1] the Lord will bring them down as a bird shot out of the sky.

It is strange, the Lord has said to me, that after all I have done for them, and all the goodness I have shown them, that they spurn me and give me only casual recognition."

Chap. 8

On another occasion, Hosea spoke at a Men's Conference sponsored by the Tribe of Israel. It was poorly attended, but Hosea said "Israel has cast away goodness, and calls on God only in emergencies. The enemies of Israel will eat her and pursue her.

Israel has elected princes and rulers that are not godly people. The rulers are greedy, they take bribes, and they worship material gods, it is just a rehash of the golden calf occasion. The Lord is angry and plans to punish Israel.

The Glad Sam Club[2] is in trouble also. It is just a snobbish way of looking out for a special group. They are sowing the wind with their big, boisterous noise, but they shall reap the whirlwind.

The tribe of Israel will be swallowed up by the Gentiles, the people of Israel act like a wild horse, they have discarded the bridle of God.

Some of the tribes have simply sold themselves to godless nations in exchange for good business, but the godless nations shall bring them only grief and deception.

The Lord has written his law to all the tribes. There is no excuse for ignorance.

Israel has forgotten the Creator the Lord God Almighty, and Judah has built some fenced in cities, but the Lord will destroy these with fire."

Chap. 9

On another occasion Hosea spoke again entreating the people in one breath and denouncing them in another, urging repentance and forecasting disaster.

"Rejoice not," said Hosea, "You people of Israel. The abundance of your riches shall not save you. Even when you interrupt your evil for a feast day to God, you use the occasion for profit. Your prophets even have lost their zeal, there is no sense of unity in the church, you divide among yourselves for money and for glory. Your leaders are phonies.

As for the people of Southern California,[3] the Lord will make

---

[1] Assyria   [2] Samaria   [3] Ephraim

gypsies out of you, wandering from one place to another, searching for you know not what, all because you have forsaken the Lord God of Hosts."

Chap. 10

Again Hosea addressed himself to the people of the tribe of Israel saying, "You are like an empty vine. You keep your gains all for yourself. You have no benevolent program.

You will find all kinds of excuses for your difficulties. You will even say you have no king, when all there is that is needed is a return to God.

The Glad Sam Club is doomed. The worthy grand master of this crowd will be cut off as easily as foam on the water.

There will be no more easy living for any of you. You will have to tread corn, and plow, and work your own fields, for you shall be as servants rather than as owners.

If you would but sow righteousness, you could reap mercy. If you will but seek the Lord, you shall find him and his understanding. If you plow wickedness, however, you shall reap disaster, and Israel shall be overcome and dishonored.

Chap. 11

Again Hosea spoke to the tribe of Israel saying "The Lord remembers well when Israel was as a child, and God loved Israel and delivered Israel from Egypt. "I blessed the people of Southern California also," the Lord has said, "in many ways, I gave them fruitful places for a dwelling. In spite of all my goodness, these people and others of my people have turned against me and worship many strange material things."

"The Lord, however," continued Hosea, "has said that he will exercise the fullness of his anger, for the Lord is God, not man, the Lord is the Holy One, and he will remain holy. Yet the Lord will sometimes roar like the lion and the cities shall shake in terror, but the tribe of Judah is still reasonably faithful with many saints, and the Lord shall bless Judah."

Chap. 12

"There is no tribe or people that is sinless," continued Hosea, "but the Lord is particularly displeased with the money mad groups. The Lord even remembers the trickery of Jacob, but the Lord accepted his repentance, and the Lord knows there is wickedness in California, and Paris, and in Reno, and little villages, and the Lord waits for the people to repent."

Chap. 13

Hosea then quoted God, "Remember that I am the Lord thy God, that delivered you from Egypt, and you shall have no gods before me. I will watch your activities as a leopard or a lion watches from the grass.

Israel has already destroyed itself, but I am still willing to help and deliver. How sad the people of Southern California do not stay in one place long enough to raise their children in a home, yet I will even ransom them in time from the grave and offer even to them redemption. The Good Sam Club crowd shall become desolate and they shall be slaughtered for their wickedness."

Finally, at a later time, Hosea pleaded again with the people saying, "Return to the Lord. It is never too late. Pray to the Lord for strength to overcome sins. There is no gain in praying to Buddha or to the Labor Relations Board, for help comes only from God.

God is ready to be as a fresh dew on the ground for Israel, the Lord is ready to spread his beauty as a giant tree, and his smell as the sweetness of the cedars of Lebanon. Those who turn to the Lord shall be under his protection and shall flourish. Even the people of Southern California shall call upon him, and forsake their greed, and he will make them as a green fir tree.

It is difficult to understand all of these things, but the ways of the Lord are right and those that walk in His ways, walk in safety, while ultimately the transgressors fall into deep pits."

JOEL

A message came to Joel from the Lord and Joel related it to the people saying, "Listen, you old codgers, in fact everybody should hear what I have to say, for God is planning some rough times for you all.

"You had better wake up, you bunch of heavy drinkers and goof-offs, for your wine is going to be gone. Tough times are really coming, for anything that the army worm leaves the locust will eat, then the cankerworm will eat what the locusts skip, and the caterpillar will bat clean up for the cankerworms. When this outfit finishes there is going to be nothing left of the vineyards.

"A strong nation with teeth like a lion will come and destroy the land on which you live. You had better start crying now, and you can weep like a high school girl who has had her steady killed in a chariot wreck.

"In the midst of all this the church will go broke. The ministers will moan to high heaven because the gifts to the church become very slim.

"The farmers will all be in trouble and all they will be able to do is howl and howl.[1] The crops of wheat and barley will be no good, and the fruit orchards will be chopped down.

"The whole ministerial association needs to go into mourning, to gather in groups and put on old clothes, and plead with the Lord, for the people will have nothing to bring to the church.

"I would suggest calling special services, organizing prayer groups, and bringing the people into the house of the Lord to plead with him and ask God for help. Destruction is close and there is very little time. I am warning each and every one.

"Unhappiness is everywhere, for desolation and depression are both at hand. The seeds are turning rotten in the ground, the barns are collapsing, and the corn is withered. The cows are perplexed. The wild beasts don't know where to go for food, the sheep are hungry and just stand around bleating.

"I, for one, am praying urgently to the Lord, for I see the brown fields and the burned pastures. The beasts join me in my cry for there is no water."

"Blow the horn, screech the siren," said Joel, "sound general quarters, for the punishment of God is at hand! No wonder it is cloudy and the day is dark, the world's atmosphere seems stifling. The enemies prepared by God are running roughshod over the land

---

[1] I have a feeling that the farmers are still howling.

and desolation is everywhere.

"The enemy seems to run like horses and yet to make noises like the sound of chariots on cobblestones — it is frightening! The people will naturally be terrified.

"The advancing army shall be the best trained outfit you ever saw, every man in his place, the lines straight, the advance ruthless, and the men will be so tough that sword wounds will seem to be scratches. All the heavens shall furnish a proper background, with the moon and the sun blocked out by clouds, and there will be no visible stars.

"Who can stand to be alive and face the appearance of the wrath of God as the army designated by God shall begin to handle the punishment for God.

"Again, however, God assures his people that it is never too late to reform and repent. Blow the trumpet again! Call for special evangelistic services, or at least some thanksgiving recognition.

"Let the ministers become very active, holding special services, leading the people in prayer. It would be a shame for the brethren to see the plight of Israel and then ask 'Where is their God'?

"When the people have repented and the Lord observes this, then God will have mercy on His people and He will see that they get food and clothing.

"God says that when the repentance takes place, then God will disperse the northern army, and the army will cease to be, leaving only a distasteful smell among the people.

"Don't you worry one minute! The Lord will do wonderful things. The land will take on new life, the beasts of the field will begin to find good pastures and the fruit trees will have good seasons.

"Rejoice, you people of Israel, for at this time the Lord will regulate your rain so that it falls moderately. As a result, there will be a great wheat crop.

"The Lord promises to make up for the time the army worms took over and the caterpillars wrecked havoc. Then will you know that God is in the midst of Israel, and the people of God shall no longer be ashamed.

"The spirit of the Lord will become active again, and the sons and daughters shall prophesy, your old men shall dream dreams, and the young men shall see visions.

"The working class of people shall be particularly blessed at this time, and God will demonstrate many wonders in the heavens,[1] there will be an eclipse of the sun, and the moon will turn real red. Let this remind you that the day of the Lord is then close at hand.

"Anybody who calls on the Lord at this time shall be saved, for the Lord has promised to deliver those who trust in him, those who

[1]UFO's?

258

know there is a city of God. There will always be that remnant of the people that shall be saved.

"The Lord has assured us that when Judah and Jerusalem are back in business and doing well, then the Lord will see that the enemies of God are gathered like an army trapped in a valley. This crowd is those that have bought and sold people as if they were cattle, sometimes selling an unfortunate girl for a drink of wine, or losing a slave in a poker game.

"The wicked cities of Tyre and Sidon are tremendously in debt to God, but even if they tried to buy themselves into God's good graces it would be useless. God remembers that the gold and silver vessels were stolen from his sanctuary and used for drunken parties.

"God remembers the selling of the Israelites. God suggests that the wicked get as organized as possible and prepare for any type of warfare they think will work, but it is to no avail. Let the heathen take their plows and make swords of them, and turn their harpoons and pruning hooks into spears. Get all the mighty men of the wicked all steamed up, but it is to no avail.

"Let all the heathen gather, trapped in a valley, for the Lord will sit in their presence and pronouce judgment. The valley is the last chance, it is the final valley decision. The sun is to be darkened and the moon will quit shining, the stars will also not be seen, and then the Lord will roar at the heathen,[1] but God's people shall know that the Lord is their hope. The Lord will want everyone to know then that God is with His people, that Jerusalem will then be a holy city in reality, and only the people of God will be allowed in the city.

"When that day comes everything will be hunky-dory. The mountain streams will flow with wine, some of the hills will flow with milk,[2] and the river Jordan will flow with water,[3] and the spirit of God shall excite the whole area.

"Egypt will be desolate because of its bad attitude toward Israel in the early days, and so shall the land be of all those who have persecuted the innocent. The children of God, such as those of Judah who have been faithful, and the believers everywhere, from Jerusalem to the fartherest corners of the earth, will be cleansed by the blood,[4] and God shall surely dwell with His people forever.

[1]Hurrah! At last!
[2]For us teetotalers
[3]For the health-kick people
[4]The blood of Christ

AMOS

Amos was a sheep herder living in Pecos and he had lots of time to sit and meditate as he sat and watched his sheep graze. On some of these occasions he began to have visions from God and one day, after several years of visions and meditations, he went to the city and stood on the temple steps and preached to the people of Israel as well as visitors concerning what God had revealed to him.

"The Lord has roared like a lion," spoke Amos. "Jerusalem itself shall hear, the shepherds shall learn from the drouth, the roar of the Lord has meaning.

"There is trouble in River City![1] The people of River City have sinned again and again and their wickedness will not go unpunished. Sometimes God will burn places like Chicago[2], wicked kings in the Middle East shall be greatly tormented, and many of the Assyrians shall become captives.

"Paris[3] is another place of sin. I will punish Paris. God will turn His hand against Moscow[4] and Peking.[5] The old Moscow Muggers gang shall be completely destroyed.

"Tyre will get it also. Tyre has long been a wicked city and its punishment is coming pretty soon.

"The Lord is going to punish England[6] also for the way it treated the Irish, and Rome[7] will burn because of its madness and sinning, and the palace of Nero will go down in flames.[8]

"The Lord will also punish areas of New England[9] because of the way some of the people have mistreated women. God will not tolerate this type of sin very long in any place. God will also use fire to punish places like Rio[10] and God will send wind to help fan the flames. The responsible leaders in such places shall have to go into captivity.

"God has roared against Moab. The sins of the land of Moab are various, including unreasonably harsh treatment of their enemies. Moab is a goner.

"Judah is also in trouble with the Lord. In spite of the preaching of some good men, Judah has refused to obey the laws of God. God will arrange for fire and pillage to work over Judah and make a shambles of Jerusalem.

"Israel has been just as bad or worse, even dealing in slavery and contract kickbacks. The wickedness of Israel has truly been terrible, disregarding the plight of the poor, ignoring the rights of good,

[1] Damascus   [2] The place of Hazael   [3] Gaza   [4] Ashdod   [5] Ashkelon
[6] Edom   [7] Terman   [8] Bozrah   [9] Land of Ammon   [10] Rabbah

260

wholesome people, and deteriorating to the point where a man and his grown son both used the same whore house. Some of the Israelites have come to church in stolen clothes and have drunk wine that was dishonestly acquired.

"God is particularly mad at the chosen people, for the Lord paved the way for their conquest of Canaan, defeated the powerful and impressive army of the Cossacks,[1] delivered the people from Egypt, and God even reared prophets and preachers from among the children of Israel to instruct you. Actually, you even influenced many of them to evil.

"You Israelites are going to be punished. The Lord will make you groan like a wooden wagon full of bricks, your swift warriors shall fall all over themselves, and your strong men will be weakened by viruses. Your bravest men will get scared to death and run for their lives, not even waiting to put on their pants or their track shoes.

"God is really hot about the way you all have acted," continued Amos. "God specifically chose you and so you will be punished more than the others. You cannot walk with God using a different path than His. Do you think God roars without a reason? Not any more than a lion roars unless it is seeking a prey, for even a young lion roars only for a reason, such as hunger.[2]

"A trap is not sprung unless it is stepped upon. You are caught. Your punishment is justified. I am sounding the alarm like a trumpet. It is time for you to be afraid. God is arranging to punish you.

"God has sent prophets to warn you. This was done long ago. Now I am telling you like it is! The lion has roared. God is at work!

"I am calling on the leaders of Egypt and Assyria to witness. Let them take a look at the armies of Israel. The Lord knows that the people have forgotten what it means to be moral. Even the homes of the people are stuffed with ill-gotten gain. The Lord has decided to send enemies to destroy the beautiful homes, after first tearing down the forts of the cities.

"There will be a remnant left of the Jews, but it will be only as if the shepherd had saved a bone and a hank of hair from a lion's mouth.[3] Not much left. That is the message God has for Israel.

"At the same time that Israel is being punished so shall the temples of the false gods fall and the affluence of the rich will be reduced to nothing. All the fine homes and comfortable chariots will be destroyed. God is going to teach his people not to build their lives on material possessions.

"God has a word to say to a small bunch of rich women," said

---

[1] Amorites   [2] All sheepherders know a lot about lions
[3] I keep thinking Amos had a lot of trouble with lions

Amos, as he continued his sermon. "God calls you 'Fat cows', you hound your husbands for more money, more money; so the stupid husbands raise rents, oppressing the poor, and charging usury interest rates on their money.

"The Lord has decided to snatch you all up like the fisherman snaps a tuna, and you will be tossed out of a hole in the wall as if you were a bucket of trash.

"God dares you to keep on as you are doing. Just continue idol worship, going through the motions of supporting some church or other, all for show, even making gifts for your own benefit and glory. Just keep at it, your time is at hand!

"God is tired of trying to teach you. For awhile you didn't need to brush your teeth because there was no food, then there was a drouth, then there was rain in one place and none in another, mildew hit your storage barns, still you did not return to God. Then the Lord tried pestilence, then some of your sons were killed in war, and your horses died in such numbers that you could hardly stand the smell. Still you did not return to God.

"Even when God tried taking isolated areas and punishing just them, this didn't seem to teach you a lesson. Because of all of this, Israel, you have had it. Prepare to meet your God!

"Be certain that he that formed the mountains, created the wind, created the mind of man, the one who made the extra darkness just before dawn, the one who overlooks all the earth, is surely the Lord, the God of Hosts is his name."

"Now, Israel, hear this song of grief, for beautiful Israel is dead, thrown upon the ground, and there is no one to help her. Poor Israel! Where there were a thousand Jews there shall be a hundred, and where there were a hundred there shall be ten.

"The Lord continues to call. 'Seek me, and you shall live', says the Lord. Don't try idols, seeking help with Buddha[1] or some Guru.[2] Seek the Lord and live, or else Israel will be destroyed as if by fire. Change your ways. Begin to be just in dealing with the poor and the disadvantaged. Seek the Lord, for he is the one that put Orion's belt in the heaven, the one who changes death into life, the one who can darken a day or brighten a night, the one who put the waters in place on the earth. The Lord is his name.

"God helps those that attack the strongholds of evil, while you careless people have no use for an honest judge or a righteous leader. You sorry outfit, you who have taken advantage of the poor and the weak, who have made money unfairly, you have homes and fine chariots, you have fine vineyards and good corn crops, but you will not get to enjoy them. The Lord knows all your sins. God knows

[1]Bethel   [2]Beersheba

how you accept bribes and disregard real needs of poor, but honest people.

"Seek good, and not evil. That is your only chance to survive. Be fair and be generous, then maybe God might ease up a bit. There will be some tall wailing at Wailing Wall. The crying shall be so great and often that the cries will become quite professional. There will be wailing in the country as well as in the city, for the Lord will tend to it.

"Be careful about praying for the end of the world, for that will be a time of judgment, of great darkness, of terrible confusion. You will be in the predicament of a man who runs from a lion and runs into a bear, or the times will seem as troublesome as if you went and in weariness leaned your hand against the wall and a snake struck you. God is thoroughly disgusted with sinful Israel.

"You cannot bribe God. Coming to church occasionally or mouthing a few pious phrases will not get the job done. God doesn't want to hear any of your silly music, either. You people are headed for captivity, and God doesn't mean just next door. That is what the Lord, the God of Hosts, has said.

Chap.
6

"God has a word also for a bunch of resort dwellers. You go from luxury to luxury, thinking only of your own pleasure. You keep putting off doing anything about a few good intentions.

"You eat well, I'll say that for you. Nice ribeyes, good lamb roasts, juicy filets, you also drink well, stretched out on ivory lounges you guzzle Scotch and rye, you listen to folk singers and walking guitarists, and you don't worry a bit about what God expects of you.

"It might interest you to know that you will be the first to go. God is fed up to here with such stuff. The men will die so fast that the family itself can't keep up with who is left. The big house will the Lord tear down with a big noise and the little ones with little noises, but they will all go. People will be terrified even to mention the name of the Lord.

"The way you Jews have acted has been as ineffective as horses trying to race on flat rock, or oxen plowing in the stone quarry. Some of you conceited ones might begin to declare how important you are and how smart, but the Lord will bring a nation against you that will grind you to pieces, from one end of the country to the other. That is what the Lord God himself has proclaimed.

Chap.
7

"God has withheld his punishment, for when in a vision I saw the destruction of crops by caterpillars and other plans of the Lord, I asked God to give Israel time to repent. The Lord agreed, and so I am preaching to you a warning which you must heed. Then in my vision I saw God planning to measure Israel with the plumbline of the Lord, to see how straight Israel might be.

"After measuring, the Lord decided to destroy a portion of Israel. There is great wickedness everywhere, especially in high places."

Even before Amos had finished preaching, word was sent to the President of the Council of Churches[1] telling him that there was a real troublemaker preaching in a way that would foul up the system. As a result, a message was relayed to Amos, who had stopped his sermon briefly for a coffee break, telling him to leave town at once. The message also suggested that if Amos had to preach, then be a foreign missionary and preach a long way away.

Amos then turned to the big cheese from the Council, for he had by this time come to the temple steps, and said, "I am not prophet, nor the son of a prophet. I am a layman. I've never been to Seminary. I am a sheepherder and I have raised some fruit, but the Lord came to me and spoke to me, and it was the Lord that ordered me to preach. Now, you big stuffed shirt, you hear what the Lord has to say. You tell me not to prophesy against Israel, but God says that you, you over-inflated churchman, shall have your wife turn bad on you, your children shall be killed, your land divided by the state, and you will be taken captive to a dirty, heathen country, and Israel will be taken into captivity."

Chap. 8

"Do you know what God said to me?" asked Amos. "God showed me a basket of summer fruit, ripe for eating, and God told me that Israel was the same way, just ripe to be eaten by an enemy. The hymns of the church shall no longer be sung, but replaced by the groans of the wounded, while the dead shall be silently cast aside.

"Now you people here today listen to this, most of you are ones that take advantage of the needy, that raise motel rates when Egyptians come to play, and all you think about is money, the market, land values, interest rates. You crummy characters, you make use of one scale to measure when you sell and another for when you buy.

"God doesn't plan to forget any of this. The land will tremble and the people mourn because of these sins. The Lord will make the occasion an awesome one for there will be an eclipse of the sun, and all your gay parties shall suddenly become full of wails and groans. It will be a bitter time and some men will turn grey overnight. The time will then come when God will send something worse than a drouth or want of food, there will be a great scarcity of the comforting word of God.

"People will wander everywhere searching for a word of encouragement. They shall travel in every direction seeking the word

[1] Amaziah

264

of God, but God will withhold his word as punishment. Idol worshippers shall perish, and many shall faint, even the young men and young women as they vainly seek the word of God."

"The anger of the Lord is ready. There is no escape from God's justice. God will get the evil ones even if they try to hide in a church, or if they dig down thinking to be safe in hell, or if they try to dodge God and rent a skylab or a space ship, God will find the evil ones and destroy them. God will not let any escape, even if God has to let a sea monster catch those who try to hide in the deep sea.

"Do you people really know who God is? God is the one who can cause the earth to melt by a touch of his hand. God is everywhere, his home may have the ground floor on the earth, but his building rises on to the heavens. God is the one who controls. The Lord is his name.

"Don't you nuts realize that God is the Lord of everyone, not just some few? You are no better in God's sight than the Ethiopians, or the Indians, or the Eskimos. Don't you know this? God brought Israel from Egypt certainly, but God delivered the Moscow Muggers a time or two, and he helped the Assyrians, the English, the French, the Germans. God is the Lord of all.

"God's eyes are on any sinful kingdom and he will destroy it. In the case of the Jews, the Lord will not destroy all the Jews, but shall save a remnant, and shall scatter them throughout the earth. The Israelites, or anybody else that says 'it can't happen to us' — look out!

"There will come a day though when God will repair the temple of David and the Jews will return to Israel. Prosperity will then return to Israel and no sooner than the harvest is gathered than a new crop will be sown and there shall be great vineyards and plenty of wine. The Jew will return and rebuild, and plant gardens, and vineyards, and fruit orchards, and again the children of Israel will have a land of their own, and God will see that they are able to keep it."

There was a man called Reb[1] and he had a vision from God concerning the fate of a small nation named Edom.[2]

In a public place Reb stood forth and made the following pronouncement. "Look out, Edom! God has created unrest against the little nation of Edom and Edom is now despised by its neighbors. People should never deceive themselves by seeking the wrong type of security. Just hiding in a rock on a high place is not security. Success has gone to your head, you people of Edom.

"Don't you puffed-up characters know that even though you soar as high as eagles, or fortress yourself in inaccessible cliffs, the Lord can easily bring you tumbling down. Actually, you would be better off if you had a few thieves and plunderers take things, but the Lord is causing your own allies to turn against you and you are doomed for real.

"Your friends in the next county will set traps for you and your wise men will lose their confidence and appear very stupid. The soldiers that protect you will be confused by conflicting orders. Why is this going to happen? The answer is simple, because you mistreated the Israelites. You are going to be exposed and then destroyed.

"When Jerusalem was in great distress you did not lift a finger to help. In fact, you aided the heathen and told the enemies of Israel where some of the Jews were hiding. The day is fast approaching when the Lord God will balance the books. What you have done and what you have failed to do will come back to haunt you, and you will disappear from history, a vague memory of a nation is all that will remain.

"Israel will again exist. Jerusalem shall be restored and shall be a refuge to the people of the Lord. The land that is now possessed by heathen tribes shall be placed under the rule of God's own people. Gradually shall this kingdom of God grow and encompass the earth, and the Lord shall be the King.

[1] Obadiah
[2] God takes a look at little nations as well as big ones

JONAH

God communicated with a young man named Jonah and urged him to go to Nineveh, a well known wicked city, and to preach reform. Jonah did not want to go and decided that he would get out of town for awhile and let the idea subside. As a result, Jonah bought a ticket on a ship bound to Bermuda[1].

The Lord, however, caused an especially strong wind to blow on the sea and the ship carrying Jonah began to groan as if it were breaking. The seamen were afraid and paused briefly to pray to some god or other before casting the cargo over the side and rigging a sea anchor. Jonah was asleep in his bunk until the captain came and said, "What are you doing asleep? If you have a special god, call on him as we are in great distress."

The sailors, being a superstitious group, decided that one in the crew was bad luck, and they began throwing dice to see who was low man and therefore the culprit. Jonah threw the snake eyes.

The sailors began asking Jonah, "What business are you in? Where is your home? What is your native state? What is your racial extraction?"

Jonah replied, "I am a Hebrew. I fear the one God, Jehovah, who made the land and the sea. I am trying to flee from God."

Then the sailors were all the more afraid and they said, "What shall we do with you to make the sea calm?"

"Throw me overboard," said Jonah.

The sailors were reluctant to do this, however, and began making a desperate effort to row to the shore.

Seeing that this would not succeed, the sailors prayed saying, "Let us not perish because of Jonah, and yet we do not like to cause an innocent man to drown, but we can't last any longer." Then the sailors threw Jonah over the side and the sea began to grow calm.

The sailors immediately made a lot of promises to God and offered sacrifices and went on their way.

The Lord, however, had prepared a giant fish to swallow Jonah and Jonah remained in the belly of the fish three days and three nights.

Now Jonah began to pray saying, "O Lord, even though I am in the belly of hell, I know you hear me. You have caused me to be thrown into the sea, in the middle of great and terrible waters, and the waves and white tops came over my head. I knew then that I was cast aside, but I yearn to look again upon the holy temple. As I was sinking, the seaweeds wrapped about my head, I felt as if I'd been

[1]Tarshish

thrown from a mountain, and was strapped hopelessly in one place, but when my soul fainted within me, I remembered God. And so my prayer comes to you, O God, in thine own holy temple. Save me, and I will be thankful and I will do your bidding for I know salvation is of the Lord."

And the great fish became discomfited by God and spit Jonah upon the dry land.

And again God encouraged Jonah to go to Nineveh and to preach as God had directed, and this time Jonah went without objection.

It took Jonah three days to reach Nineveh but he did not postpone his preaching. Immediately he began to exhort the people to repent and to tell the people that because of their wickedness God would destroy the city in forty days. Jonah poured it to them in brilliant and moving fashion.

The people believed and acknowledged God, repenting of their sins. The people began to fast, put on clothes proper for worship, and then the king of Nineveh set aside his royal robe and joined the people. The king then published a decree of worship and repentance, calling on every man to quit eating and drinking, not even should a man feed his animals, but everyone should concentrate on calling on God in the hopes that God would no longer be angry and would not therefore destroy the people of Nineveh. The king also called on everyone to desist from evil and from any form of violence.

And God saw their new works, and noted their change from their evil ways, and God did not destroy them.

Jonah, however, was greatly irritated, as he didn't like the people of Nineveh and he had wanted to see them destroyed; so he prayed to God a lament saying, "You went to a lot of trouble, God, to get me here, and I went through a lot. I have always known, of course, that you are merciful and compassionate, slow to anger and of great kindness but I, Jonah, am disgusted. I wish you would take my life as I'm mad enough to want to die."

And God said, "Think about it a bit, Jonah, why are you so angry?"

Jonah then went out on the east side of the city, and built a small booth, and sat in it and sulked, watching to see if God might perhaps destroy the city.

And God pitied Jonah, and caused therefore a gourd to grow on a vine near Jonah to give him some shade and cool him down a bit. Jonah rejoiced over the gourd and felt better, now that he was getting a little attention himself.

The next day, however, God prepared a worm to eat part of the gourd so that it withered. After this God prepared a strong east wind, and the sun shone full on Jonah and he felt hot and miserable. Again Jonah began to feel that life was not worth living, and he mumbled to himself, "I'm better off dead than alive."

"Is it sensible, Jonah, to be irritated about the gourd?" asked God.

"Yes," said Jonah, "I'm sick to death of the whole thing."

Then God reasoned with Jonah saying, "You were sympathetic with the gourd, a plant which you didn't make or cause to grow, why should I not bless the city of Nineveh which has some 120,000 people in it, most of them not even having had a third grade education, not to mention all the cats, dogs, and cattle?"

There was a man named Mickey[1] who was born in Utah[2] and he was a prophet, a man who prayed and meditated, who observed life around him, and who spoke forth for God, putting things right bluntly.

"Now hear this, everybody," spoke Mickey,[3] "The whole world should know how God deals with evil people and evil places. When the Lord takes the notion, he visits the earth, he flattens out the mountain tops,[4] and he cracks open the valleys. God is planning to do such things because of the sins of Samaria and Jerusalem.

"Samaria will become a pile of stones, the foundations of the city will be uprooted and the place will look as if it is a deserted vineyard. The precious images and keepsakes that the strayed-from-God worshipped shall be broken to pieces. There is nothing to do about it except wail and moan and run around the house naked in misery and discomfort.

"Eventually evil gets its comeuppance. Take Monte Carlo, Las Vegas, the dens of Panama, they will suffer. If a person was smart they would get the fastest car[5] available and drive away from such places at once. Some people keep thinking better times are ahead and that evil scheming will finally help them, but God says 'No'. Find a righteous place and take your children there or they will become slaves to evil or to evil people."

"Woe to you, you evil men. God knows what you do," spoke Mickey. "You lie awake at night plotting and scheming to take away another man's land or his money. Some of you lawyers cheat on handling a will, but God is planning to fix you plenty. In the long haul, you will get what is coming to you, for the cheater will get cheated. You may even wonder why God has done this to you. You asked for it!"

"You want me to hush, don't you? You don't care to hear such talk. Well, the righteous don't mind. They are comforted to know that God is tending to his business. God doesn't like to threaten people, but it is one way of trying to get you on the right road. In spite of all God's pleas you skin your neighbor, you will take the shirt off his back, you pay no attention to the plight of women and children. Because of this, the people of Judah must leave their land.

"You don't like that kind of sermon, do you? You'd rather have me encourage you to drink wine and get stoned. Well, you'll have to get another prophet for that. The time will come, however,

---

[1]Micah   [2]Morash   [3]Maybe at a Rotary meeting
[4]Sometimes God has army engineers who save him the trouble   [5]chariot

when for the sake of his own name, God will gather you again, those that are left, and under a new leader with a new covenant shall there be a new kingdom.

"Now a word to the leaders of Israel. You are supposed to know right from wrong, but you seem to love evil and care nothing for good. You are incessantly taking advantage of God's people, the poor, and the disadvantaged. You treat people as dirt under your feet and then you piously pray to God for deliverance from hard times.

"Do you think God is going to listen to you? You forked tongue leaders, God is going to completely disregard you. Your system is to bless those who pay their church pledges and punish those that don't pay as you think they should.

"One thing that will happen to you is that you will lose contact with God, and your preaching shall be practical hogwash, you will be speaking in darkness, and there will be no revelation to you. When this happens you will come apart at the seams, and go to visiting local shrinks.

"I speak, however, with confidence, for God has empowered me to declare to Judah and Israel their sins. I speak without fear. Now listen, you prosperous leaders, who deal unfairly and simply dwell on making a profit. You are murderers and money grubbers, and yet you tell the people that God is with them and that all is well. Well, because of you God will make a mess of Jerusalem and even the place of the temple will become a place of ruins.

"Toward the end of time, however, there will be a change," prophesied Mickey, "for the holy mountain of God shall be a place where tourists come from all over the world to see where God declared himself to be Lord. In those days all the world will be ruled by the Lord, and the place of his headquarters will be Jerusalem.

"The new king of this new kingdom[1] shall judge and rule, and the nations of the world shall adopt a disarmanent plan, and instead of weapons of war, the nations shall make tractors and all forms of farming instruments. There will be universal peace as God has promised.

"At this time the righteous shall be brought forth by God, and they shall be the leaders and for once goodness shall be synonymous with prosperity. God will bless his people and restore their power, and the center of this operation will be Jerusalem.

"For the present, however, you've got it tough. Your king might as well be dead and your ministers have chickened out. You have reason to groan as a woman in labor, and so groan away. You must leave this wonderful city and this delightful countryside. You

---

[1] I think this refers to Christ

271

are going to be captured.

"Nations continue to plot against you, but the time will come, far off as it may be, when God will not allow anyone or any nation to tamper with his people.

"The day will come when the Lord will make the righteous appear to have horns of iron and feet of brass, and there will be no people who can contend with them. The wicked nations and people shall then be subservient to the people of God.

"Try getting organized. At least begin to prepare for a great new kingdom. For out of Bethlehem shall come a new king, one who was with God at the very beginning. Greatness shall come from the tiny little town of Bethlehem. There will be, however, a period of time when the people of God will seem to be fighting on their own, but God plans to correct all of this.

"The new king will feed his people with the food of the Lord and his name and his kingdom shall gradually encompass the earth. In time there shall be specially appointed leaders, seven or eight of them, and at the proper time these leaders will save the people from the Assyrians, and the spirit of God's people shall be refreshing to the world even as morning dew refreshes the grass, and God's people shall be as strong as a lion.

"Another sign of this time will be that God will do away with weapons of war and walled fortresses, and tanks and the like, and all the worship of material things shall end and man's selfishness will perish. Those who do not conform to this plan will be destroyed.

"Now listen. The Lord has a complaint to file against his people and the Lord has a plea to make to Israel. God wants to know what you have against God? Where has God wronged you? Speak up! Didn't God bring you out of Egypt, furnish you with leaders such as Moses, Aaron, and Miriam, did not God confound the king of Moab?[1] What do you think God wants in return for all his goodness? Do you think God wants a bunch of sacrifices? Or a new church building? Or airconditioned temples? God has already said what he requires, it is for you to do justly, to love mercy, and to walk humbly with your God.

"God calls to all Jerusalem. If you've got a dime's worth of brains, listen to him. Armies are already heading this way. Are you going to continue cheating, using loaded dice, and measuring cloth with a short stick? Is there no end to your wickedness?

"You are so accustomed to falsehood that you don't know how to tell the truth. Because of this God will make you pyschologically ill, even your food won't taste good, and your puny savings and

[1] Omri

272

so-called securities will be confiscated by the enemy. You'll plant and have lousy crops, and olive oil will turn sour on you. You follow the rules of the Playboy Club and you use as your example for living ole Henry VIII.[1] Just for that I will make you a pain in the neck to the people of the world and you shall be constantly despised. People will snicker at you and make fun of your plight.

"It is a tough time for me," groaned Mickey, "for I continue searching for honest, upright men, and they are scarce as hen's teeth. It seems as if all the good men are dead, it is like looking for a fig after the pickers have finished with a tree.

"The money-mad people are scrambling for the dollar in a pitiful manner. The people bribe judges, the rulers take kick-backs, how skillfully they connive and cheat. Justice almost doesn't exist. A man cannot even trust his own kinsman, they squabble over inheritance, and tell lies about one another even though they serve the God of my salvation. I'm certain God will in time hear me.

"Don't count me out, you foolish, wicked enemies. I may get knocked down, but not out. I'll come back, for God is with me. When I sit in darkness, God brings me a light. I know I am a sinner and that I deserve punishment, but I have repented and I will be restored. Some of you may taunt me by asking where my God is, but you just wait. When God decides to act, you are going to be in big, big trouble.

"The cities of the people of God will be eventually rebuilt, bigger and better than ever, and then people will come from all over the world to visit and to recognize your success. Before that happens, however, you must suffer terrible destruction because of your sins.

"Naturally, I pray to God for all of us, asking God to come and establish his rule, to make the people live in peace, and bring prosperity again to the Holy Land. I have prayed to God for a return of the good old days.

"God has answered and has promised to do mighty miracles, like those the Lord did when he delivered his people from Egypt. Everyone will be astounded, some shall put their hands over their mouths in awe and some shall plug their ears so as not to hear, but to no avail. The wicked will be as worms crawling helplessly around, and they shall fear God.

"How could there possibly be such a great God as our God. Surely he pardons sins, he allows his anger to last for only a brief period, our God delights in mercy and is full of compassion. God will take the sins of the repentant people and cast them into the depths of the sea. At this time God will fulfill his wonderful promises to Jacob and Abraham."

Amen.

[1] Ahab

273

NAHUM

Matty,[1] from Pensacola,[2] was a theologian who in his study of God had some visions and insights, and as a result he made some significant pronouncements.

"God is not one to accept second place. When a person or a city places good less than first, God takes a dim view of the situation and he always punishes wickedness and disregard of God's power or his commandments.

"The Lord doesn't have a short fuse, and he angers very slowly, but once his wrath is aroused then things begin to really happen. You must realize that God is in charge of the whirlwinds, the sea, the earthquakes, and God is not subject to General Motors[3] or the Senate Foreign Relations Committee.[4] God has the control over all the earth.

"Who thinks he can stand up against God? Doesn't God control landslides? God particularly loves those who trust completely in him, and the Lord is a good, strong refuge to the faithful in time of trouble. The enemies of God, however, may be washed away in a flash flood or they may just live in mental darkness. The enemies of God don't have a chance, they will be folded up like a blanket and put away. That's the way it will be with you, you wicked city of Nineveh. Who does your mayor think he is defying God? He must be nuts for sure! Your stupid king could gather an army of tremendous numbers and they would be nothing to God.

"As for the people of God, they have been punished enough and God plans to free them. The Assyrian king that holds the people captive, however, is on the way out. God will destroy him, so thoroughly that not even one of his sons will inherit the dynasty.

"Look up! There coming down the mountain you can see the feet that bring good tidings, that tell of peace. Be happy, Judah, and keep the commandments of God and follow his statutes. Nineveh is already handled, and she will no more be a source of trouble to Judah.

"Do anything you wish, try gathering together your strongest men, but it is a waste of time. Nineveh, you've had it. You have previously desolated the land of God, but not any more. The Lord has prepared an army that flashes as scarlet, and pandemonium should reign. The chariots shall be in a traffic jam rushing uselessly back and forth and even though the king calls forth his ablest men to man the walls, it will be in vain.

"The incoming army shall descend as a flood breaking through

---

[1] Nahum   [2] Elkoshi   [3] Bashan   [4] Carmel

the gates of the city and the palace itself shall be over-run.

"The beautiful Queen Liz[1] shall be made captive and she will be led forth practically naked with all her handmaidens following along crying and exposing their own breasts in shame and sadness.

"The soldiers of Nineveh suddenly become yellow bellies and begin to sneak away and hide so that the city appears to be a leaky bucket. Some of the leaders call for the men to stand their ground, but they don't, and shamefully flee.

"Looting will begin immediately. There is great wealth in the city and soon it is gone, for those seeking spoils take everything. Soon all is gone, and the glory of Nineveh exists no longer. You can see the pathos on the faces of the defeated people. You can't help but wonder what happened to the fierce young warriors, the strong men of Nineveh. The answer is that God has turned against Nineveh, and God is the real reason that the chariots are broken in pieces, and there is no more respect for voices that come from Nineveh for her power is gone forever."

Chap.
3

"God repeatedly denounces Nineveh. Woe to such a city, or any city, that lives on violence, crime, and lust. The men of Nineveh have had no respect or concern for people, and they have needlessly slain others just for practice. It is almost unbelievable the number of dead that you can see in the streets, and nobody cares.

God has seen this and God doesn't like it. As a result, God will expose Nineveh as simply as pulling a skirt over a girl's head exposes her nakedness. God will cause other nations to despise Nineveh and to detest its existence. In fact, when Nineveh is destroyed no one will regret it and there will be no sad resolutions passed by the United States. Because Nineveh was a completely wicked city the Lord decided to destroy the city, and to ruin its reputation as a place to visit or a business center.

"The people of Nineveh will be captured, the leaders will become slaves, and Nineveh will reel under her hardships as a drunken man, with no direction or stability. Other wicked cities and countries have perished because they became ungodly in their conduct.

"The city of Nineveh will seemingly have an army of women, and the city will be destroyed by fire and by pillage. You can prepare all you wish, store water, assemble arms, man the walls, strengthen the barricades, but the Lord will manage the destruction of all these devices just as simply as moths handle cloth or worms gnaw away on the wood.

"There is no escape for you people of Nineveh. Your sins are

[1] Huzzab

275

about to catch you. Your leadership is rotten and when the trouble starts you will find that your princes and your rulers have deserted. There is no cure for your plight and your destruction and your loss will not be mourned as other nations will be glad you no longer exist. Wickedness has its day, but it has its sad end."

HABAKKUK

There was a prophet of the Lord and his friends called him Hub.[1] Hub became greatly distressed by the existing conditions in the world and he prayed to the Lord saying, "How long, O Lord, must I pray? How often I have told you of the violence in the land and yet nothing happens. Everywhere I look I see evil at work. Why is this? The law is real slack. The judges let people go, they postpone trials, they give all kinds of extensions, and the courts turn free criminals regularly. Why?"

"Just keep your shirt on, Hub," replied the Lord. "You are going to be amazed at what I plan to do. My plan is to bring a bunch of heathens, worse men than you ever saw, and turn them loose on the sinners you are seeing every day. These Cossacks[2] are fierce and mean. Their horses are swifter than leopards, they make their own laws to suit themselves. These warriors will descend on your area like an eagle swoops down on its prey.

"These Cossacks are unbelievably terrible. They love violence, they disregard kings and princes, and they only leave a pile of dust behind them. These toughies claim to receive power from some strange god, but it is a god of their own making."

"Wait a minute, now, O Lord. You don't mean you are sending this awful outfit down on us, do you? You are only going to use these people to punish and correct us, certainly not to eliminate us," prayed Hub to the Lord. "For one thing, we are bad, but these Cossacks are worse. Certainly you don't plan to sponsor them. I know you dislike sin in any form; so how can you let these Cossacks crush us?

"The way you talk, we will be just like fish caught in the Cossacks' nets, or snared on their hooks. When they have captured or killed all of us, the Coassacks will bless their equipment, they will not acknowledge God. Do you plan to let them get away with their cruelty? Will the Coassacks punish us, and then go unpunished themselves?" asked Hub.

After this Hub climbed to his meditation seat on top of the wall and waited for God's answer.

God then spoke to Hub and said, "You can print my words. Put them on a public bulletin board. The things that I have planned will not come suddenly, but will gradually through the years work to the fulfillment of my plan. Have a little patience, Hub.

"The man who puts his trust in man like a Cossack does, these kind eventually fail, but the man who puts his trust in God, who has

---

[1]Habakkuk   [2]Chaldeans

faith, and pursues righteousness, such a man in time really lives.

"The Cossacks fill themselves with wine, and with vainglory, and they are never satisfied, but pursue one endeavor after another, never knowing where they are going.

"The very people that the Cossacks mistreat will in time rise up and crush them. Because the Cossack type spoils many nations, so shall it work around that these nations shall eventually destroy the Cossacks. The desires of evil are very perishable. Such things only look successful, but eventually all evil is to be crushed.

"If the stones or bricks would talk, they would tell you that a wall or building built at the expense of the blood of innocent people is a construction that will definitely tumble. Godless nations can work as hard as they wish, but it is in vain. God will not always tolerate evil doings of evil people.

"Woe to you who tempt your neighbor or your friend with strong drink," says the Lord. "Particularly is this evil if you use it as a means of taking advantage of a girl. Shame on those who do such things! God's judgment will come down on all sinners. There are plenty of you in the area where Hub lives," God continued, "who have cut down trees needlessly, in fact, who have often made idols to worship from the wood. Woe to those who pray to idols of wood and stone, expecting them to do something. Idols covered even with silver and gold are worthless."

"Remember all of you, the Lord is in His holy temple and all the earth should keep silence before him," spoke Hub to the people.

On another occasion Hub voiced a prayer to God which was also a song of hope as he said, "O Lord, when I hear your pronouncements I am filled with wonder. Let us again see you in action, God, mingling wrath and mercy. I can see the manifestations of God in every direction, his glory in the heavens and his handiwork on the earth. God shines as a bright light and power is in his hands.

"God has complete control of disease, God knows everything there is to know about the earth. The hills themselves stand in testimony to the Lord, people of all nations are impressed, even those nations of Russia[1] and China[2], whether they admit it or not.

"Sometimes when you see the sea in great upheaval with monstrous waves and whitecaps on the rivers, man wonders if God is angry with the waters, while actually this is just the way God made things. God made the rivers to divide the land.

"God created the sun and the moon and he started them on their regular rounds, just because God ordered it that way. God sometimes paces the earth in indignation and beats the wicked as

[1] Anshan   [2] Midian

grain on a threshing floor.

"God continues to arrange to save his chosen people, those who believe on his name. The manifestations of God in nature are truly impressive. Particularly is this true of the sea, for when the sea is terribly rough one thinks that God has his own horses thrashing in the deep, and it is a fearful sight to behold.

"I know this though, even if hard times come, if there are no figs, if the olive crop fails, if the grain fields have no yield, and the cattle perish, yet I will rejoice in the Lord, I will be delighted to know that in God is my salvation, for the Lord God is my strength, God will give me speed when I need it, and will make me capable of climbing mountains."

Hub suggests that the above song be sung accompanied by stringed instruments.[1]

---

[1]If he had known, he would have added with volume down.

ZEPHANIAH

There was a prophet in the land named Sim[1] and he was a great grandson of ole Hez.[2] As a prophet he spoke forth for God and he addressed the people of Judah with the following exhortation.[3]

"The Lord has decided to clean out the land of Judah. The Lord is angry and he will destroy fish and game, man and beast, and God will avenge the sins of Jerusalem, and everywhere that Baal was ever worshipped will be punished. Men who have served strange gods or simply neglected to worship the true God, these will be punished as God will vent his wrath on the area.

"The day God has appointed for His vengeance is close at hand. Those men who wear the garb of the heathen, the leaders of Judah who are selfish and phony, the criminals, and those who take advantage of the weak and innocent, on all such God is ready to pounce. Don't worry, you'll hear about it. From the front gate to the back the cry of terror and alarm shall be yelled. Death is bearing down on the money grubbers and the conniving merchants.

"There will be a period of great distress, so that men will wander around in a daze wondering what has happened to them. Some of the fellows will try to buy their safety, but they will find it is not for sale. The Lord is going to burn the whole place and the people of Judah will suddenly disappear."

On another occasion[4] Sim arose, and inspired by God, spoke to the people saying, "In God's name I urge you to gather yourselves together and turn to the Lord in prayer, for the Lord is extremely angry over your disgraceful behavior. Seek ye the Lord. Strive toward righteousness and study the ways of God so that you might follow in his path. It is still perhaps not too late to abate the anger of God and avoid his punishment.

"Look out, you wicked places! Las Vegas, the Riviera, the dark haunts of Panama, perhaps even Acapulco shall be shredded. Woe to the wicked coastal cities, the French Quarter, all the habitations of sin, for God in his own time will utterly destroy such places. All places shall finally come into the hands of the people of God.

"God knows about places like New York or parts of Mississippi or Nevada where those who served God are ridiculed. God has decreed the same treatment for all such places as that of Sodom and Gomer. God's people will in due time control all these places. The people who have made fun of those who worship God shall get it in

---

[1]Zephaniah   [2]Hezekiah
[3]Probably a family night supper speech that no one liked
[4]Would you believe a Rotary program?

the neck, but plenty! The Lord will be a terror to them, God will eliminate the effectiveness of all other gods, and men will worship the living God.

"God is not limited. God will make Ethiopia desolate and reduce Assyria to a nothing nation, and eliminate Nineveh. This is what finally happens to the wicked. The wicked city Ninevah that bragged of its greatness, that distributed tremendous brochures of self-praise, this wicked city shall be a place for ground hogs to burrow, for wild animals to use as a habitation, while owls and buzzards roost on the remains of the city. People will pass by the ruins and talk of the shame of the place and denounce it with words and chariot stickers saying 'Long gone Nineveh!'

Chap.
3

Since Sim had spoken to Rotary he was shortly thereafter asked to speak to the Kiwanis Club. On this occasion, again inspired by a revelation of God, he spoke about the city of Jerusalem.[1]

"Woe to Jerusalem! God has clearly seen that this is a wicked and corrupt city. The people have not obeyed God. Apparently the attempts of God to show the people how God works has made no impression, although God has destroyed a number of wicked places seen and known by the people of Jerusalem.

"The leadership of your city is rotten, most of your judges are crooked, and your preachers are dull, dreary reciters of stale platitudes.[2] The so-called godly church people are among those that pay no attention to the laws of God or man. The people go about in a corrupt city as if there was no God at all. Yuk!

"God is in no big hurry. Just you wait," continued Sim. "The day is coming when God is going to give a mighty whack to all the wicked nations and wicked places at once. The whole earth will feel the impact of the anger of God. At that time, God will begin to give all those that believe on him a new importance. The people of God will have one common language, and the people of God will be worshipping God all over the earth, even throughout all Africa.

"A great nucleus of these believers will be among those normally considered poor and ignorant, or disadvantaged, but the whole operation of God's people shall be honest, sincere, truthful, and their word of greeting shall be 'peace be with you all.'

"Sing, rejoice, be glad, all you believers. Your day will have arrived. Where you were accustomed to be treated shamefully, you will be honored, God will bless all his people, and the name of the people of God will be great throughout the whole earth, and the spirit of the Lord will constantly be living in the midst of his people. Amen."

---

[1] This was not well received. He was not asked back to speak again.
[2] This turned some of the preachers against him, too.

281

HAGGAI

There was a prophet of the Lord known as Haggy[1] and he was inspired by the Lord during the second year of Darius the King to go to the governor of Judah[2] and to the Archbishop[3] and speak to them.

"Governor and bishop," said Haggy, "the Lord has asked me to come to you and inquire as to the reason for letting the church get so rundown and neglected."

"The people say that now is not a good time economically to do any building or add to the present church,"[4] was the reply.

"Well, God suggests that you take a look at the situation. You plant a lot of seed, but you get a poor crop. You eat all right, but you don't get enough. There is some wine, but not near enough. You all have some clothes, but not enough to stay warm on a real cold day. You all have jobs and get some income but the deductions leave you under the impression that you are bringing your pay home in a bag that is full of holes."

"Now God knows all this. God says though that now is the time to get with building the church. Go up the mountain and cut wood and build on to the house of God. Do you know why your economics are in bad shape? That's God's way of telling you that your worship of him is inadequate. Because you have been more concerned with your own house than with the house of God, the Lord has encouraged a drouth and brought on a recession."

Then the governor, the bishop, and the people repented and recognized the truth of what Haggy said to them. As a result, the Lord was pleased and he encouraged the leaders of the people, and everyone pitched in, doing each his own thing for the building program of the church, and all was well.

A few months later Haggy, again inspired by God, called on the governor and spoke to him.

"God appreciates the work which the building committee is doing. God is also aware of the fact that this building program is nothing compared to the great temple of Solomon. God, however, does not want you or the people to be discouraged because of this.

"The time of the great renewal of all the people of God is coming. You must remember that all silver and gold, and all precious things, all these are the Lord's. God doesn't need such, but in time all these things will be under the care of the believers. The wicked are doomed!

"God doesn't want you to worry about the inadequateness of

---

[1]Haggai   [2]Zerubbabel   [3]Joshua of Josedeck
[4]I've heard that song before

the present work, for the future splendor of the temple of God will be caused by the peace which God will bestow on his church."

A couple of months later Haggy again received word from God and this time he was sent to speak to the bishop.

"Bishop," said Haggy, "let me ask you a question. If a holy man is carrying a holy object, and his pants leg brushes against a table or touches a loaf of bread, does the table or the bread become holy?"

"Not on your life, Haggy. What a stupid question. Holiness is not contagious," replied the bishop.

"If, however, a person touches an infection or hangs around measles, now that will be apt to spread to the person, isn't that right?"

"Right on, Haggy, right on," said the bishop.

"In just such a manner will the Lord bless his people and his spirit in time will spread from one to the other like measles."

Haggy then visited the governor and spoke to him for the last time.[1]

"God wants me to inform you," said Haggy, "that eventually he will get with his program at full speed. The whole earth will be aware of what God is doing. God will destroy all the wicked kingdoms, and chariots, horses, and armies will be as nothing before the power of God. God says that you are a good man, Governor, and because of your faithfulness you will be rewarded, and you shall be among those who sit on the right hand of God. Amen."

[1] As far as we know

There was a young man living during the reign of Darius named Izzy[1] and he was a preacher's son, and he made his first public speech at a family night supper at the church. At this time he spoke to the people telling them that he was inspired by God and that God was urging the people to repent. In fact, Izzy told the people that if they would turn to God, that God would bless them.

"Why don't you learn a lesson from your fathers?" shouted Izzy. "God warned them and pleaded with them, and they paid no attention. That's why we are all in trouble now. Your fathers finally realized this too late."

Several months later Izzy had a vision in which he saw a man riding a red horse and behind him there were black horses, white ones, and speckled ones, each with a rider.

Izzy in his dream then cried, "What is all this?"

"I'll show you," spoke forth an angel. "These men on their horses have been commissioned by God to patrol the earth in the interest of peace and good times."

Then an angel of the Lord prayed publicly to God asking, "How long will your anger against Jerusalem last, O Lord? Hasn't Jerusalem been suffering now for 70 years and isn't that enough?"

Then the Lord replied in such a way that the angel was comforted. As a consequence, the angel encouraged Izzy to speak out and to say to the people that God did care, that God felt kindly toward his people and the city like a man feels about a wife who has been taken into captivity.

The Lord revealed to the angel and thus to Izzy that the Lord was exceedingly angry at the nations who as heathens conquered Israel. The Lord decreed that his temple shall be rebuilt, that the cities of God will again prosper, that they will be restored, and God shall bless his people and their habitation with His own presence.

Then Izzy, who was still dreaming all this, dreamed of four horns and so Izzy in his dream asked the angel, "What gives with these horns?"

"These four horns," said the angel, "represent the four great powers that are reponsible for scattering my people and for destroying Judah, Israel, and Jerusalem."

Then Izzy saw four carpenters in his dream.

"What gives with these?" asked Izzy.

"These are the powers that will punish the horns and their power, and do away with them."

[1] Zechariah

Izzy continued in his dream state, and he saw in his dream a man with a measuring line.

"What are you planning to do?" asked Izzy.

"I am going to measure Jerusalem," replied the man.

"Why?" asked Izzy.

"To see if it is big enough to hold the crowd that will some day be there."

Then Izzy saw an angel in his dream go to another angel and say to him, "Go to the young man with the ruler and tell him that Jerusalem will not be large enough for all the people, but there shall be many who will live outside the walls, and they shall create suburbs and rural communities and there shall be great prosperity. There will be no need for a wall, as the Lord himself will serve as a wall for his people, and the glory of the Lord will be in the midst of the people."

The Lord then revealed to Izzy that God was pleased with the way the people who had been taken north into captivity had conducted themselves.

"The Lord says it is a time for rejoicing. Get with the program!" said Izzy. "The fulfillment of the promises of God is not too distant. Sing with joy! All the earth will be silent before the Lord, and the glory of God will again fill the earth with gladness."

As Izzy continued dreaming or dreamed again on another occasion, Izzy saw Joshua, the great leader and high priest of the early days, standing in the presence of God and standing opposite the devil.[1]

God spoke to Satan and said, "You are not to get your way. I am going to deliver Jerusalem, just as man would pull a log out of the fire."

Now Joshua was in dirty clothes[2] as he stood before one of the angels, a Mr. Clean,[3] who said, "Get some clean clothes for this man. Just as the Lord has forgiven your sins; so also will your clothes be made clean."

Then Izzy interrupted and said, "Don't forget to get him a clean hat." As a result, Joshua was suddenly spic and span.

Then one of the angels spoke to Joshua and said, "The Lord has authorized me to tell you that if you will obey his laws, and if you will encourage many other priests, ministers, and teachers to do the same thing, then you will be cleared to pass back and forth in his presence."

"You see," the angel continued, "all of you who will speak and teach in this manner, you will represent and will continue to represent the Branch that the Lord will bring forth to save his

[1] I continue to think of him as being red with horns
[2] No drip-dry clothes then   [3] Zerrubebel

285

people. There will be an event in one day which will remove the sin of the world, just as has been illustrated to you. When that day comes, the equality of man shall be pronounced, and rich or poor shall all be neighbors."

Then an angel came and awakened Izzy and asked him, "What did you see?"

"This last time I saw a candlestick of gold, with a bowl on it and seven lamps, with seven pipes, with two olive trees on each side. What in the thunderation does such a vision mean," asked Izzy.

"You don't know that?" said the angel.

"No, I don't," said Izzy.

"This vision is the word of the Lord to the Christians saying 'not by might, nor by power, but by my spirit,' saith the Lord of hosts, you will succeed this way regardless of your few in numbers or your strength.

"Even the mountains will flatten out before the Christian movement. Nothing can stop this. The Christians shall build to the glory of God and through the church, and with mighty shouts shall proclaim God's mercy, and shall credit all these things to the grace of God."

Then Izzy received another message from God saying, "It is the Christians, acting as the hands of Christ, who have laid the foundation. Do not be upset by the small number at the beginning, or the slow growth, the eyes of the Lord, represented by the seven lamps, are everywhere, seeing the worth of God's people, and watching how the will of God progresses."

"What about the two olive trees?" asked Izzy.

"Don't you know?" asked the angel.

"Absolutely no," replied Izzy.

"The two olive trees represent the annointed ones who watch over all the earth for the Lord."[1]

Izzy dreamed again a few weeks later[2] and in his dream he saw a flying blackboard.

An angel then turned to Izzy and asked, "What did you see?"

"A flying blackboard about 25 ft. long and 14 ft wide," replied Izzy.

"This blackboard represents the word of God being made known everywhere to everybody. It declares that it is wrong to steal or to lie. The Lord has ordered this to be a conscience that shall torment everyone who does wrong willfully."

The angel of the Lord then said, "Izzy, look up again."

"What is that thing I see?" asked Izzy.

---

[1] Christ and Holy Spirit   [2] Certainly not the next night

286

"It is a container. There is a woman sitting in the container, and the whole thing represents evil and man's abuses of God's gifts."

Then Izzy saw two women with great wings fly by and seize the container of wickedness and fly off.

"Where are they going with the wickedness?" asked Izzy.

"To the city," said the angel. "There it is easy for it to survive."

Izzy had another vision and in this dream Izzy saw brass mountains and there came forth from between the mountains four chariots, one chariot had red horses, another black, a third white, and the fourth was pulled by dappled greys. Izzy then turned to the angel who was present and asked, "What are these?"

"These chariots represent four spirits which come from God," replied the angel. "The black horses and the white horses represent spirits that for the most part deal in the northern areas and the dappled greys were assigned to the south. The Lord was soon pleased with the work of the spirit in the north area."

The Lord informed Izzy in a vision that he would soon be visited by representatives from the north and that he was to accept their gifts, and then take the silver and gold contained in the gifts and make a crown, and then to put the crown upon the head of the son of the high priest.

Then the Lord instructed Izzy to speak to Joshua, the son of the high priest, and to tell him that although he wore the crown, he was merely symbolizing the king and high priest who was yet to be born. The great one to come will be known as the Branch.[1] In time, the Branch shall be the real ruler, both ruler and priest, and there shall be peace and understanding between church and state.

Izzy then instructed Joshua to place the crown in the temple as a memorial and a reminder of what was to come.

The Lord further revealed to Izzy that people would come from all over the world to acknowledge God and that the Lord has promised all these things, contingent upon man's diligently obeying the word of God.

A committee from the Jewish community at Bethel came to Izzy with Leo the Lip[2] as chairman and spokesman.

"We have come to inquire if it might be permissable for us to drop the fasting and mourning period during the month of August. We really don't understand what it's all about anyway."

"The Lord has often questioned the sincerity of the observance of your fasting. God is certain that many of your observances were conducted for appearance's sake, and not as an act of worship. Maybe you need to brush up on the pronouncements of God when

[1]Christ   [2]Sherezer

God instructed the children of Israel during times of prosperity."

"Do you know what God has always sought?" asked Izzy. "God says for you to execute righteous judgment, to show compassion, to deal with mercy. It is not the performance in the temple that impresses God, but the way you deal with widows, the disadvantaged, the poor, and strangers. God is concerned more with your heart than your liturgy."

"Your fathers would not listen to this fine preaching," continued Izzy, "and they shrugged their shoulders and hardened their hearts. For this, the Lord became angry. As a result, you find yourselves scattered, the enemies of Israel prospered, and the good land was made desolate."

Chap
8

Izzy again received another message from God, this time pointing out that the Lord was real hot over the way the enemies of Israel had taken advantage of her. Because of this, the Lord told Izzy that Jerusalem would be some day restored, there would be a place in the city for the young as well as the senior citizens. God announced plans to gather the scattered people of Israel and restore them in fact as well as in prestige.

As surely as God punished as surely will God restore. Prosperity will return and such sayings as 'poor as a Jew in Judah' will be outmoded.

In order that these things be accomplished, God has asked everyone to begin speaking the truth, to use fairness, to promote peace, and to think of good things to do rather than evil ones.

The Lord also indicated that the more people observed the teachings and commandments of God, the less need was there for liturgy.

Because of all this, God has declared that some day Jerusalem shall be truly the holy city, a great center for tourists, many people, some church groups, some prayer groups, and many leaders of great nations shall come to Jerusalem to praise the Lord. At this time there shall be an organization of ten great nations and they shall choose a Jew to lead them, and they shall choose him because they will have heard that God is with him.

Chap
9

Further word from God came to Izzy and he passed along the information that in spite of the craftiness and cunning of such evil places as Tyre and Sidon, their doom was sealed. The Lord will not allow wickedness to be permanent. Disaster will come to the nations and the cities that defy God and that persecute God's people.

"The word from God," said Izzy, "is to rejoice. There is a great king coming, unlike any ever born, even though the king may be seen riding on a lowly donkey, the king is real. The king will carry with him salvation.

"This great new king who will come will pronounce peace and gradually his influence and his kingdom shall spread from sea to sea, and from the nearest river to the ends of the earth.

"The people of God will be leaders in this great movement and victory, though gradual, shall be a sure thing from the very beginning. This new kingdom will finally bring peace and prosperity, and the abundance of food and drink shall provide health and cheerfulness to whole generations."

Chap.
10

"God will send rain when rain is requested, and the earth shall be a blessed place. Why do people depend on weird rites, or strange charts, when all the powers of existence reside only in God?

"The Lord is angry that people go to fortune-tellers, that they seek odd ways of success through man devised programs. God plans to restore Judah and Israel and to let them be part of the great rehabilitation program of peace on earth.

"Even though the scattering of the Jews has been cruel and effective, the Lord will re-build from the remnant. In time the Lord will gather the Jews again, bringing them from England, Russia, Germany, Syria, and even some from the U.S., and the land will be crowded with them. At the proper time, the Lord will dry up the river Nile as a protection for his people.

"The believers in God will grow in strength, and their power will not be the power of men, but the power of God. It shall be known that they live as witnesses to the power of God."

Chap.
11

According to Izzy, the Lord revealed to him the fate of Lebanon. "It is a wicked country, and it will be destroyed. It will be as if a great fire comes raging and burns the whole place."

Then Izzy was urged in a vision to go out and get a job as a shepherd; so that not only would he know about what was going on, but also as a means of teaching God's message visually.

As a result, Izzy took the job as a shepherd of a flock that was being fattened for the butcher. The owners did not save any sheep, they were poor stewards, and they sold only to make the most possible money.

Izzy then spoke to the people and said, "You are not mindful of God's things, but are only interested in your own wealth; so as you have done to the sheep, the Lord will do to you. You will be completely destroyed. Even as I broke the staff marked to point out the sheep to be saved, so has God broken the staff which could save you."

After this Izzy turned to his employers and said, "Pay me for what you think I'm worth."

289

As a result, Izzy received 30 pieces of silver and the Lord instructed Izzy to donate it to the church, as it was obviously a means of scorn for the work of a prophet.

The Lord then told Izzy that he had illustrated the punishment part of God's plan and now he was to take a job as the shepherd for a poor man, and to give the appearance of being a poor and worthless leader.

When this was done, Izzy said to the people, "Now this recent act of mine illustrates to you that God will provide a worthless leader for you, one that cares not for individuals. It is this type of leadership that will bring Israel to trouble, but the Lord will punish such a leader who does not care for his flock and shirks his responsibility."

Izzy came to the people again with another message.

"The Lord God, the one who laid the foundations of the earth, who stretched out the heavens into limitless space, who created man and breathed into him a living soul, this Lord of All," said Izzy, "has announced that he will eventually bless Jerusalem. It will again someday be God's holy city, and the city itself will be the focal point of all international relations. Anyone who attempts to destroy Jerusalem in that day shall be destroyed.

"Because of this, the people of Judah shall wonder and be impressed, and they shall seek to join again with the people of Jerusalem. The power of God will be with the people of Judah at this time and their strength shall be great. The Lord will deliver Judah first, in order that the people of Jerusalem may not become too self-impressed.

"In that distant day, a feeble person living in Jerusalem shall feel protected, for the strength of the Lord God of hosts shall be in the city.

"In that day, God will begin to destroy any nation that turns its strength against Jerusalem.

"At this time there shall be a great revival in Jerusalem, and a tremendous feeling of repentance shall fill the mind and heart of everyone, for they shall know that the one who was pierced and crucified was their saviour.

"There shall be a great period of worship, of mourning for sin, and each person will try to find a place apart and pray fervently in private to the Lord."

"In that great day to come," continued Izzy, "people will understand forgiveness, and it will seem as simple as washing at a fountain. False gods will no longer exist, and those who do not follow the Lord and believe in his messenger shall be denounced. A father or mother will even denounce a son for this in that day.

"There will be no distinction between minister or priest and the laity. All will live under the spirit of God. In fact, if a man ask another where he received certain scars, he would lie and say 'in a brawl,' rather than admit that the scars came from falling down the library steps at the Seminary.

"There is a great deal of trouble ahead for the people of God, but a good nucleus will always be retained, and they shall be blessed by God and protected. God will say to such "You are my people," and they shall reply, "The Lord is our God."

"About all I can say is to tell you," Izzy said, "to watch carefully for the coming of the time of the Lord. Now here is what is going to happen. The enemies of God and of Jerusalem shall attack the city, they shall steal treasures, rape women, and take away captives by the hundreds. About half of Jerusalem in men and materials shall be left.

"Then the Lord God of hosts shall go forth in his power against the warring nations. First God will create a mammoth earthquake which shall split the land open, creating a great valley running east and west, and the believers in God will begin to gather in this valley. It will be an awesome time, for there will be neither darkness nor light, but everything will be gray and murky, and only God will know what time it is, and whether it be day or night.

"As a result, living waters shall flow in every direction, through the saints of the Lord, and there shall be one God, and only one name worshipped. Jerusalem shall again be safely inhabited.

"For all the people who fought against Jerusalem will be struck with a plague of such horror that it destroys tissue, tongues shall shrivel to nothing, and people will seem to melt. There shall be such suffering and confusion among the non-godly that they shall begin to turn against each other. The plague will also affect the animals. Judah and Jerusalem will assemble most of the confiscated wealth.

"There will be those people in enemy nations who worship God, and they shall come to Jerusalem each year on a holy pilgrimage. If there happens to be a nation that does not properly represent itself in the worship of God, the Lord will simply withhold rain from that nation.

"Should Egypt not come to be represented, another punishment will come to Egypt, as it doesn't rain there anyway.

"The whole atmosphere of life in the city will be changed in the time of the rulership of God on earth, and bumper stickers in Jerusalem will say such things as "Holy Property," and trash cans will be marked "Sacred Bowl." In fact, everything in Jerusalem will be considered a holy object, and this is for the convenience of the pilgrims coming to the holy city. In this great day, there will be no money changing or trading in connection with the Lord's temple, but the church of God shall be a holy place for the worship of the Holy God."

MALACHI

There was a man named Edwards[1] who was the guest speaker at a lecture series in Israel. Inspired by God, Edwards spoke to the people saying, "The Lord has loved his people always. How has he shown it? By choice. God didn't have to bless Jacob from whom you are descended. God could have just as easily blessed Esau, but instead he made a curse of all that Esau did, for he was selfish and anti-godly.

"It will always be this way with the wicked. Every time wickedness prospers God in his time comes along and wipes it clean. You will someday see the glory of God throughout all Israel.

"You yourselves teach that a son should honor his father. Why then don't you honor God? Even your preachers are not free from blame.

"What do you do wrong? I'm glad you asked! For one thing, you bring gifts to the church, leftovers to the family night supper, and stale bread for the communion table. How does that grab you?

"What's more, you pay your church pledge with blind animals, or sick doves, and you claim more deductions than you give. You wouldn't try to cheat the IRS, would you? Why then do you try to cheat God?

"Why don't you ask God for forgiveness? If God closes the door on you, it is for a reason, just as you have a reason for closing a door. God is rightly disgusted with you and God will not accept gifts reluctantly given.

"Even the gentiles are beginning to acknowledge God and the name of the Lord will grow in importance everywhere. You have made fun of the worship of God and trifled with the holy symbols. You have complained about being bored with the services and you have reflected this in your church giving. For those who are guilty there is trouble, for the Lord is the one Great God of all."

On another occasion Edwards was invited to lecture at a ministers' retreat, and he spoke to them saying, "The Lord will punish you if you do not begin to emphasize more the need to glorify the name of God. You are far too much concerned with your own image and your own problems.

"God promised life and peace to the members of the ministry who follow the Lord and preach in his name. The priest or minister should be knowledgeable in the law, for he is the one chosen by the Lord to teach the law of God. You have strayed from this, and you have tried to water down the law and mislead the people.

---

[1] Malachi

"You have violated the arrangement God made with Levi and therefore you will be held in contempt by the people, some of whom will sneeringly refer to you as 'just another preacher.'

"God has explained that there is only one father and we are all brothers, how can you teach otherwise? Yet you are careless with the law of God.

"Didn't God warn everyone about marrying heathen women and then following their strange gods? A lot of you have done this, not only the general populace, but even some of the ministers. Then you wail to high heaven when there is a drouth or you do not receive all the blessings you think you should have.

"Another thing that God dislikes is the way so many of you are unfaithful to your wife, in spite of your vow in the presence of God. There is no excuse for this! Stay with your wife.

"Finally, you have bored the Lord with all your creeds and liturgy, for you have not followed your own testimonies. You even intimate that God won't punish you because God doesn't care that much. You are wrong again!"

On still another occasion Edwards was invited to speak to a men's conference[1] and he spoke strongly saying, "God says that he will send a special messenger ahead to prepare the way of the Lord. Then suddenly there will appear the great one for whom you have always been looking.

"He is coming. There is no doubt about it. It will be difficult to be in his presence, for he will search your soul. He will be like a refiner of silver, one who removes all sham and all blemishes.

"This great one shall purify the ministers of God and they will once again serve him because of their love for God. Then again will the Lord be pleased with the worship services and the gifts of the people.

"The Lord will then move quickly against the wicked, the witchcraft crowd, the adulterers, the cheaters, those who take advantage of the poor, who shun the stranger, and who do not worship God.

"Repent. God is always willing to forgive. Return to the Lord, and the Lord will return to you. Then you say, 'When did we ever leave God?'

"Let me ask you, will a man rob God? Yet you have robbed God. Do you want to know how?

"In tithes and offerings. The whole nation has neglected the fulfillment of this requirement. God says, however, to test him, just try it, bring the full tithe to God's house and see if God doesn't open the windows of heaven and pour out such a blessing that there shall

---

[1] Apparently he was never invited back

not be room to receive it.

"If you give properly to the Lord, God will bless the land for your sake and the whole nation will prosper and be respected by other nations.

"You know, you have actually spoken against God often. You immediately say 'when?'

"Well, you've often said that it didn't pay to serve God, that the wicked seem to prosper, that they get rich and are often voted into positions of leadership.[1]

"God noticed all this and God had the names of all those put in a book who did not do this. You better believe that God has a record! The day will come and the righteous shall be rewarded and the wicked punished. God will care for the righteous as for his own son.

Chap.
4

"The day is coming for judgement, and for the wicked it will be an experience like being thrown into a furnace, while for the righteous it will be as if crippled wings were healed and a person could fly as free as a breeze. The righteous shall be separated from the wicked, who will be as ashes under their feet.

"Remember the law of Moses. Also I will send to you a prophet like Elijah[2] who will preach before the coming of judgment day, and he shall convert many and save many and be a great and helpful influence, for the people will sense that they must respond or the Lord will smite the whole country."

[1] You can say that again

[2] Maybe Billy Graham